THE HAINDL
TAROT

VOLUME I:
THE MAJOR ARCANA

BOOKS BY RACHEL POLLACK

SEVENTY-EIGHT DEGREES OF WISDOM,
   PART 1: THE MAJOR ARCANA
SEVENTY-EIGHT DEGREES OF WISDOM,
   PART 2: THE MINOR ARCANA AND READINGS
GOLDEN VANITY
SALVADOR DALI'S TAROT
THE OPEN LABYRINTH
TEACH YOURSELF FORTUNE-TELLING
AQUA DREAMS
UNQUENCHABLE FIRE
THE NEW TAROT
TAROT TALES
THE HAINDL TAROT, VOLUME I: THE MAJOR ARCANA
THE HAINDL TAROT, VOLUME II: THE MINOR ARCANA

THE HAINDL

TAROT

VOLUME I:
THE MAJOR ARCANA

RACHEL POLLACK

NEWCASTLE PUBLISHING, INC.
NORTH HOLLYWOOD, CALIFORNIA
1990

Dedicated to
Maeve Moynihan

Contents

FOREWORD

Artistic vision registers and prophesies the expanding consciousness of man. I am not speaking only of works of art, but the artistic vision wherever it imbues living acts. Artistic imagination creates what has never before existed. To live artistically is to embody in social forms the unique individual and the intuitions of union.

—M. C. Richards

THE HAINDL TAROT captures the essence of artistic vision and honors the true meaning of the word *craft*, which comes from the German word *Kraft*, meaning power and strength. The collaborative team of Rachel Pollack, award-winning writer, and visionary artist Hermann Haindl demonstrates the power and strength of two people committed to the combined craft of Tarot.

Artful in their respective crafts, Pollack and Haindl live with a special immediacy to the questions of technique and the questions of meaning and how they apply to Tarot. Through art, Haindl addresses the questions of technique; and through writing, Pollack addresses meaning. Using different means to achieve a combined result, Pollack and Haindl illustrate how perennial and ancient wisdoms can be applied in contemporary times. Haindl, through his contemporary style and Tarot deck, renders traditional archetypes with modern symbols. Pollack skillfully interprets the many layers of meanings found within the symbols. She brings together multiple spiritual and esoteric traditions and demonstrates their relevance and varied applications in modern themes of ecology, politics and ways of developing human resources.

The Haindl Tarot and Pollack's interpretations reveal the power of the creative arts in their capacity to bridge visible and invisible worlds. The rich matrix of the Tarot provides a symbolic map of consciousness which can serve as a visual affirmation and a synchronistic mirror of an individual's experience and life process. Combining the oracular traditions of the *I-Ching*, Runes, astrology and the influence of ancient cultures and the Kabbalah, these two volumes synthesize multiple doorways in which mainstream people and scholars can access invaluable information.

The challenge of the twenty-first century is how to integrate ancient and modern themes that will create synergetic visions and applications which can further the expanding consciousness of humankind. Perhaps Cezanne described this process best when he said: "Any craft is a harmony parallel to nature." Rachel Pollack and the Haindl Tarot remind us that symbols provide a harmonious mirror of our own nature and craft; and that it is time, as M. C. Richards states, "to live artistically . . . to embody in social forms the unique individual and the intuitions of union." In many ways, Pollack and Haindl have paved the way in their joint effort in bringing forward the Haindl Tarot.

Angeles Arrien
San Francisco, California
Spring 1990

AUTHOR'S PREFACE

THE WORD "TAROT" is a French word for a card game known also as "Tarocchi" or "Tarock." Nobody really knows the Tarot's origin. Many people have put forth theories, some of them mundane, others esoteric or frankly legendary. At one end of the scale we find the idea that the Tarot began simply as a game with no deeper meaning until occultists invented fantasies about it in the eighteenth century. At the other end we read of secret congregations of Atlantean masters who wanted to encode their wisdom for the dark ages after Atlantis's destruction. As far as historical information tells us, the Tarot first appeared in Italy in the mid-fifteenth century. Contrary to what we might expect, cards of any kind do not get mentioned in European documents until the late fourteenth century. Among the earliest cards that have come down to us are the Tarot cards painted by Bonifacio Bembo for the aristocratic Visconti family of Italy.

The Tarot has remained remarkably the same throughout its history. From the time of Bembo the deck has consisted of seventy-eight cards ("seventy-eight degrees of wisdom," as Charles Williams called them), in two main parts, referred to by esotericists as the Major Arcana and the Minor Arcana (*arcana* means "secrets"). The Major Arcana are twenty-two trump cards, usually numbered 0–21 and displaying names, such as "The Empress" or "The Fool." The Minor Arcana contain four suits of fourteen cards each, ace through ten and four "court" cards: page, knight, queen, king.

Though the structure has stayed the same, the pictures on the cards have changed a great deal. The images most people think of as traditional, or classic, the images found on the famous Tarot de Marseille, became fixed fairly early, around the seventeenth century. Nevertheless, many of them vary quite strongly from the pictures left to us by Bembo. People who know the Tarot may look at the cards created by Hermann Haindl with some surprise, for he has radically redesigned almost all the images. And yet, we can consider such alteration as part of the Tarot's tradition. Interestingly, the card that remains closest to the older decks is the famous Hanged Man.

This same card probably has varied the least throughout the Tarot's many transformations.

Many people have put forth esoteric theories of the Tarot's origin (see also the introduction to the Major Arcana). The fact remains that as far as we know, the occult interest in the Tarot did not begin until the late-eighteenth century when a man named Antoine Court de Gebelin declared that the Tarot formed the "Book of Thoth," a supposed compilation of ancient Egyptian wisdom created by the God Thoth for his disciple magicians. In Classical times people considered Thoth the equivalent of the Greek Hermes, or Roman Mercury. Hermes' name has been given to the "Hermetic," or esoteric tradition. In the correspondence of the Tarot trumps to astrology, the planet (and god) Mercury belongs to the card of the Magician. Following Court de Gebelin, various people began to create occult Tarot decks. The most important of these was the Grand Etteilla deck, "Etteilla" simply being the artist's name, Alliette, spelled backwards.

Probably the most significant development for the Tarot came in the mid-nineteenth century, when the occultist Eliphas Levi (whose real name was Alphonse Louis Constant), connected the Tarot to the body of Jewish mysticism known as Kabbalah (a word which means tradition). Ever since the Middle Ages Kabbalistic ideas had fertilized the wider Hermetic and magical philosophies. By noticing a remarkable correlation between the Kabbalah's structure and that of the Tarot (see the Major Arcana introduction) Levi set the Tarot in a direction that has remained important to this day.

In 1888 a man named MacGregor Mathers, who had written about the Tarot and fortune-telling, joined with others to found the Hermetic Order of the Golden Dawn. This organization continued for only a few decades but its influence remains strong today. It carried Levi's ideas further, formulating complex correspondences between the Tarot, Kabbalah, astrology and ceremonial magic. It also led to people using the cards as aids in study, meditation and ritual. The Golden Dawn urged its members to create their own decks based on the group's doctrines. This idea of individual creation may have helped foster the modern renaissance in Tarot, with literally hundreds of new decks, many of them vastly different from earlier designs.

Apart from the poet William Butler Yeats, the two most famous members of the Golden Dawn were Arthur Edward Waite and

Aleister Crowley. Both designed their own Tarot decks. The one by Waite, known as the Rider deck (after its London publisher), and painted by Pamela Colman Smith, has become the world's most popular deck, probably because of Smith's vivid images. Crowley's Book of Thoth Tarot went further than most other decks in directly incorporating esoteric and sexual symbolism. Because of this—and because of the stunning pictures painted by Lady Frieda Harris— the Book of Thoth has influenced a great many Tarot artists of the last forty years. One of these is Hermann Haindl, who consulted Crowley as a source when he decided to paint his own cards.

Though the Haindl Tarot contains much esoteric information, including Hebrew letters, Runes, astrological symbols and I Ching hexagrams, we should not think of it as an occult deck, not in the sense of Crowley. We do not find here the precise details of Hermetic symbolism, the references to doctrines and rituals, the complex use of magical signs and formulas coded into the pictures. Rather than an occult work, Hermann Haindl has created a sacred Tarot, one which reaches back to ancient spiritual traditions of many cultures.

The Haindl Tarot certainly contains a great deal of information. Most importantly, however, it opens our minds. It leads us to see the world in a new way (or perhaps a very old way), as a vessel filled with spiritual power and truth. To do this, the deck does indeed draw on Crowley and other representatives of the Tarot's occult teachings. It also draws on the mythologies and the religions of different peoples, from Europe to Native America, to India, to China, to Egypt. And it takes inspiration from sacred art, from prehistoric statues and temples to Wagnerian opera. None of these things becomes a doctrine, not in the narrow sense of a fixed ideology. As an artist, Hermann seeks to create an inner understanding rather than promulgate a particular theory.

The deck certainly does contain ideas. Though Hermann Haindl worked to a large extent unconsciously—not planning the symbolism so much as allowing it to emerge in the painting—the pictures present to us a complex and, at the same time, unified vision. We will explore this vision and its concepts in the individual cards. Here, we can describe the central theme of the Haindl Tarot as the renewal of the Earth—not just the material resources, but the spiritual Earth. For thousands of years people have seen the Earth as a living being. All over the world She was worshipped as an aspect of the Great Goddess, the Mother of Life. The Goddess is the Earth, and She is also the Sky. She rules as well over the mythological realms of Heaven and the Underworld.

In recent years we have become conscious of two great dangers facing our world. One is the possibility of nuclear war ending all life in the fire of explosions and the darkness of nuclear winter. The other is the threat to our planet's environment. Various groups, including the Green Party in Germany, have attempted to push for disarmament, as well as to stop the acid rain, the cutting down of forests, the destruction of the ozone layer of the atmosphere. Hermann Haindl, like many others, sees this as a spiritual struggle as well as an ecological and political one. For Haindl, the roots of our current dangers originate in a male-dominated mentality, one based on hierarchies and dominance, rather than cooperation and mutual respect. When patriarchal ideologies banished the Goddess, women became seen as primarily vehicles for producing babies—and the Earth became an object rather than a Creator, an object created solely for human exploitation. Hermann Haindl is not a feminist. Nor does the Haindl Tarot attack men. Rather, it seeks a balance between different qualities. And it roots this balance in the ancient view of the female as the primary principle of creation.

Though Haindl has worked in the Green Party, he has come to his ideas more through his own experience, primarily with the native peoples of North America. Hermann Haindl and his wife, Erica Haindl, have traveled among the Native Americans; they have stayed in their homes and taken part in their rituals. They did not go to the Native Americans out of curiosity. They went to learn, and to awaken in themselves a genuine respect for the Earth and for the Spirits who share our world.

The Haindl Tarot does not spell out Native American teachings any more than it does occult doctrines. Haindl's American experiences form an influence in the deck, along with his travels in India and other lands, his knowledge of European mythology and traditions and the Tarot itself. Above all, he has created a sacred work of art, one which speaks to us through the power of its images.

At one time, the symbolism in a Tarot deck counted more than the pictures. People concerned themselves less with the quality of the art and more with specific references to some teaching, such as Kabbalah or Freemasonry. This may help to explain why relatively

few professional artists have created Tarot decks. Perhaps the subject struck them as too restricted, even for those with esoteric interests. In recent years, however, the vast number of new decks have
returned the image to a primal place. The Haindl Tarot re-works the
old designs in a radical way, but it does not do so alone. Other people have begun to re-imagine the Tarot, creating new pictures out
of their own lives and beliefs. The strongest of these pictures have
gone beyond the personal to archaic and mythological levels. We
find this kind of power in the Haindl Tarot, especially in such cards
as the Chariot, or the Star, or the very beautiful Court cards, derived
from religious traditions around the world. Once again, trained
artists have begun to explore the Tarot. Along with such figures as
Salvador Dali and Niki de St. Phalle, a whole group of young artists,
particularly in Italy, the home of Tarocchi, have created their own
decks. The Haindl Tarot goes deeper than most, for it forms the life
testament of an artist dedicated to spiritual understanding.

The Haindl cards are obviously symbolic. Each card, but
especially those of the Major Arcana, contains an entire structure
of symbolism, based on a set of ideas and images derived from tradition, but finally belonging to this particular deck. Because Haindl
is first and foremost a painter, the meanings become part of the picture, rather than the picture being formed only to serve a theory.
Many cards show what we might term an "economy of symbolism."
A single gesture, or an object, or a color pattern, will appear simple,
but will actually convey a whole range of ideas. These ideas then
create a new relationship with each other. The card has brought
them together. We find this technique in many of the trumps, not-
ably the Fool, but also in the Minor Suit and Court cards.*

I first heard of the Haindl Tarot when Hermann Haindl's German publisher called me on the telephone to ask if I would like to
write a commentary for a new deck. I asked him to send me some
of the pictures. The moment they arrived they struck me with their
conceptual beauty, their daring designs and their sense of mystery.
I had recently done some writing on the Runes, so it seemed to me
a wonderful idea to bring this ancient system into the Major Arcana.
Shortly afterwards, I met Hermann and Erica Haindl for the first

---

*See *The Haindl Tarot, Volume II.*

time. They came to my house in Amsterdam, arms laden with paintings, and we sat for several hours, looking at the cards, talking about the symbolism, discovering the many ways in which we all shared the same concepts—of the Tarot, of politics, of mythology and archaic beliefs. When they left they gave me a kachina doll, a sacred image to bring favor to the house. In return, I gave them a rock I had found containing a natural Rune. The next time I saw them, in their home in Germany, they presented me with a rock from a beach in Tuscany. The rock had a six-pointed star etched by nature into its surface; Hermann had searched among the pebbles on the beach until he found one containing an appropriate symbol.

In describing these cards I have attempted to follow Hermann Haindl's statements as closely as possible. At the same time I have brought to them my own ideas and experiences, not to contradict the message in the pictures, but to explore them and their possibilities. Hermann Haindl and I come from different cultures, different generations, different genders, different religious backgrounds, different creative disciplines. Yet we can experience the world in a similar way. Working with the Haindl Tarot has taught me a great deal. I hope that this book will enable others to enter this new and ancient labyrinth.

Rachel Pollack

INTRODUCTION TO THE MAJOR ARCANA

THE MAJOR ARCANA of the Tarot consist of twenty-two cards not connected to any particular suit. From the earliest examples the Major Arcana have always shown a variety of vivid scenes and characters: popes and nuns, carnival jugglers and alchemists, mythological figures such as Hercules, love scenes, religious teachings such as the Last Judgement and so on. One theory of the Tarot holds that the trumps, as the Major Arcana cards are called, began as a gallery of typical early Renaissance characters, plus moral virtues and lessons. However, certain images would seem to suggest some sort of esoteric, even heretical message. The alchemist may have been a stock character, but alchemy is the occult art par excellence. The nun in some early decks metamorphoses to a female pope. Medieval legend tells us of a Pope Joan, a woman who disguised herself as a nun, entered the Church and rose to the top position only to have a mob attack her when she gave birth during an Easter procession. More significantly, perhaps, an heretical group named the Guglielmites elected a woman pope toward the end of the thirteenth century. In 1300, the Church burned this woman to death. Her name was Maria Visconti. Some of the earliest Tarot decks— approximately one hundred and fifty years later—were painted for the Visconti family.

An emperor would also seem an obvious figure for a card game based on social types. Europe had once again discovered the Classical age, and the Church had always used Latin as its common tongue. There was also the example of the Holy Roman Empire. Quite early, however, the card of the Emperor developed a certain esoteric quality, showing him in profile (some Kabbalists tell us you can see the "Ancient of Days" from the side but not the front), and seated with the legs crossed to form a four. The number four in occult philosophy represents divine law and the four worlds of creation.

And from the beginning the decks have always shown a certain strange image—a man hanging upside down, usually by one foot

1

with the other crossed behind him, again in that figure four. Now, Italy has a tradition of hanging traitors upside down (Mussolini was hanged upside down at the end of the war). However, the Tarot Hanged Man usually displays a radiant face. He might remind us of a yogi standing on his head. St. Peter was crucified upside down, supposedly so he would not commit the sin of imitating Jesus. In an interesting essay on the Vita Merlini, a twelfth-century manuscript about Merlin, Robert Stewart points out a story known as the "three-fold death," which ends with a man hanging upside down by one foot from a tree, with his head in a river. Stewart sees this story as a screen for ancient Celtic rebirth rituals. Whether this can be proved or not, the story itself predates the earliest Tarot decks by more than two hundred years.

The Kabbalist case for the Tarot rests on the number of trumps —twenty-two, always twenty-two. The Hebrew alphabet contains twenty-two letters, and this forms the basis for the Kabbalah's mystic explorations (possibly the oldest Jewish mystic text, the Sefer Yetzirah, describes the mystic properties of the alphabet). We must, however, recognize that the Kabbalist theory of the Tarot did not appear until the nineteenth century. In all the thousands of pages of Kabbalist writings we find no reference to any sort of pictures or cards.

Many people have put forth theories of the origin of the Major Arcana. It is interesting to note that most theories of the Tarot deal only with the trumps, as if the four suits, the Minor Arcana, were tacked on later. One suggestion for the trumps connects them to processions of "triumphs" (the word trump derives from triumph) honoring important people. The poet Petrarch, who spent time at the court of the Viscontis, wrote a poem called "I Trionfi," describing six allegorical triumphs. An historian named Gertrude Moakley has suggested that these might have inspired early Tarot cards. More esoteric theories include picture panels in an Egyptian temple, twenty-one stages in the rites of Tantra (the Indian esoteric tradition), different steps in the alchemical "Great Work," or even (recently) twenty-one stations of the Moon in ancient Chaldean astrology.

In a certain sense all the theories are true. For what matters most to us today, and certainly what matters for the Haindl Tarot, is not the Tarot's original purpose but the meanings and values it has acquired along the way. Whether or not it came out of Tantra, writers such as Barbara Walker have allowed us to make that connection. In recent years people have reinterpreted and redesigned the images of the Major Arcana, joining them to Mayan mythology, Native American beliefs and social traditions, pantheons of ancient Goddesses, the Arthurian legend and so on. All these influences and more have come into play in the Haindl Tarot. If Hermann Haindl had deliberately planned to include these various ideas his cards might have ended up a hodgepodge. They present a unified version because he draws on these various traditions—and his own direct experiences of them—in order to set his deck, his vision, within the ongoing tradition of the Tarot.

The earliest Tarots display no numbers on the cards. If they did originate as a game (at least on the surface) we can assume they must have had some ranking. Quite early, however, the names and numbers became standard, more or less as they appear in the Haindl Tarot. The only exceptions are cards 8 and 11, which Haindl has switched, following a modern practice that began with the influential occult group, the Order of the Golden Dawn. The Fool, however, presents something of a problem. As card 0, it would seem to belong before card 1. In the Tarot card game, however, it does not occupy a fixed place. Some esoteric commentators place the Fool as first, others last, and others between cards 20 and 21.

The sequence becomes important when we see the cards as links to the Hebrew letters. Some of the other esoteric links contain twenty-one stages, so that the Fool becomes the pilgrim, or initiate. However, the Hebrew alphabet has twenty-two letters, and therefore twenty-two paths on the Tree of Life, requiring the Fool to occupy a particular place. If that place comes at the end, then the first letter of the alphabet, and the first pathway, belongs to the Magician, the second to the High Priestess, etc. But if we make the Fool the first letter, then the second goes to the Magician, the third to the High Priestess, and so on down the line. Haindl has followed Aleister Crowley and made the Fool the first letter.

There are two basic approaches to interpreting the Major Arcana. One is to see each card for itself, with its own special qualities. The other is to see the cards as a sequence, building up a kind of story. Often this story depicts the Fool as a journeyer through the cards, or as an incarnate soul making its way through life. When we look at the cards as a sequence, the meaning of each card depends not only on its own qualities but on its place. The Tower, for instance, card 16, depicts an explosion. We often interpret this explosion as coming from the pressures built up in card 15, the Devil. We also look ahead, saying that the explosion leads to the openness and renewal of card 17, the Star.

This method of interpretation resembles the way we look at the cards in Tarot readings. There we examine the position of the card as much as its meaning. For example, the Lovers in the position of Past Experience may mean something very different than the Lovers in Near Future, and something else again in Hopes and Fears. Also, in a Tarot reading we look at all the other cards to see the meaning of a particular one. In recent years Tarot readings have become much more complex—and more popular—than ever before. At one time serious students and writers on the Tarot tended to dismiss readings. Now, some of the best writers focus almost entirely on readings. It is probably not a coincidence that the sequential method of interpreting the Major Arcana has become almost standard.

The Haindl Tarot (like most really valuable decks) combines the two approaches. Hermann Haindl painted these cards as individual images, each with its own themes. In each painting, however, a definite story developed, as if by itself. This story combines history and politics with the Tarot's spiritual ideas. Haindl did not plan these stories deliberately. Nor did he plan a certain line of images that develop step-by-step, from the Fool to the Universe. The themes and pictures emerged because they came from an artist with a very clear and coherent vision. Hermann did not have to plan what he wanted to say. The ideas came out of his experiences, his spiritual studies and deep conviction.

Many people interpreting the Major Arcana separate it into two or more parts. People who see the cards as two halves usually describe the first half as looking outward in life and the second as concerned with introspection and spiritual development. This is often a theme with Jungian interpreters. People sometimes debate which card is the turning point. The most obvious candidate is the Wheel of Fortune, card 10, which carries us upward through the first half of life, and then, when we reach middle age and our powers begin to decline, carries us downward, toward death (and for some, reincarnation, a new turn of the wheel). The Hanged Man, 12, also can serve as a turning point, for it symbolizes a reversal of previous values. And card 11, either as Strength or Justice, can mark the mid-point, for strength implies a readiness to go beyond past achievements, while Justice shows past and future balanced in the scales.

Another method of dividing the cards sees trumps 1–21 as three groups of seven (with the Fool as the pilgrim going through all of them). This approach gains meaning from the ancient symbolism of numbers three and seven. Three signifies a whole range of ideas, many of which we will look at with trump 3, the Empress. One of the most important of these is the three phases of the Moon, new, full and old, which represent youth, maturity and old age. We can see these in the cards. The first seven show the concerns of youth learning about the world. The second depict the problems of maturity: self-knowledge, psychological transformation, an awareness of deeper values. The final cards go beyond the individual personality as the soul becomes aware of universal principles. In traditional cultures, such attitudes often go with old age, when the woman beyond childbearing age, or the man too old for hunting, concern themselves with wisdom.

In ancient times people could see seven "planets" in the sky: Sun, Moon, Mercury, Venus, Mars, Jupiter, Saturn. Seven, therefore, becomes a number of completion. In the Tarot, card 7, the Chariot, signifies "Victory." This meaning carries over to the higher multiples of 7, 14 and 21. In other words, the end of each sequence shows a victory, for the soul has confronted various challenges and passed through them.

In the musical scale each octave contains seven notes. The eighth note repeats the first at a higher level. Therefore, we sometimes refer to each group of seven cards as an octave. We also say that card 8 is the "harmonic" of card 7, or that card 18 is the harmonic of 11. This is not just a figure of speech. Very often, special meanings link the harmonics. Strength and the Devil (8 and 15) both bear a relation to the Magician, card 1. The Lovers, 6, foreshadows Death, 13, for the ego dies "a little death" in sex, and in fact, people used to refer to orgasm as exactly that—dying. Card 20, Aeon, then goes beyond Death to indicate a rebirth (shown in traditional decks as the dead rising from their graves for the Last Judgement, and in the Haindl Tarot as a baby floating down to Earth in a cosmic egg).

We can also link the cards through "reducing" the numbers. The Devil is15, or 1 + 5 = 6, the Lovers. Therefore we can see a link between the Devil and the Lovers. The link is sexuality. Similarly, we call the Hermit a lunar card, partly because the Hermit is 9, and the Moon is 18.

People often try to connect the Major Arcana to some specific doctrine—Kabbalah, or alchemy or Tantra. It fits all of these because it does not really belong to any one concept or set of values. The trumps show us the story of the soul, as it confronts life, develops consciousness and ultimately finds mystic enlightenment.

The story begins with the Fool as the innocent. The 0 trump symbolizes an ideal state, a lost paradise. The first two numbered cards, the Magician and the High Priestess, depict the two poles of existence: male and female, light and dark, action and stillness, conscious and unconscious. This sets up the basic structure of the cards. In a way, we can describe all the other trumps as the means of bringing these two poles together. The baby of card 20 represents the new unified consciousness, while the final card, 21, shows the way this consciousness experiences the world.

This, then, is the great theme of the Major Arcana. The Haindl Tarot, like all others, acts out this ancient story. At the same time, it develops its own themes. They reach beyond the individual to the suffering and redemption of the Earth itself.

Haindl painted these cards "unconsciously." That is, he absorbed the ideas for each card, and the traditional images, and then he began painting, allowing himself to discover what emerged. He then refined each picture when it became clear what the card "wanted" to say. We might expect such a method to produce chaotic work. This is clearly not the case. These cards ar very organized, usually around a vertical structure or in terms of distance, with a central image in the foreground and then others farther back. This organization comes from several sources. The first was Haindl's experience and skill as a painter. Second, he had his own themes, which came through in the images. Just as important, the Major Arcana itself has such a strong message that the cards could be said to have guided him. Several times he chose images that seemed right to him, only to discover later that the images traditionally belong to the specific card. For instance, he painted the camel on the card of the High Priestess before he knew that the Hebrew letter for this card means camel. The same thing happened with the hand in the Wheel of Fortune.

The cards also contain a great deal of conscious design as well, especially in recurrent symbols. The use of color, of left and right, of diagonal lines, of aged rock, of rivers, of male and female, all these carry the ideas from one card to the next. The images are highly symbolic. The shape of the swan's wings on the Fool, the crystal on the Empress, the arrangement of feathers in Justice, all these convey particular meanings.

Haindl painted each card separately. When he looked at them as a group he discovered a clear development. If you have the Haindl Tarot at hand, lay out the trumps in a row, beginning with the Fool. Notice that card 11, in the middle, displays two balls, one above each of the scales. The scales themselves form half circles. In the next card, the Hanged Man, we see another half circle, in the shape of the Earth. This half circle appears at the bottom. At the end, card 21, we again see the Earth as a half circle, but now at the top of the picture. The number 21 is 12 backwards. In card 21 we see that great half circle but also a number of smaller circles. These balls are actually planets. Now look back at the Fool. There we see planets but also cosmic bubbles, symbols of spirituality and new life. On the High Priestess we see a great sphere of light. This sphere/bubble also represents the full Moon. Other smaller bubbles fill the air. We find a similar image in the Empress.

The Emperor holds a gold ball. The image has become solid, losing its cosmic meaning. For several cards we lose the image. It returns subtly in the Hermit, card 9, where we see him looking up to a half-circle of light. The bubbles return in card 10, filling the card as in the High Priestess. In card 11, as we saw, we find both whole circles and halves. The two halves, the two poles of existence, make a unity.

In card 12 we find the half-circle of the Earth, and then in card 13 the round eye of the peacock, with its rainbow colors, similar to God's eye in the Empress. In card 14 we find interlocking circles, as the poles begin to move together. In the Devil, 15, we find another half-circle, this time a dark hole at the bottom. On card 18 this changes to a circle of light at the top, a full circle in comparison with 9 ($9 \times 2 = 18$).

Card 19 traditionally shows a boy and girl holding hands. Here we see two circles, the Sun and the rose, symbolizing Sky and Earth. On card 20 we find the egg, and then in card 21 the Earth joins with the Sky by appearing above the dragon.

The images in this Major Arcana may appear radical to those

who know the traditional cards. They are radical, of course; Haindl has reimagined all the images. However, he has not done so with any desire to overthrow the past. Some cards contain subtle references to traditional symbols, as in the Grail emblems on the Magician. In describing the cards' meanings I have now and then referred to the older versions, for these cards grow out of the Tarot's ancient history.

We have mentioned that the Haindl Tarot contains its own story. This becomes clear in the explanations (as they became clear, I suspect, to Hermann Haindl himself, through working with the pictures). We can describe these themes briefly as a return to ancient wisdom and respect for nature, a need to renew the Earth as well as a need to restore the female principle to its true place—in daily life, in society and in the cosmos. The Empress shows us Woman as dynamic and creative, as Mother, but also as Thinker.

The story of the Haindl Tarot deals with the rejection of this figure. The Empress symbolizes the Great Mother, the Triple Goddess as source of life. The young Emperor denies Her, setting himself up as the sole power and authority. Historically, this represents the "new" patriarchal religions which conquered the much more ancient Goddess religions. Like a great many people today, Hermann Haindl sees our twin dangers—destruction of nature and the arms race—as connected to the masculine principle conquering and denying the feminine.

The Emperor shows us the God Odin, from Scandinavian mythology. We see him as young and arrogant. Later, Odin returns as the Hanged Man. He has become an old man, a figure of wisdom. And now he returns to the Earth. This is the great reversal. It overturns past mistakes and restores the balance. We then see this image of reversal echoed in the Star, where the woman bends forward; in Aeon, where the baby descends upside down (and remember that a baby has to emerge from the womb head first); and in the Universe, where we see the bottom half of the Earth. The movement of the cosmic bubbles described above tells the same story in abstract images.

With each card we find a Hebrew letter, a Rune and an astrological symbol. The Hebrew letter and the astrological connection have become traditional. We saw above how the twenty-two Hebrew letters match the twenty-two trumps. Similarly, modern astrologers describe ten "planets" and twelve signs. For each of these Haindl consulted previous decks and commentaries. The borders around the cards join them to the four medieval elements, Fire, Water, Air and Earth. This, too, connects with astrology, for each of the twelve signs belongs to a particular element. In extending this to the planets Hermann Haindl has made his own choices based on the qualities of the cards.

The use of the Runes is an innovation in the Haindl Tarot. He had several reasons for doing this. First of all, he wanted to show how the Tarot expresses various traditions. The teachings do not contradict each other but work together. A similar impulse led him to set his Court cards in different cultures. He also chose the Runes because they expressed a German esoteric tradition, native to his own people. Finally, Haindl wished to place the Runes alongside the Hebrew letters as a sign of hope for a reconciliation between Germans and Jews.

The Runes go back in Germany, Scandinavia and England to at least the early Middle Ages. They form an alphabet, actually several alphabets, for they varied from country to country. We can use them just like ordinary letters, to spell words (see the Runic spelling of TAROT on the Father of Cups). Unlike our modern alphabet, each letter carries a particular meaning. These meanings were quite literal, such as "Cattle" or "Property" or "Man." However, they also referred to symbolic and esoteric meanings. In this, they are exactly like the Hebrew letters, which mean such things as "ox" or "head" but also have esoteric, Kabbalistic meanings. More than the Hebrew letters, the Runes were used for divination. A Runemaster carved them on wood or stone, and when someone asked a question the master cast the Runes, similar to laying out Tarot cards. Since each Rune carried magical properties, people also used them for protection, or as charms, for love, strength, protection, money. People inscribed Runes on swords, or boats, or the frames of their houses.

The Rune connects us to the mythology and worship of Odin, known also as Wodan, the Father of the Gods in Germanic myth. According to the myth, Odin brought the Runes out from the dark well at the base of the World Tree. To do so he "sacrificed" himself, giving up an eye and hanging from the World Tree for nine days and nights. The poems do not tell us his position but we can assume that if he reached down to snatch the Runes from the well, he must have been hanging upside down. This moment in the story of Odin becomes a central myth as well for the Haindl Tarot. We see its traditional form in the Father of Cups. In the Hanged Man, however, we see Hermann Haindl's transformed version of the myth.

At one time a major feature of Northern European culture, the Runes faded from use and public interest until the beginning of the twentieth century. At that time Pan-Germanism had become popular, as well as an interest in the occult (including Tarot). In 1902 a writer named Guido von List had a kind of vision of the Runes. Following an ancient poem called the Havamal, in which Odin describes the Runes, von List developed an eighteen-Rune alphabet. The idea spread, and soon societies grew up to study and work with Runic lore and magic.

Along with its cultural interests, Pan-Germanism developed ultra-nationalist, racist and especially anti-Semitic doctrines. When the Nazis extended Pan-Germanism to such horrible proportions, they also adopted and corrupted the Runes, which by the 1930s had become very popular. Some of their most terrible groups and programs used Runes as symbols. In bringing the Runes into the Tarot Haindl has sought to help cleanse them of this corruption.

After the war, an esotericist named Karl Spiesberger sought to rehabilitate the Runes, following von List's eighteen-Rune alphabet but taking out any racist connotations. While Hermann did consult Spiesberger, he worked more closely with a contemporary system, that of his friend Zoltan Szabo, author of *Book of the Runes*.

Szabo, too, uses an alphabet, or "futhark," of eighteen letters. Haindl has assigned these in sequence to cards 1–18, the Magician to the Moon. For the other four cards, the Fool, the Sun, Aeon and the Universe, he consulted Spiesberger as well as the older alphabets. In following Szabo he discovered a close correlation of the Rune meanings with the meanings of the cards. The only place where he changed Szabo's order was for cards 8 and 11. Rune 8 appears on card 11, and Rune 11 on card 8. However, the cards themselves are switched around from their traditional order. Haindl switched them partly because of the meaning of the Hebrew letters for those cards. Therefore, we can say that Kabbalistically, Strength is 8 and Justice 11, while for the Runes Strength remains 11 and Justice 8.

In my own interpretations for the Runes I have followed a number of books which go back to the medieval literal meanings for each of the letters. To this I have added Haindl's comments on the Runes, derived partly from Szabo and partly from his own observations. The Runes are a vast subject, much of it still unexplored. Where I may have made mistakes or given a particular Rune a distorted interpretation, I apologize. As with all other aspects of the Haindl Tarot the Runes will inspire others to much deeper explanations than those I have described here.

Most people who work with these cards will wish to read them. For each trump I have outlined "Divinatory Meanings," the ways we interpret the card when it appears in a reading. These involve a certain shift in perspective. The images on the cards portray universal spirituality. For divination we need to see how they might describe moments in a person's life. The cards become more psychological, more personal. For example, card 21, the Universe, depicts the realization of a new consciousness and a restoration of the Earth. In readings, however, we say that this card means "success."

Many books on Tarot give only a few catchwords or a few simple sentences for each card's divinatory meaning. We have attempted to go a bit further, showing something of the complex ways the cards influence each other in actual readings. Other people will make fresh discoveries, not only in readings, but in the cards' esoteric meanings as well. This is part of the Tarot's power. Like genuine myths they will never yield a final, absolute interpretation. Hermann Haindl has created these pictures. Following his guidance I have interpreted them. Both of us hope and expect that each person who enters their world will find a fresh meaning.

0

THE FOOL

THE KABBALISTIC LETTER for the Fool is Aleph, the first letter of the Hebrew alphabet. Aleph means "Ox" or "Bull," a sacred animal in many parts of the world. By its curved horns the bull symbolizes the Moon, and so the bull became known as the male partner of the Moon Goddess (see the High Priestess and the Empress). The bull represents active life energy.

Unlike all modern letters, Aleph is actually silent, a carrier for vowel sounds. This means that it symbolizes the mystery of the spirit, which cannot be described in ordinary words. Aleph begins the Ten Commandments, whose first sentence reads, "I am the Lord, thy God." In Hebrew, "I am" is "Anokhi," beginning with Aleph. Thus, when God declares Himself to humanity, the first letter is silent, symbolizing that knowledge of God cannot be spoken in human terms.

The Rune for the Fool is Wynn, or W, meaning "Joy." The Fool is a child, rejoicing in life. To look at the world as the Fool means to delight in existence, to dance through the challenges of the trumps. The Rune also means to bind forces together, or to bind people into a community. The Fool, the Aleph, is the silent force that binds together all the varied experiences of the Major Arcana.

The Fool's astrological planet, Uranus, emphasizes the unexpected, the joy of surprise which moves the Fool through the different steps of life, forever daring to move on into the unknown. The white border around the card indicates that the element is Air. Usually Air means thought, but it also symbolizes Spirit.

Though the card is filled with symbols and ideas, the image is direct. We see in the foreground the Fool himself. He stands outside the border, as if he has not yet entered the world of the trumps, with all their challenges. He wears a multi-colored coat with one sleeve all brown. He also wears six bells. Behind the Fool and slightly above him we see the swan, and beyond that six planets in a night sky.

When we think of archetypes we tend to imagine stories, or

The Fool

dreams or encounters with mysterious old men or strange children.
In fact, we call an idea or an image an archetype because of its importance to daily life. We find archetypes not only in mythology but
in social and cultural institutions.

Countless myths and fairy tales present to us the image of the
Fool, someone innocent, who lacks education or worldly sophistica-
tion, yet ends up winning the treasure or the princess because of a
pure heart and an instinctive sense of what to do in every situation.
But virtually every society has made a place for real-life Fools as well.
The Haindl Tarot card of the Fool shows us a medieval court jester.
The jester's job required him to entertain, but it also allowed him
to criticize the powerful, to speak truths no one else would care to
express. Further, the jester's position as an outsider allowed him to
see truths that everyone else, in their fixed place in the social hierarchy, missed or avoided.

In our time we see the archetype in the television comedian.

While some rely on clichés or slapstick, others, surprisingly many, fulfill the archetype with observations on contemporary life and sharp attacks on the powerful.

The jester and the comedian represent one aspect of the Fool. In many cultures the archetype takes a more basic, perhaps more powerful, form, that of the sacred clown who breaks down all rules and social conventions. In medieval Europe the lord of the carnival, chosen for his foolishness, presided over a temporary disintegration of the rigid rules that governed society. In some Native American cultures the society of clowns deliberately broke the most fundamental laws, dancing naked, telling jokes during the solemn ceremonies, cross-gender dressing, even defecating in public. Through their bizarre behavior they reminded people that the rules and customs of society, even the holy rituals, merely form a set of conventions, like clothes we put on as we grow up. Reality remains underneath, strange and unknowable. In Hermann Haindl's card of the Fool, the court jester wears colors sacred to the Lakota of North America.

Maybe because we become more conventional, more rigid, as we get older, the Fool in fairy tales usually appears as a child. In the Haindl Tarot we see a young person, eyes wide with wonder at life, yet without emotion, for the Fool touches something deeper than ordinary feelings. We describe the Fool as "he" but the figure is neither male nor female. The Fool's innocence takes us beyond that most fundamental split, reminding us that masculine and feminine roles are cultural institutions.

The Fool launches us into the Major Arcana. Traditionally the Fool represents the child, the seeker about to journey through life, the soul as it incarnates into a body. The other twenty-one trumps then signify the various challenges of life, practical as well as spiritual. Like the child in fairy tales, the Fool moves from one task to the next, until he reaches the unification, the final *triumph* (trump) of the Universe.

The Fool bears the number zero. This sets him before and apart from all the other cards. It also symbolizes that intuition of the sacred clowns, that we are not any of the things we think we are. Reality can never be pinned down to any specific explanation or philosophy. Therefore it remains—nothing. Where the other Major cards, with their fixed places in the sequence one through twenty-one, represent particular states or stages of life, the Fool, zero, can become anything. In modern number systems we write zero in the shape of an egg, 0, indicating that all life, all experience emerges from an unknowable nothing. Originally zero was written as a point to signify the same idea. In Kabbalist tradition creation begins as a point of light from a Nothingness beyond all comprehension (see also the Sun). And in modern cosmology we can trace the universe back billions of years, almost to the precise instant of the Big Bang. But what existed before that moment?

The Fool symbolizes instinct and innocence, a sense that we contain within us something pure, something that reaches back before culture, before conditioning, before ego, even before personality. We think of ourselves as particular people, with character traits that make us different from everyone else. The Fool, with his blank expression, reminds us that something lies below all those visible characteristics, a universal life energy, beyond thought, beyond individuality, shared by all life.

In the fairy tales the older brothers or sisters plot and scheme. Their plans fail because life does not run according to their expectations. But the Fool plans—nothing. He or she does not know how to scheme. The Fool can only respond to life as it is.

The sacred clowns break all the rules in order to remind us that human beings made those rules, that reality remains something else. Culture is to humanity what personality is to individual humans— something constructed, yet something that becomes so ingrained we confuse it with the essence of life. We become so used to our images of ourselves that we think of all those character traits as the sum of our individual existence. Similarly with culture, we learn our cultural assumptions so deeply we consider them universal truths, refusing to believe that in other times and places people have believed differently. Personality and culture become like masks we wear over our faces. And since we never take them off—and everyone around us is wearing a similar mask—we consider them our true faces. But the Fool reminds us that we can never hold life to a set of rules. Life remains always something else. No specific thing. Nothing.

All this does not imply that we should think of the Fool as perfection. If the Fool represents freedom it also carries its own limitations. We cannot maintain such a state. In reality we cannot dance through the world, reacting purely on instinct. There are times when we need to plan, think ahead, even to scheme. And something else about the Fool. He can never know himself. This is his paradox.

Because the Fool is not separated from the world around him, he cannot step back and look at himself. Therefore we cannot stay with the Fool, but must travel through the different stages of the Major Arcana—through life—carrying the Fool inside us as the instinct that pushes us onward, the reminder that reality is always something different, yet learning, through each step, to become conscious of ourselves and the universe.

In virtually every culture we find a myth of the Fall. The human unconscious produces a story of some lost paradise, when no one died, no one suffered or quarreled, no one had to work or go hungry. Sometimes, as in Genesis, the Fall comes through disobeying the gods. In other, less moralistic cultures, a simple mistake loses paradise. Somebody goes to sleep at the wrong time, or drops something, or eats from the wrong basket. These stories reflect more than a complaint that life is too difficult. They spring from a sense that we have lost something true and perfect. Probably in reality no such perfect innocence ever existed. Most likely, human beings were always pretty much the same as now, bound to their egos, struggling with each other and with life. But if paradise never existed, that does not make the myth a lie, or a simple wish fantasy. The truth of the story does not lie so much in its picture of perfection as in the image of loss. We carry within us that intuition that life can be different, spontaneous, joyful, loving. To believe we have lost it allows us to hope we can get it back.

The Tarot goes beyond regret or nostalgia. It says that we *must* fall into consciousness and separation, so that the individual self can emerge. The Tarot teaches that we can travel through consciousness to a state where we become conscious of the Fool's unconscious energy. At the end of the Major Arcana, in the Universe, the yearning for innocence becomes transformed into wisdom.

In Hermann Haindl's card of the Fool the wounded swan represents the Fall. In many cultures the swan symbolizes purity and love. The Hindu creation gods, Brahma and Saraswati, rode upon swans. People have often linked the swan to the planet Venus, and thus to the Goddess of love (the Empress). More particularly, a wounded swan appears in the legend of the Holy Grail, a myth vital to the Tarot, for the symbols of the Minor suits*, Cups, Wands, Swords

---

*See Volume II.

and Disks are exactly the symbols connected to the Holy Grail. We see these symbols in the trump of the Magician.

In the Grail story the innocent hero, Parsifal, shoots a swan. Parsifal wounds the swan, but himself as well. He becomes conscious of suffering and so begins the quest that will result in the discovery of love and redemption.

The presentation of the Fool and the swan exemplify what I have called Hermann Haindl's "economy of symbolism." Let us look first at the card's structure. The picture appears in layers, the Fool himself in the foreground, behind him the swan, and farther back the stars and planets, some of which are obscured by clouds. If we take the Fool as ordinary reality then we see that beneath or behind daily life lies a level of animal desire. Now we tend to think of the animal in us as savage and cruel, but in fact, humans become most destructive when they separate themselves from the animal level of feeling. Nuclear bombs, concentration camps and the extinction of vast numbers of species (one an hour at the current rate) have all been done in a mood of cool rationality. So the Fool points to a wounded beast to remind us that we must heal that broken connection between ourselves and our animal existence, between ourselves and the world.

Western culture has long held the notion of animal instinct beneath our rational surface. Christian moralists have taught that we must overcome the animal, modern psychologists that we need to acknowledge it and ecologists that we must somehow embrace it. But the esotericists, and the mystics of all religions, speak of a further level of awareness, a direct connection between each being and the cosmos. Isolation is an illusion, for we are linked to every atom, to the most distant stars. And so, in the Fool, we see the swan behind the jester, but the heavens behind the swan.

Medieval theology described humanity as halfway between the angels and the beasts. Through rejecting passion and following "right reason" humans could move towards the angelic. The Tarot turns this around. We must discover and join with the animal in us in order to go through to cosmic awareness, for only by exploring hidden truths in ourselves can we find the truth in creation. Therefore, the animal lies between the human and the stars.

We can view the card vertically as well. At the bottom we see the green-brown mass representing the Earth. The swan rises from this shapeless area and in turn reaches above, to the sky. This movement follows the evolution of life and consciousness. The first creatures arose from the seas and the dirt. As animals evolved and became more complex, consciousness evolved as well, leading finally to that sense of unity with the heavens. This movement forms a circle, or a return, for the Earth itself emerged out of material thrown off by exploding stars.

We might also describe the vertical ascent as the development of individual awareness. We begin without any real sense of who we are. We do not separate ourselves from our parents or the world around us. And so we see a vague mass of color. As we mature we gain more of a sense of uniqueness. The sexual instinct plays a large part in this, showing us our own needs and leading us away from our parents. Therefore we see an animal sacred to the Goddess of love. But the animal is wounded, for we cannot fully understand love until we experience the reality of suffering.

The wound is vertical. It points upward (and downward) toward that universal knowledge. This symbolizes the double-sided quality of suffering. While it helps forge the individual personality it also links us to humanity (the Fool's finger touches the wound) and to the world, finally lifting us beyond individuality to a union with all life.

We see the connection between the wound and evolved consciousness in the swan's body. Though the neck twists in pain it forms a spiral curling into the sky. Consciousness does not "ascend" in a straight line, but spirals upward, like the whirling dances of the Sufi dervishes. The golden beak, however, does point almost straight up, a kind of arrow directing us to the stars and planets. The swan's left wing arches upward, creating both a frame for us to view the sky, and a kind of staircase, as if we could climb to heaven through the experiences of love and pain.

The Fool's costume, apparently the simple clothes of a jester, shows the same density of symbolism as the swan. The squares on the jacket symbolize the social function of the jester, to give a direction to the rulers of society. This is because in esoteric symbolism the square signifies the material world (the circle signifies the spiritual, and the circle is another way of writing zero).

The Fool wears six bells. We see six planets in the sky. This reminds us of the Greek myth of the music of the spheres, representing the harmony of existence. (The number six also connects us to the Lovers, card 6.) The Fool, in his aspect of the innocent, perceives this harmony, but only intuitively. Before he can grasp the truth he must "fall" into consciousness. Three bells line the crest of the Fool's hat. Haindl has said they signify the three crows of the rooster when Peter's human weakness led him to betray Jesus. Just as the swan indicates wounded nature, so Christ, the junction of the spiritual and the physical, redeemed the suffering world through his own pain. It also links the Fool to Parsifal, who became a figure of Christ in his search for the Holy Grail.

An unclothed hand emerges from the voluminous sleeve. In the Middle Ages and the Renaissance, European culture saw the awakening of individual consciousness out of the great dream of myth and theology. The value of personal experience, the worth and difference of each human being, the possibility of individual action and responsibility—these things have led to modern ideas, such as democracy and liberation. But as we have seen, they have also separated us from nature and led to the very edge of annihilation. And so that naked hand touches the wound in the breast of the swan.

The ecological dangers of our time probably derive in part from the Western belief in humanity as separate from, and even opposed, to nature. Our theology has taught us that God expects us to dominate nature, to use it for our own comfort and wealth. This attitude had led to the wonders of technology and medicine, giving vast numbers of human beings a far better life than ever before possible. It has also led to unchecked destruction, and the death of species as well as whole bodies of water and huge stretches of land. Many non-European cultures, such as the Lakota (Sioux), whose colors appear in the Fool's jacket, have seen themselves as vitally connected to the land and the plants and animals around them. We cannot turn our back on everything we have made in the last centuries; nor should we want to. Like the Fallen Fool, we must travel through the crisis, to bring together the achievements of individual consciousness and that sense of union with nature and the divine.

The brown hood and sleeve suggest the Christian monastic orders, with their vows of humility, their renunciation of wealth and power. More specifically, they connect the Fool to St. Francis of Assisi. Like a shaman or a Lakota visionary, St. Francis went out into the wilderness where he learned to speak to the animals. St. Francis could serve as a symbol for contemporary culture struggling to unite the concept of the individual with the older truth of harmony with the world around us. St. Francis was driven into the wilderness where necessity brought him to join with the animals. Necessity—the danger of disaster—has led modern women and men to the realization of ecological union with nature.

The Fool's mouth, a horizontal line, appears at the same height as the swan's vertical wound. Together they form a cross. The corners of the mouth turn down, symbolizing his Fall and his sadness at the wound in himself and in the world.

The image of talking with the beasts, and especially with the birds, forms a further archetype. Around the world we find stories of people learning "the language of the birds." Because birds fly they symbolize heaven and "higher" consciousness. The beasts of the Earth, on the other hand, symbolize the "lower" or unconscious levels. To speak with both joins human consciousness—for speech, language, is very much a human attribute—to all these levels. In the Haindl Tarot we see the union as well in the swan, whose feet vanish into the brown-green mass of the Earth and whose wing arches upward while its neck spirals among the planets.

Despite his link to St. Francis, the Fool does not actually speak. His mouth remains closed. We can look at this symbol in two ways. Language belongs to consciousness. Existing in a pre-conscious state, the Fool has not yet learned to speak. Through speech he will become more human. In the Parsifal legend, Parsifal encounters the Grail at an early stage but loses it because he does not say anything. The journey through the Major Arcana is a journey of learning to speak.

But we can also look at silence as a form of speech that reaches beyond words, beyond human language, to an instinctive communication with life. As a creation of cultures, words limit our understanding to the ideas embedded in whatever language we happen to speak. They also tend to limit us to a rational explanation of life. Silence, as an aspect of Nothing, contains the potential for all languages, plus an understanding of experiences and intuitions that cannot be expressed in any language. Remember the Aleph, the silent beginning of God's speech.

With his Rune of Joy, the Fool embraces all life, including suffering. He dances through experience, finding the secret joy in the heart of all existence.

DIVINATORY MEANINGS

When we encounter the Fool in a reading we look at how the complex ideas relate to a person's immediate situation. The Fool indicates a situation where planning ahead is not possible or not desirable and the person needs to react intuitively. Sometimes this means following a "foolish" impulse, such as quitting your job, or moving to another country, without any certainty of what comes next. Other people may point out the craziness of such plans. The Fool says to follow your instincts rather than someone else's wise advice or the norms of society.

More generally, the Fool indicates a time in life when a person needs to act impulsively, to follow her or his feelings. It advises us to leap into new experiences, to trust that things will work out in a good way. The Fool can signify a time of surprise, of wonder and excitement at life. If opportunities come, the Fool says to take them. Do it. Do not hesitate.

The Fool insists on acting on impulse. But the Fool is only one card. The meaning of a reading depends on all the cards taken together. If the outcome appears undesirable, and other cards, such as Temperance, suggest a more cautious approach, then the person might think again about following the Fool.

REVERSED

Reversed, the Fool indicates finding it hard to believe in your own instincts. The person may desire to do something but doubt the value of it, especially if it appears foolish, or others point out practical problems. The person may fear to step into the unknown. Alternatively, depending on the other cards, the reversed Fool may warn against recklessness.

I

THE MAGICIAN

THE NUMBER ONE traditionally symbolizes the male principle. This comes from the phallic shape, but also from the idea of masculinity as single-minded, direct, forceful. One signifies will-power and directed consciousness.

The Hebrew letter is Beth, which means "House." A human creation, a house, symbolizes culture, civilization, creativity. But a house can also isolate us from nature. Cities began as collections of houses. In the Tower we will see the image of the skyscraper as expressing a desire to separate from the Earth.

The Rune is Peoh, P. It means cattle, and by extension, property, wealth. Peoh was sacred to the God Frey, a Norse God of sexual potency and peace. Weapons were not permitted in Frey's temple. He received no sacrifices. Frey was a God of the Vanir, the original Gods of Scandinavia. The Vanir were overthrown by the Aesir and their chief, Odin. We will look more closely at this change in the Emperor.

Peoh signifies cosmic fire, the male principle of creative force. In Norse myth the world begins witih fire melting ice. It will end in the fiery destruction of Ragnarok (see Aeon and the Universe).

The German for Peoh is *Pa*. Haindl has discovered various word plays with this syllable. Pa is father, *fa-che*, German for torch, *fa-cere* (doing, thus action) and pha-llus for maleness.

The astrological planet for the Magician is Mercury. Mercury was the God of magicians, but also healers, writers, swindlers and thieves. In other words, Mercury represents mental and magical power. In his Egyptian form, Thoth, he invented writing as well as magic, supposedly giving his Book of Thoth to the first Egyptian magicians. One of the first modern occultists to work with the Tarot, Antoine Court de Gebelin, believed the Major Arcana was the Book of Thoth itself. Aleister Crowley used the name as the title for his own set of Tarot cards, painted by Lady Frieda Harris.

The Magician

When the Romans encountered the Germanic tribes they interpreted Wodan (Odin) as their own Mercury. Thus, the Magician signifies both Frey and the more aggressive God who overthrew him.

In the Middle Ages Mercury became the patron of esotericism. The magical tradition in Europe bears the name "Hermeticism," after a legendary magician named Hermes Trismegistus, "Hermes Thrice Great." But Hermes is the Greek name for Mercury, so that Hermes Trismegistus is the God in human form and the book he was said to have given his followers was the Book of Thoth.

The element for the card is Air. The Magician represents the creative power of intellect.

We see in this card various axes crossing each other. A vertical axis runs from the four symbols at the bottom to the face of the

Magician above them, and a dark shapeless face rising from the Magician's forehead. The spear and the sword create diagonal axes as they crisscross each other. The symbols represent the four suits of the Minor Arcana* and the four elements, Fire, Water, Air, Earth.

The symbols are also ritual objects for the Holy Grail. In traditional versions of this card the four lie on a table before the Magician. Here they occupy the forefront of the card, and instead of lying apart they join together, the male sword and spear penetrating the female stone and cup.

To the left of the Magician we see a field of crystals, and above that the Sun. To the right we see a group of eyes set in a nighttime sky. Above them shines a crescent Moon.

The occultist sees the universe as built upon polarities. These include light and dark, conscious awareness and unconscious energy, intellect and instinct, action and stillness, the positive and negative poles of electromagnetism, and of course, male and female. The occult description is actually more complex, for it recognizes as well the trinity of body, mind and spirit, as well as the fact that forms of matter, such as stars and one-celled organisms, lack sexual polarity. More important, the poles are ideal abstractions. In reality they never exist separately, but join together, with one side more dominant than the other. The day is never entirely light, and the night is never entirely dark.

The Fool bore an androgynous quality. But the Fool exists outside normal experience, in a kind of perfect innocence. When we "fall" into the ordinary world, we need to deal with the opposites and contradictions of life. And so, the numbered cards of the Major Arcana begin with the Magician and the High Priestess.

Traditionally, the Magician signifies light and consciousness, the ability to analyze and create, while the High Priestess represents darkness, the unconscious with its sense of wholeness and mystery. When we look at the Haindl cards we see a more subtle blending. For while the High Priestess shows a night scene, the card is filled with light. And even though the Magician's face is radiant, and we see a field of white crystals, the card carries a dark brooding quality.

---

*See Volume II.

This suggests that the Magician, the creator, must struggle with the dark mass of matter in order to release the light hidden within it.

In the early days of Christianity the Gnostics (the word "Gnosis" means "knowledge") formed an esoteric alternative to conventional Christianity. Though the official church stamped out organized Gnosticism, the Gnostic ideas remained as an underground influence on such later teachings as Kabbalah and the Hermetic tradition in Europe.

The Gnostics taught that God, and all existence in its true state, consisted of pure light. This light became broken up and trapped in the gross darkness of the physical universe. Gnosis consists of recognizing the truth and attempting to release the light so it can return to God. And so we see in the left-hand corner of the Magician, a formless mass of dark brown changing to green, while from the Magician's forehead emerges a dark lumpy face, as if the light could sink back into being trapped in the material world.

What must we make of this strange figure arising from the Magician's head? The Magician wears a tiara, symbol of the crowning power of the intellect. As the principle of light and creation, the Magician represents thought, while the High Priestess represents intuition. But out of this mental crown we see the dark figure, as if the Magician has not integrated his own darker emotions with his intellect. His ideas can become distorted, he can lose his ability to perceive the pure forms of existence, here symbolized by the field of crystals radiating from the Magician's left eye. Notice that the dark face looks the other way. The Magician can fall from the truth, perhaps through temptation, such as a desire for power over knowledge, or through the distractions of physical needs, such as sexuality, which he may think he has left behind or overcome.

The lumpen face bears a scarred hole, as if something were torn from its forehead. When the archangel Lucifer fell he lost the emerald that had blazed light from his face into the heavens. The name Lucifer means "light-bringer" and his fall symbolizes the Gnostic myth of creation as an imprisonment. The light existed as a pure force, an archangel, but when it entered into the physical world it became buried, and the beautiful Lucifer devolved into the shapeless lump we see in the card. In the figure's sad, downward-looking eyes we see the sense of loss as well as the confusion that results from being separated from the truth.

Apart from the rituals and the complex theories, what does the Hermetic magician try to do, and why? Human beings possess a desire for joy, a desire to transcend the problems of life. But the world resists our efforts with the sluggishness of a great mound of dirt pushed at by a small child. We find ourselves hungry, weak, prey to sickness, loneliness and death. Our efforts to join with others become misunderstood, and no one seems to understand us, or recognize the truth about us. More subtly, we find we cannot know ourselves, for that most basic knowledge remains locked in the unconscious.

Like a scientist, a magician seeks to become a master of the physical universe. The four objects in the front of the card symbolize the elements of creation. They are also the tools used in magical rituals. Many magicians, like many scientists, seek power for its own sake. In orthodox Christian mythology non-Gnostic Lucifer fell because his lust for power caused him to rebel against God. But the true magician, like the true scientist, works to master the world simply because the world is what's there. The magician seeks truth—an awareness of the inner nature of reality, a confrontation with the self, and finally a re-union with the divine presence that lives hidden within all existence. Think again about Lucifer's fall. How could he have rebelled against God if he had recognized himself as a part of the divine? So the Fall (the great mistake) is not just the desire for power, but rather the separation of the ego from the rest of existence. Therefore, the magician seeks to overcome the illusion of isolation.

Like the court jester (or modern comedian) with the Fool, the ritual magician is a person acting out an archetype. The archetype appears in the card as a wise old man. We can think of him as Merlin, master of wisdom, King Arthur's teacher, counselor to the knights seeking the Holy Grail (such as Parsifal, the Fool). The Grail itself appears as the cup in the front of the card.

At the end of his story Merlin allows the sorceress Nimue to imprison him—some say in a cave, some say in the heart of a tree. Either way, we can see this as the light imprisoned in matter. A master of prophecy, Merlin knew this would happen. Yet his lust for Nimue made him powerless to stop her. The intellect alone cannot deal with life. If we separate thought from unconscious desire then we may discover all our knowledge useless.

If Merlin's weakness seems strange, the experience with Tarot readings may show the truth of it. Very often a reading will indicate that a person's current course of action is leading to some unpleasant outcome. The reading will outline this explicitly, so that the person can understand and agree with what's said. And yet, most people will continue in the same direction. Desire overpowers knowledge.

The Magician seeks to become master of his destiny. But he cannot do this simply by willpower or intellect. Instead, he needs to raise up the unconscious, become conscious of its power and transform it into liberating energy. The Gnostic methods involved sexual magic (possibly influenced by Tantra, an esoteric branch of Hinduism), and their teachings included the idea that rebirth into heaven demanded a psychological merging of male and female. We will look at these ideas again in the Empress and the Lovers.

So far, we have viewed Merlin's story as an allegory of thought (light) imprisoned in matter (darkness). But there is another, perhaps older, interpretation, one that returns us to the Fool's theme of harmony with nature. Imprisoned in a cave—a cave symbolizes the womb of Mother Earth. Imprisoned in a tree—in the pre-Christian religions of Europe trees were worshipped. Some, such as the oak, were seen as symbols of male potency and creative force, yet these masculine trees "belonged" to the Great Goddess of the Moon and the Earth.

The Grail objects of the Magician derive originally from Celtic mythology. So do the stories of King Arthur and Merlin. In his famous book *The White Goddess* Robert Graves described how the ancient Celts in Britain practiced a system of magic—and a philosophy and a poetics—based on trees. Not only did the trees represent the life force, they also formed a language which the magician learned in order to compose poems to the Goddess. Thus we see a vital connection between thought—for poetry means speech, and speech, remember, comes from the intellect—and nature. Merlin's "imprisonment" by a woman becomes a distortion of a deeper allegory. Nimue symbolizes the Goddess as well as physical existence, and Merlin submits to her, indeed becomes joined to her in the form of a tree. In the card, the Magician's face appears gnarled, almost like the bark of a tree. And if we look again at the dark face above him we will see that it indeed metamorphoses into a tree trunk.

When we first glance at the crystals on the left side of the card they suggest intellect released from the physical world, for they appear cool and abstract. Yet many contemporary people have begun to explore the ancient healing power of crystals, while among some Native Americans crystals were known as the "brain cells of Mother Earth."

Notice that the dark face separates the Sun and Moon, the day and night. These stand for all the polarities described above, light and dark, male and female, etc. For the Fool to become a true Magician he must overcome this false polarity, created when intellect separates from nature. Eyes appear in the dark below the Moon. Perhaps they symbolize instinctive knowledge, and a yearning for truth and release, for they look up toward the blocked sun.

The four Grail symbols dominate the card. The lance and the sword create diagonal movement, one upward, the other down. Crossed, they also form two triangles, one pointing down, the other up, meeting at the apexes. We will see, in the card of the Lovers, that the two triangles signify matter and spirit, the Earth and the sky, female and male. At the same time the lance and the sword form phallic symbols and therefore signify the masculine principle, while the cup and the stone disk represent the feminine. In each pair the two symbols have interpenetrated, again showing the necessity of union. King Arthur, Merlin's protegé and successor, proved his mystic right to rule by drawing a sword out of a stone.

In Christian legend the Holy Grail was the cup used to collect Christ's blood as he suffered on the cross. In older versions of the Grail story, however, the Grail was a stone rather than a cup. In Wolfram von Eschenbach's poem the Grail is a green stone— perhaps Lucifer's lost emerald. In later centuries it came to symbolize the presence of the Holy Spirit giving life to the world of matter. Christians saw the lance as the spear that wounded Christ in the side. In the card the spear's fiery tip (Peoh as creative fire) can also indicate blood. And so we return to the Fool's theme of wounded nature.

Many people believe that the cup and the spear go back before Christianity, that the cup symbolizes the Goddess and her gift of life pouring onto the world, while the spear symbolizes her male consort. We can say the same for the sword and stone.

The four symbols form some of the tools used by the Hermetic magician, with a wand substituted for the lance, and a disk or pentacle for the stone. The four also stand for the suits of the Minor Arcana, and the four elements which make up the physical world. We find the four elements in the zodiac (four elements of three signs each) and the four-letter name of God in Hebrew, the Tetragrammaton, YHVH. This name can be spelled but not pronounced and so signifies the unknowable, that which cannot be reduced to words or explanations. At the same time tradition tells us that God used these four letters to create the physical universe. The sword of spirit penetrates the stone disk of matter.

In many Grail stories a woman appears carrying the cup on a disk, while others carry a sword and a lance. We have already seen that the appearance requires a response and that Parsifal failed by keeping silent. We cannot expect that we will automatically move through the different steps of the Major Arcana to evolved consciousness. We must make an effort. On a more mundane level, the problems of the ordinary world will not simply go away. We must not hold ourselves back like Parsifal, but commit ourselves to life. By doing so we will find that life responds and we will learn to recognize the divine spirit that lives within nature and our daily existence as much as within the exalted realms of the Magician.

DIVINATORY MEANINGS

The Magician is a card of power. For both men and women it signifies feeling strong, in control of your life. This does not mean rigidity or "control" as repression. Rather, it means the power to direct your life in positive ways. Magical power means transforming old situations and bringing new ones into existence. If a person has gone through a stagnant period in which nothing seems to happen, the Magician in a reading will point to a burst of energy and the ability to make things happen.

The Magician signifies creativity. Artists instinctively look upon the card as their "patron." In fact, in the twentieth century, many artists and performers have deliberately investigated Kabbalah, Hermeticism, and other disciplines involving magic. They have understood that art and magic share an underlying experience—that of a spiritual energy literally flowing through the body. Musicians, writers and others often say that they do not create their works. A force works through them to bring the work into the world.

This creativity is not just for artists. The Magician tells a person that he or she can begin new projects or develop things already started. The card signifies imagination, the ability to take a fresh approach to problems, to come up with new ideas.

The Magician is a card of focused will. It shows someone persuasive, dynamic, able to excite others and bring them along on her or his projects and ideas. The Magician overcomes resistance in other people, but also in himself. The magical power transforms situations. It breaks down obstacles.

The Magician is a card of wisdom. Merlin's power came partly from his understanding of people and events. But it is also a card of service to others. Merlin was strong when he used his magic for the sake of Arthur and the kingdom. When he cared only about himself—when he gave up his duty for Nimue—his power vanished and he became trapped.

REVERSED

The Magician reversed indicates a block to the natural expression of a person's energy. This may happen if outside resistance stops the person from realizing his or her potential. The reversed card may also show an inner resistance. The powerful Magician energy requires openness, and if the person carries repressed fear or emotional pain, these may close off the flow of creative force. The trapped energy may show itself as physical troubles, or depression or anxiety. Notice that the repressed material itself does not cause the trouble, but rather prevents the Magician archetype from its natural expression. At another time old fears or long-buried pain might not disturb the person in the same way. Just because the Magician shows a time of power, that power needs to flow openly.

Alternatively, the reversed Magician can signify arrogance, or the misuse of personal power to dominate others. The person has the magical power to overcome resistance. However, he or she lacks the wisdom to use it for a good purpose.

II

THE HIGH PRIESTESS

IN OCCULT TRADITION the number two signifies the female principle. Just as one is phallic, so two, or II, suggests the vaginal lips.

The Hebrew letter for this card, Gimel, means "Camel," the animal we see crouched at the woman's legs. A symbol for timelessness and patience, the camel, which carries its own liquid as it crosses the desert, links the elements Water and Earth. But this camel is filled with light, radiating upward, reminding us of truth found in animal instincts. The camel looks away, into the past. The images and myths implied in this card belong to humanity's most ancient memories.

The Rune, Ur, or U, means either "Aurochs," a prehistoric European bison, or else "Rain," an image seen in the card. As the bison, the Rune connects to the Norse creation myth of a primordial cow which licked a block of icy salt into the shape of Buri, an androgynous being (like the Fool). The Rune therefore symbolizes the patterning power in the universe, giving form to basic energy.

The modern word Ur means "before all," the original pattern. The ur-mutter is the Great Mother, source of life. The ancient Egyptian Goddess Nut is an ur-mother. She is usually pictured as arching over the Earth, her body forming a shape similar to the Rune (see also the Mother of Swords and the glyph for Leo, in Strength). Some other ur terms are ur-quell, the source of existence, and ur-licht, the first light at the beginning of the world. This is the light we see in the card.

The Rune also means the mythical lands of Ur, Thule or Avalon. An island, inaccessible to ordinary ships (everyday consciousness), Avalon was sacred to the Goddess, a place of everlasting life. When King Arthur lay wounded, after the Grail had left his kingdom, he instructed his servant to throw the king's sword into a lake. This action can symbolize surrendering the ego. As soon as the servant had done this, a boat appeared with three women to take Arthur to Avalon. We will see in a moment that the three women were one, the Triple Goddess of the Moon.

The High Priestess

The astrological planet for the High Priestess is the Moon. The element is Water. We will look at the associations for both of these.

Traditionally this card shows a female pope, or, in some modern decks, a priestess of Isis, the Great Goddess of Egypt. The Haindl Tarot presents us with an image of the Goddess herself, who manifests in the natural world as the Moon, the seas, the night and the Earth. We see her as a transfigured woman with a sphere floating before her. Though we associate the Goddess with darkness and mystery, light fills the card. It rises up from the camel crouched at her feet, it radiates from her palms, it pours down from a globe above her head. Along with light, water suffuses the scene. It fills the air with mist and bubbles. Her dress seems to pour down like rain on the camel and the dark land below. Rivers run in deep channels.

When we put the High Priestess together with the Magician, we develop a symbolic picture of the polarities of existence. The Magician signifies action, the High Priestess stillness and receptivity. A magician, after all, seeks to act upon the world, while a priestess is a figure of devotion and understanding. As number one the Magician signified unity and directed consciousness, while the number two suggests balance and therefore calm. The traditional High Priestess sits between two pillars, one dark, one light. We see this image subtly preserved in the Moon diadem over her forehead, with one horn bright and the other dark. We spoke of the number two as suggesting the vagina. The vagina opens to the dark of the womb, the mystery of creation. It receives the energizing sperm which awakens the eggs hidden inside (see also the astrological glyph for the Sun). The Bible tells us of "darkness on the face of the waters" until God sent down a beam of light. But the vagina also opens to allow the newborn child to emerge. The Goddess, the Mother, is not passive but creative. We will see this idea developed more fully in the Empress.

We should recognize that even though we speak of the Magician and the High Priestess as masculine and feminine principles, they apply both to women and men. The psyche knows no boundaries, not even male and female. At different times in his life a man will experience aspects of the High Priestess, while a woman may act with the creative force of the magician. In alchemy, and in many traditional Tarots, the perfected human is depicted as a hermaphrodite. "Hermaphrodite" means "Hermes-Aphrodite," a joining of the male god of intellect—the Magician, with the female god of emotion—Aphrodite (also known as Venus), the Empress.

The Magician signified the development of human awareness, the High Priestess represents the divine life principle (present in the Magician as the Holy Grail, a feminine symbol). Connected to this idea the Magician represents intellect, the ability to make distinctions. The High Priestess symbolizes the unconscious, formless, with all possibilities for future development. She gives us an intuition of unity beneath the wondrous forms of existence. Our single planet contains millions of separate species of plants and animals. Yet they all belong to the same ecological system.

The High Priestess takes us back to the pre-individual state, the feeling "I am a part of everything." Indeed, if we truly merge with the High Priestess we may lose the sense of "I" entirely. This represents a danger in the card, symbolized by the dark streams running between the clefts in the rock. Like the Fool, the High Priestess shows no emotion. Emotion, like thought, develops out of individuality (ego).

To many people the idea that people once worshipped the Moon, or that they believed in links between the Moon, the seas and individual women, seems extremely naive. But in fact, the realization of a single life principle in all these things forms one of humanity's greatest achievements. The seas surge and fall back under the gravitational pull of the Moon (and of the Sun as well, but the Moon is much closer and so more powerful). The average menstrual cycle runs about the same length as a lunar cycle. When a woman is pregnant the fetus floats in water, which "breaks," like rain falling, at the start of birth. Life originated in the seas. Some scientists believe that life started when lightning—the masculine principle of sky and fire—struck the waters and quickened certain molecules into proto-organisms.

The Moon passes through three distinct phases, new, full and old. The female body passes through three phases as well; childhood, which ends with the onset of menstruation; the fertile period; and the post-menopause, when she can no longer bear children. Men have pre- and post-fertile phases as well, but not so clearly marked as with women. Moreover, when a woman becomes pregnant her belly takes on the shape of the full Moon. Is it any wonder that people have depicted the Moon as a unity of three Goddesses, a maiden, a mother and a crone?

Many modern people can acknowledge all these correlations. They may even believe that the Moon's gravity somehow "scientifically" affects a woman's childbearing potential. But the ancient peoples saw it differently. They looked on the Moon, the seas and women as all the same thing, a mystery of life which they worshipped through Moon rituals and statues of pregnant Goddesses.

In the Haindl Tarot we see the three phases of the Moon subtly brought together. The maiden appears in the woman's face, the full Moon in the sphere, and the crone in the dark waters at the bottom of the card, as well as in the dark horn of the diadem.

The astrological symbol for the High Priestess is the Moon. The element is water. We have seen the connection between these two in the tides. But water—formless, yet surging with energy, continually shifting, impossible to cut or break into pieces, impossible to grasp yet able to overwhelm, never the same from one moment to the next, with no fixed surface yet with hidden mystery—water represents the unconscious.

The unconscious is energy. If we try to separate ourselves from it we become arid of feeling. So the life-giving rain pours down from the woman's hair and dress. Feeling connects ideas to experience, the ego to the outside world and to inner truth. Therefore, the mist and the bubbles blur the distinction between air (intellect) and the land (the "real" world). But the unconscious is dark and even dangerous. At the bottom we see the blue-black streams flowing through clefts like cliffsides. Mythologically this water symbolizes the River Styx, which souls crossed from the world of the living to the land of the dead.

Some people become very drawn to the stillness and mystery symbolized by the High Priestess. They withdraw from others, they enter deeply into meditation or some similar discipline, they avoid any involvement with the world. The High Priestess has seduced them, and as they lean too far over the cliffs, trying to see into the water, they run the danger of falling into that river which obliterates personality. The Tarot teaches us of the necessity to balance the High Priestess with the Magician, and vice versa.

We have spoken of the Goddess as the Moon and water, but the Earth belongs to the Great Mother as well. Agriculture depends on the Earth's giving birth each Spring to the young plants. The cycle of growth links the Earth and the Moon. The new Moon symbolizes the Spring. We see the full Moon in Summer, and the old in the harvest. Winter connects to the dark period when the Moon has died. And since women and female animals give birth (out of the dark waters of the womb), we see why people have always viewed the Earth as female. And so the cycle of the Moon, the seas, women and the Earth becomes complete. In the Tarot we see the Goddess as Mother and Earth most fully in the following card, the Empress. The High Priestess symbolizes the "virginal," withdrawn aspect.

The camel sits below the woman's root chakra. The chakras form the body's centers of energy, the root being the base of the spine. The "kundalini," or life energy, lies coiled, like a snake (or a crouching camel) at the root. Through yoga, meditation or some other discipline, we uncoil the kundalini snake (see the Empress) and move it up the spine, through the chakras. The pineal gland chakra, traditionally pictured as a third eye, functions as the seat of revelation. When the kundalini reaches the pineal level we experience the light of truth, as if the third eye has opened. The final chakra, the crown of the head, connects us to that divine oneness sought by the Magician. In the card we see the Moon diadem, with its polarity, over the third eye. When the eye opens the opposites become united. Above her, at the crown, we see the glow of cosmic energy, the source of the light coming from the camel. The stigmata of light in the High Priestess's palms do not signify suffering, like the holes in Christ's hands. Rather, they show the life-giving energy within the unconscious. We describe the unconscious as dark, because it is hidden from us, a mystery. And we gain a sense of it through stillness and darkness, for the clear light of day brings us back to the outside world. But if we enter that unknown world we will discover the dark unconscious blossoming into infinite light.

The great sphere floats before the woman, joining the camel to the higher chakras, uniting heaven and Earth, showing us the possibility of perfection through bringing together the varied elements of existence. If we meditate with this card or look at it a long time, the sphere seems to be gently turning. Traditionally the second trump shows us an image of stillness, for the kundalini remains coiled. We still see that stillness in the card, with its fairly strict vertical axis, its motionless woman and crouching camel (compare it to the dynamic movement of the Magician, with its diagonal axes). But the unconscious, and life itself, can never remain motionless. Slowly, almost majestically, the sphere turns.

DIVINATORY MEANINGS

The High Priestess signifies a time when the person needs to be quiet, to look inward. This does not mean barricading yourself in your house and refusing to speak to anyone. Instead, it means to take life slowly, to spend time alone, not distracting yourself with television or other entertainment, but keeping still, feeling a sense of returning to who you are. For someone who has been very active, in business or social life, the High Priestess says to step back, look inward for awhile. Instead of trying to conquer the world, seek peace with yourself. Under the influence of the High Priestess, patience and calm are more important than action.

During a time of the High Priestess the person finds a sense of wholeness in life. She or he does not try to separate existence into pieces. It is a time for intuition rather than analysis, for feeling rather than thought (for a contrast see Justice). The person may experience deep feelings which she or he cannot put into words. More important, perhaps, the person will not want to put these feelings into words. The High Priestess advises resisting any demands to "explain yourself." The person needs time.

For people with commitments, to business or children or other demands, withdrawal may be difficult. Often, if the person receives the High Priestess and the reader explains it, the person will say, "That sounds great, but I can't right now. I'm too busy." But is this really true? Often, at least part of a person's busyness is habit. If there's work to be done the person must do it, but afterwards, instead of going out, or scheduling something else, the person might spend some time alone. Even in a frantic day of errands the person can try to develop a distance, an inner calm. Sometimes, when people say, "It sounds great," they do not really mean it. The idea of doing nothing, of letting the inner life awaken, frightens them. But the High Priestess is a card of peace and joy.

One way to join with the High Priestess is through meditation. Just as the Magician is the patron of ritual magicians, so the High Priestess rules meditation.

As a virgin, the High Priestess does not indicate a time for romance or passion. If a person is asking about a lover and the High Priestess appears, then it says that the lover (or the subject of the reading) needs time alone or is avoiding a commitment.

REVERSED

The High Priestess reversed indicates a time when the person should not withdraw from the outside world. It is a time for action, for involvements with other people. In connection with romance the High Priestess reversed may suggest commitment, especially if it appears with the Lovers. In work, the reversed card advises taking the initiative, especially with the Fool or the Chariot.

Depending on the other cards the reversed trump may suggest that the person is finding it difficult to be alone or to slow down. This may come from other people making demands on the person, or because the person is afraid. The High Priestess can lead to self-knowledge, and for many people this is a disturbing possibility.

III

THE EMPRESS

THE NUMBER THREE is the sum of one and two, the basic poles of existence. Three therefore symbolizes nature, which is formed by the two poles acting together. Three also signifies birth and motherhood, for a baby is the "sum" of its parents' genes mixed together. And of course three is the number of the Triple Goddess.

The Kabbalistic letter for card three, the Empress, is Daleth, which means "Door." The Rune is "Thorn," Th, which relates to thunder and the Norse God Thor, as well as the thorns protecting a rose bush (see the rose in the Lovers, and the Sun). It also, however, means door. We see this union of the two symbolic systems, the Hebrew letter and the Rune, in the door on the lower left, opening to a room filled with light.

Thorn is a Rune of eternal return. The "return" of the Goddess forms one of the major events of our time. As a thornbush the Rune recalls the story of "Dornroselen" or "Thorn of Roses," known in English as Sleeping Beauty.

There is another Rune present in this card, that of Hagall, in the form of the crystal above the woman's head. As the Rune belonging to the Chariot, Hagall links the two cards, showing that the Empress is a triumph of the human will as well as a symbol of mother love and sexuality. Hagall means "Hailstone." A hailstone is a frozen crystal, water frozen into a fixed shape. Hagall was said to contain the primal pattern of life in the universe. In the cold wintry climate of northern Germany and Scandinavia life begins again each spring, when the ice thaws and the snow and hail change to rain.

The planet for the Empress is Venus, Goddess of love. The Empress stands, however, on a Moon crescent, which in turn floats on the water. The Moon links the Empress to the High Priestess.

Despite the dominance of water in this card, the element is Earth. This shows up the difference with the High Priestess, whose element is water. Where trump 2 symbolized the unlimited potential of life and the unconscious, the Empress indicates the life force,

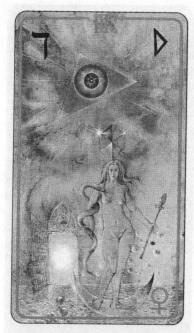

The Empress

manifesting itself in the "real" world of nature, motherhood, sexual desire and finally, individual consciousness.

Unlike some other cards, the Empress is not organized around axes or levels. We see a single scene, though in two parts. Above, a bluish triangle radiates yellow beams of light. Inside the triangle we see concentric circles. Together they form an eye staring out at us.

Below the eye we see a woman, and behind her a doorway. The open door appears layered or ornamented, giving the appearance of fish scales. Above it rises an arch, suggesting a church. Within the arch, a red spot appears in a triangle of circles.

The woman stands on the crescent, which floats on the water. Her weight rests on one leg, a motif from Greek and Roman sculpture. The pose also recalls Botticelli's famous painting of Venus rising from the sea. Her left hand holds a golden scepter topped by a pine cone. In her right hand she holds a snake which wraps itself around her arm so that the snake's head comes over her shoulder to above her breasts. Around her head she wears a band of light, set with three emeralds—three for the trump number and for the Triple Goddess, green for the Earth. A golden bird flies toward the woman's ear, as if to bring her the word of heaven. The image links her with the Virgin Mary, for the Holy Ghost came to Jesus' mother in the form of a dove.

We have seen how the six-sided crystal above her head contains the Rune Hagall. The colors come from the Lakota nation of North America. Black refers to lightning which lights up the black night (this color links the hexagram to the Rune of thunder). White represents clear thought and purity. Red, the color of blood, symbolizes life, yellow the Sun, blue the sky, and green the Earth. Light shines on either side of the hexagram, though more strongly on the left, the side of intuition and wholeness. The six sides and colors link the card to the Lovers, a proper connection for the Goddess of Love. Six is also 2 × 3, a further connection to the High Priestess.

Dark spheres float out from the room and into the air. They symbolize potential creation. The light from the room radiates out to illuminate the spheres, the water and the crescent. The woman, however, shines with her own inner light, warm, yellowish like the Sun, like the beams radiating from the triangle above her head.

Traditionally the Empress signifies Venus—Aphrodite in Greece —goddess of love and passion. She symbolizes motherhood, for that, too, is a kind of passion. And we have seen that she represents nature, the physical universe formed by combining the polar opposites one and two (the Magician and the High Priestess) into three. The Haindl Empress represents all these attributes. Her voluptuous form suggests sexuality, her maturity indicates motherhood. The crystal, too, symbolizes motherhood, for Hagall, when enclosed in a hexagram, is called "the Mother of Runes." This is because we can form any Rune from either the lines or the sides of the hexagram. There are also hints of masculinity—the phallic scepter, and the snake, whose phallic yet curved and sinuous form symbolizes male and female mixed together.

But if the Empress here represents Venus, she is also Psyche, the lover of Eros, whom we will find in the following trump, the Emperor. In the Greek myth Psyche, a mortal woman, was so lovely that she angered Aphrodite, who, like the queen in Snow White, could not tolerate competition for the title of most beautiful. Aphrodite sent her son Eros to kill the maiden. Eros, however, fell in love with Psyche. Afraid to openly defy his mother he hid Psyche in a secret palace removed from the world. When Aphrodite discovered Psyche still lived she set her a series of tasks in order to prove herself worthy of loving a God. Partly with the help of a bird (birds are messengers between the Gods and humans—see the Hanged Man), Psyche survived these tests and became united with Eros.

Modern culture has adopted the name Psyche to represent the mind and soul united as the self (the Greek word "psyche" means "soul"). The character Psyche begins as a figure of desire (in modern terms, a "sex object"). Through the tests she discovers herself as a person. At the end, Zeus (king of the Gods) raises Psyche to the level of an immortal so that she can face Eros as an equal. The human will can triumph, but only if it is connected to love. Suffering and love bring Psyche to immortality.

The tale shows us the progression of awareness. We begin as simple physical beings, directed by desire. The hardships of the world push us to develop a sense of individual personality. But if we do not lose our connection to sexual energy, to love, we may come to discover that this same energy—the kundalini—can transform itself into divine revelation. The Empress's snake is the kundalini (see the High Priestess), asleep in the unconscious of every human being. But the kundalini is also the Goddess herself, Shakti, who is said to give life to her consort Shiva, God of yoga. Without Shakti's energy, we are told, Shiva would only lie unmoving, like stone. The kundalini is the Shakti energy in each of us. And so we learn that the Goddess is not a person, but divine energy, and that this energy lives in us as much as in Shiva. We gain glimpses of it in sexual arousal, and moments of religious intensity. But these are only glimpses, and in our state of ignorance we think of sex and religion as opposites. In normal experience they are simply two manifestations of the same energy. If we work with that energy, if we uncoil the Goddess's snake, then, like Psyche, we will discover our own immortality.

Water dominates this scene, as it did in the High Priestess, though here the rough water symbolizes the emotions more than the depths of the unconscious. We also see a symbol of mind—the crystal, and creative achievement—the room. Far from pure emotion, the Empress thinks, makes decisions and acts upon the world.

Our male-dominated culture describes men as thoughtful, women as intuitive. Men are said to create in art and science, while women create only in the passive sense of having babies grow in their bellies. Other cultures have recognized that the Goddess is creative in all ways, through giving birth and through intellect. Paula Gunn Allen writes of Thought Woman, the Goddess of the Keres Indians. Allen links her to Spider Woman,* the Mother of Stones in the Haindl Tarot. Thought Woman is described as the mother of the universe, which she has created from her mind. Thus the universe is a thought, a dream of the Goddess (see the Wheel of Fortune). In Keres culture, creative humans, whether female or male, receive the title "Mother." In the following card, the Emperor, we will look further at the question of creativity.

The room and the doorway symbolize culture, a creation of intellect. The churchlike arch represents religion, another human creation. The red dot (red is the color of life) indicates that religion becomes empty (the churches literally emptying out) when it detaches itself from love and people's physical needs and desires. Notice that the curves in the arch suggest the vulva.

The straight lines of the doorway symbolize the mind. Straight lines do not exist among plants and animals and rivers. Compare the door to the curved body of the Empress herself, symbol of the physical world. The fact that humans turn curved trees into straight boards, or build right angles on the round Earth, shows the human urge to abstraction. The doorway, therefore, represents philosophy.

We see a great light shining within the room. According to Jewish myth, when God ordered Moses to create the Ark of the Covenant, He sent a portion of His light to dwell within the Ark. God took on a physical presence in the world, like the Holy Grail of Celtic and Christian myth. This presence became known as the Shekinah. The Kabbalists took the idea of the Shekinah and changed it to a feminine aspect of God—the Empress. In the movement of the Tarot picture from background to foreground we can say that the light changes into the woman.

Straight lines do sometimes appear in nature, as the rays of light seen when the sun shines from behind a cloud. This is another reason why people sometimes associate geometry with divine intellect. Above the woman the light radiates from the triangle, the same shape as the Rune in the upper-right corner. The rays appear in groups of three, the number of the card. Though the eye within the triangle stares out at us, it also seems to draw us inward, through the

---

*See Volume II.

different layers of existence to the point of light within the dark center.

We have described the crystal as Hagall, the Rune that contains the framework of the world, the primal pattern of creation, and therefore, cosmic harmony. All these ideas suggest a similar image, the Kabbalistic Tree of Life, which takes the form of

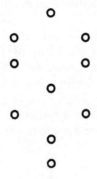

similar to the hexagram (see also the Lovers). The bottom circle, or Sephirah, symbolizes the physical world. And so the Empress stands beneath the crystal.

As the Mother of all the Runes, Hagall connects us to the God Odin, who first brought the Runes into the world. We find Odin in the Hermit—3 × 3, and the Hanged Man—4 × 3. The six sides of the hexagram suggest the Lovers, trump 6—2 × 3. The snake connects to the Devil—5 × 3, and the Universe Dragon—7 × 3, while the woman stands on the Moon—6 × 3. Finally, the crystal contains the colors of the Fool's jacket—0 × 3. In the Empress we find the entire range of the Major Arcana.

The snake, as we have seen, represents transformation and enlightenment. European culture, built on the Bible, sees snakes as evil. Part of this view comes from the desire of patriarchal religion to attack all aspects of Goddess worship, for around the world the snake was sacred to the Goddess. Snakes have symbolized rebirth, for the snake periodically sheds its skin. Also, the venom of some snakes, such as the cobra, can act as a hallucinogen, bringing people divine visions.

In trump 21 (2 + 1 = 3) we see the divine snake, the dragon. Dragons, too, are seen as evil. St. George's victory over the dragon can indicate consciousness triumphing over unconscious energy, civilization triumphing over nature. But why oppose these things? The battle with the dragon might also indicate a historical event: patriarchal power defeating the Goddess. In the Babylonian version of St. George, the hero, Marduk, kills the monster, Tiamat. The official religion described this victory as the beginning of creation. But Tiamat was Marduk's mother .

A culture that sees nature as an enemy will also see women as evil, or as passive "Earth mothers," dependent on men. Nature and intellect become opposed. Compare this to the Keres, where nature and intellect combine in the figure of Thought Woman. In the Haindl version of the Empress we see symbols of nature, sexuality, motherhood—but also decisiveness, intellectual creativity and power. In many ancient cultures the king derived his power from his service to the Great Mother. Haindl's words in describing this card and the next card form a key to the entire Tarot. "The Empress creates the Emperor."

DIVINATORY MEANINGS

The Empress signifies passion. It shows that this is a time in the person's life to experience the world with great feeling. The two prime ways for this feeling to express itself are through enjoyment of life, especially sexuality, and through mothering. Before looking at these in detail we should consider the link between the two. We tend to think of sex and motherhood as somehow opposed. But of course they belong together, for women cannot become mothers without sex. And yet, we tend to think of mothers, especially our own, as "pure," that is, sexless. This attitude may result partly from the child's possessiveness toward its mother, and infantile jealousy at the prospect of Mommy giving her body to someone else. Such patterns may stay with us as we become adults . But the sexless view of motherhood also comes from Christian culture, which presents the ideal of the mother as literally a virgin. Christianity splits women into two Marys—the Virgin, and Mary Magdalene, a whore.

The Empress reminds us that motherhood and sex belong together, not just because of biology, but because both represent fulfillment and maturity. Therefore, in readings the Empress signifies someone who is actively sexual, but in a responsible way. This contrasts with the Devil, where sexuality can become oppressive and disturbing. It also contrasts somewhat with the Lovers, which emphasizes a relationship. The Empress stresses the person's own sexual expression.

The Empress may apply to a man as much as to a woman. If so, it will show him expressing himself in a "feminine," yet powerful way. The Empress may also signify a passionate woman who is important to the subject of the reading.

The passions are not only sexual. The Empress also may show a love of nature, of growing things, of being outdoors, of all sorts of joyous activity. The Empress cares deeply for her friends as well as her lovers.

The Empress means motherhood. This may be literal, showing the importance of being a mother for the person. For fathers, it might imply acting in a more "motherly" way. The card may also signify the subject's own mother. Or the Empress may refer to mothering friends, or nurturing an idea.

More than most other decks, the Haindl Empress signifies creativity. She shows an ability to give birth to ideas, to bring things into the world. This aspect becomes stronger with other creative cards, such as the Magician.

REVERSED

The reversed Empress shows passion being blocked. The person finds it difficult to express herself or himself. The block may be sexual, or it may be emotional, saying that the person cannot express feelings easily. Or it may be creative.

The reversed Empress may indicate problems with the person's mother. The person may experience her mother as unloving, or distant. Or the person might feel distant from her own children at this time in her life. If the person feels guilty, the card may help her acknowledge that she needs this distance for now. The same can apply for resentment toward the person's own mother.

Rather than showing blocks, the reversed Empress may show that this is not the time for passion and involvement. The person may need to rest, to withdraw from others. This meaning becomes reinforced with the Hermit, or especially, the High Priestess.

IV

THE EMPEROR

THE EMPEROR BEARS the number four, traditionally seen as masculine. The Hebrew letter, Heh, means "Window." The Rune, Ansuz, or A, symbolizes the stag, the powerful horned beast who has always symbolized masculine power. Ansuz also symbolizes two sacred images which to some extent conflict with each other—the Horned King, consort of the Mother Goddess, and the Aesir, the young gods of Scandinavian mythology. Led by Odin, the Aesir conquered the older Vanir. Historically, this myth describes the patriarchal conquest of a culture focused on worshipping the Earth as Mother.

The Rune is also called Ansur, which means "Mouth." This implies speech and the invention of language. The Rune is sometimes drawn as a diamond, an image we find in the crystal. A diamond, with its four equal sides, symbolizes the rule of law. It also signifies stable structures. These qualities—language, law, stability, belong to the positive side of the Emperor as ruler of society.

The astrological sign for the Emperor is Aries, the ram, the first sign of the zodiac, the sign of spring, and therefore of vitality, new energy and sexual potency. Spring also suggests attractiveness, optimism and courage. All these qualities belong to the appealing side of the "young" masculine gods, the Aesir. However, the ram also symbolizes aggression, lack of subtlety, intolerance, dominance through force. The red border of the card indicates the Emperor's element, Fire. Fire, too, represents vitality, energy, but also aggression.

Looking at the picture we notice first of all how simple and naturalistic it appears in contrast with the abstract, highly symbolic images that came before it. The Emperor contains symbols, such as the crystal above his head; overall, however, we see the plain scene of a man standing in the forest. There are no vertical levels or varying worlds. We do see three layers, the man himself in the foreground, the great tree behind him and then the forest. In the

The Emperor

forest we see light, and green leaves, a suggestion of springtime. But the large tree appears dark, and very old, with a different kind of power than the young forest or the young man. Because he stands under the tree, the Emperor remains in the shadows, even though we see him stepping away from it.

The tree is Yggdrasil, the world tree of Scandinavian myth, with its roots deep in the mysterious origins of life, and its branches reaching up to the stars and beyond. Odin hung from this tree in order to receive the Runes (see the Hanged Man), but Yggdrasil is far older than the chief of the Aesir. It belongs to the Great Mother, the first principle of life. And yet, as we saw with the Magician, the tree also symbolizes the male, for the hard trunk is like the phallus, and the branches resemble the horns of the stag. Yggdrasil links Earth and sky, darkness and light. In the picture, Hermann Haindl has created a unity of the tree and the man, for the gnarled trunk and roots mirror the contours of the man's legs and feet. At the same time, if we look on the left of the tree we see that the roots become like the legs of an animal. This suggests an animal force in the Emperor.

Everything about the Emperor suggests youth and vitality. He stands powerfully, full of energy and health, ready to stride forward. The naturalistic image implies simplicity, a theme we see in the symbolism. He wears four jewels, red for fiery energy. In contrast with the Empress's hexagonal crystal of sacred colors (symbolizing all levels of existence) his four-sided crystal contains the colors of humanity: red, black, yellow, white. The rod of power contains no crossbar like the Empress's. Phallic, it suggests masculine energy, direct and forceful. His gold ball symbolizes the material world.

In many Tarot decks the Emperor card shows a traditional ruler. He represents society, laws, fixed structures. In their positive sense, these ideas are suggested in the Rune. However, human laws can take people away from nature. Originally, Hermann Haindl painted a picture of a shriveled old man sitting on a narrow throne and clutching the emblems of his power. He named him Amfortas, the injured ruler of the Wasteland in the Grail stories. For Haindl, Amfortas symbolized the repressions of a society ruled by masculine authority, rather than by the natural laws of nature. When Haindl looked again at the Empress he realized that she needed a more dynamic partner. And so, the picture changed, from the old king to the young god. However . . . .

The Emperor holds his rod in his right hand. He has received it from the left hand of the Empress. The left side gives subtlety and sensitivity, the right, logic and power. The angle at which he holds the rod, rising from lower right to upper left, introduces a motif we will see in the later cards, especially the Hanged Man, the card in which Odin reverses himself to rejoin with the Mother. Psychological tests have shown that when people view a picture with a diagonal from lower left to upper right (like the rod of the Empress in the previous trump), they experience a subtle sense of calm and well-being. But when the diagonal moves the other way, like the Emperor's rod, people experience agitation. The rod of the Empress roots itself on the left, the side of wholeness. The Emperor's rod roots itself in the right side of force and single-mindedness. And yet, looking at the pictures we see the Empress's rod in the right side and the Emperor's in the left side. In this way, the qualities merge together.

Inseparable from the card's vitality we find undertones of aggression and arrogance. The Emperor strides away from the tree, denying his origins in nature and the female. His feet overstep the border of the card. In this gesture we see that combination of dynamism and force. When we look at our culture's image of heroes—in movies and on television, in politics and war—we often see the same mixture of simplicity, singlemindedness, vitality, sexual potency, arrogance, self-assurance and aggression. Our conditioning teaches us to admire these qualities. Some women find themselves drawn to men who treat them badly, as if the lack of sensitivity, or even of kindness, increases the animal power.

In our discussion of the Empress we said that she "creates" the Emperor. The female principle comes before the male. The Emperor—the young patriarchal religion and society—denies this, claiming that creativity belongs to him alone. A great many people today believe that this denial has brought about our twin dangers of nuclear and ecological devastation. Therefore, in order to understand the Emperor, but also the history of our culture, we need to look more closely at Haindl's idea of the Empress creating the Emperor.

For millions of years life on Earth was single sex, reproducing by cell division, so that a mother divided into two daughters. The creation of sex difference—the entrance of the male principle—made greater variety possible through the combination of genes from mother and father. Yet the male derived originally from the female. In the early stages of growth all humans are female. A male fetus develops when the Y chromosome triggers changes after the first weeks of pregnancy.

This information comes from scientific research. Early human societies may not have known about one-celled organisms or fetal development, but they did recognize that all babies, human and animal, grew in their mothers, and that our first food comes from the mother's breast. For many thousands of years, therefore, religion centered on the power of the female to create life. The very earliest statues all represent mother figures, usually with large hips and powerful breasts. The earliest and little-known cave paintings show female figures dancing in groups. In its image of the Empress, the Haindl Tarot restores the picture of woman as wholly creative, culturally (with the complex door a symbol of art and science) as well as physically.

Patriarchal society denies the reality of this ancient female-centered religion. We learn in our schools that the statues represent "fertility cults," as if they concern only a narrow aspect of life. (In 1977, *National Geographic* magazine described a statue of the Great Goddess in Malta as the "headless 'fat lady.'") When we read of cave paintings, we rarely learn of the earliest ones, with dancing females. The ones commonly studied have male figures, often as hunters. Most significant, perhaps, we still tend to think of giving birth as somehow not "creative," but rather as cow-like. Creativity means poetry, painting, music, science—and these things, we learn from our histories, belong to men.

But the histories begin too soon. The evidence of archaeology suggests that women invented agriculture, women invented the first calendars (based on lunar and menstrual cycles) and women created the first art. Yet any popular book or television show about early "man" will always show men as the inventors of everything important. They will describe human culture as beginning with male hunters, as if the female food gatherers contributed nothing significant. And they will describe those hunters as praying to their "gods" when they more likely prayed to their Mother, the Earth.

This habit of denial comes from the "young gods," the patriarchal tribes who substituted their male-centered religion for the worship of the Goddess. In doing so, they attempted to wipe out all previous human experience, and to claim that creative power belongs to the male alone. The Bible insists that a male God created the universe out of nothing, and that this happened only 5,700 years ago. Many researchers believe that this period of some 5,000 years marks the beginning of patriarchal power.

When the Aesir conquered Scandinavia they, too, claimed ultimate creative power for their father god, Odin. Odin indeed embodies wisdom and mystery, with his discovery of the Runes. Yet even the Runes derive ultimately from the Mother. Our figure of the Emperor would deny this. He steps over the boundaries of the picture as if he would step out of history, as if the world began with him. He does not look back at the great Tree of Life.

In his arrogant denial of the source the Emperor can lose sight of the deeper levels of existence. The material universe becomes everything. Thus, while the naturalistic image of the card conveys its freshness, it also suggests the illusion that nothing exists but the so-called real world. The Hebrew letter Heh means "window." In the history of architecture windows derive from doors. The door of the Empress opened to the light of spiritual consciousness. In the card of the Emperor the tree appears something like a window, but it remains closed, dark.

Traditionally the number four, and the square, symbolize law, the physical universe, masculine authority. Esoteric symbolism pictures the square as the "opposite" of the circle, the image of spirit. The Emperor holds a sphere, but unlike the cosmic potential of the bubbles on trumps 2 and 3, his gold ball signifies only his domination of the world. As the Rheingold of German myth, it represents great power but also greed, and the desire for total control.

Patriarchal culture sets up written laws and rules. People become detached from a way of life that follows rhythms of nature. When patriarchal invaders overthrew cultures that worshipped the Great Mother, as in the Middle East, or the Celtic lands of Europe, or the American continents, they set up strict codes of law, describing the sexual worship of the Goddess (including love between women and love between men) as "crimes against nature." But the true crimes against nature are such things as pollution, mass extinctions of animals and plants, and genocide against such peoples as the many tribes living in the Amazon rain forest.

How can we return to the image of the Emperor as vital, alive, connected to the young forest, but also to the ancient Tree? We need to abandon the arrogant image of the all-powerful God the Father, and remember that other image of the male, as the lover and son of the Goddess. Remember that the Rune can mean "stag-king," the Horned God as modern witches call him, whose potent sexuality joins with the Mother to create life. For many people the forest in spring came from this union of the stag-king and the Earth. Such a change in the idea of masculinity does not deny the importance of fatherhood, or the love real fathers show for their children. On the contrary it brings fathers more into harmony with the physical world.

We saw how the Empress represents both Psyche and Aphrodite. As Eros, the Emperor signifies the Goddess's son as well as her lover. Eros, or Cupid, as the Romans called him, usually appears as a youth. At the same time he signifies the power of sexual love (the word "erotic" derives from Eros). This love surges most powerfully in the spring. And so we find ourselves with the young god—not the conqueror supplanting the Mother, but the irresistible image of desire, the joy of new life.

DIVINATORY MEANINGS

In most Tarots the Emperor will indicate the influence of society, of law and social structures. But these meanings derive from the old man sitting on his throne. By changing the image to the young god in the forest, the Haindl Tarot gives the card fresh meaning, that of vitality and energy. It can indicate a time of beginnings in a person's life, a resurgence of energy. These meanings will be especially valuable if the card comes after a time of illness or depression.

For women as well as men, the card may indicate sexual potency, being driven by desire, and at the same time irresistible to others. These meanings apply if the card represents the self. It may also represent someone else with these qualities. Some women will tend to look at this very masculine image as automatically signifying a lover—either a real person or a fantasy of someone attractive, physical, non-intellectual, someone simple and direct, with an overpowering animal energy. Though this image (or fantasy) may be important, women who get the Emperor should consider the possibility that the card refers to themselves—just as men should do with the Empress. One valuable aspect of Tarot readings is the opportunity they give us to see ourselves in different ways.

When the Emperor describes someone else, especially a lover, the person will appear irresistible. He (or she) may also be dangerous, for the Emperor follows his own desires, without sensitivity to others. Part of his appeal rests in his tremendous confidence. He knows his power and charm and doesn't hesitate to use them.

As a picture of yourself, the Emperor also carries certain dangers: arrogance, insensitivity, a habit of manipulating others through charm and magnetism. More subtly, the Emperor may signify a delusion. He may believe that everything depends on him. Just as the patriarchal conquerors tried to wipe out history, so the Emperor in a reading can indicate a desire to wipe out personal history. This may mean ignoring people who have helped you. It may also mean trying to ignore the experiences that have made you who you are. The card of Justice may appear, calling you to examine your life.

At its best the Emperor represents energy and desire.

REVERSED

On the most basic level any reversed card indicates a blocked possibility. When the Emperor is reversed, the person has the chance to experience that vitality or sexual energy, but somehow it is not happening. The other cards will show the problem.

Alternatively, the reversed Emperor will signify the development of sensitivity. The person may listen more to others. It may also indicate complexity, an awareness of the underlying causes of things.

To find the best interpretation you will have to look at the other cards, and finally, follow your intuition.

V

THE HIEROPHANT

THE HEBREW LETTER for the fifth trump is Vav, which means "Nail," a shape we can see in the form of the letter. A nail joins things together, and this introduces us to the card's theme of religious tradition, for tradition unites a culture. However, by its phallic shape, the nail also signifies a particularly masculine tradition.

The Rune belonging to this card, Radh, or R, means "Wheel." It represents ritual, an essential quality in any tradition. Ritual serves several functions. Firstly, it gives an outer form to religious teachings. Ritual takes concepts and spiritual insights and puts them into words for people to say and actions for them to perform. In the Jewish tradition represented by this card, one primary ritual consists of removing the Torah (the first five books of the Bible) and placing it on a special table for the reading of the Law. When the ritual occurs people experience a surge of spirituality in their emotions and bodies. Christian tradition centers even more on ritual, especially the communion, in which the bread and wine miraculously change into the body and blood of Christ.

Ritual also connects people to history. The circumcision of a Jewish boy and the baptism of Christian babies serve their spiritual purposes, but they also join people to the tradition. Ritual can also bind people to each other, forming a community. Again, we find this very much among the Jews, where a service requires ten men for a "minyan" or quorum. Someone alone, away from a synagogue, may pray privately, but proper prayer requires that minimal community of ten.

Finally, ritual carries people through crises. When someone dies, those mourners who do not follow any rituals or religious tradition often feel incomplete, or guilty, unable to leave the experience behind. Those who do mourn according to some ritual will feel they have done what needed to be done and can continue with their lives, carrying their memories with them.

54

The Hierophant

The astrological sign for card 5 is Taurus, and the element is Earth. Both of these indicate manifestation, that is, concrete reality. In most Tarots, this card connects with the High Priestess. Some decks call this card the High Priest. Older Tarots designate card 5 as the Pope, and card 2 as the Papess, or female Pope. Card 2 signifies the inner or secret truth, the mystery at the heart of religious experience. Card 5 signifies the concrete ways in which this mystery expresses itself in the world—in other words, religious tradition. In this sense, it does not actually matter whether the card refers to ordinary established religion, or to occult teachings (such as the Hierophant of Aleister Crowley). Either way, the image symbolizes specific teachings derived from the intuitive wisdom of the High Priestess ($2 \times 5 = 10$, the number of the Jewish minyan).

Taurus means bull, symbol of male power and sexuality. Yet we have seen how such animals actually "belonged" to the Goddess as her consorts, bringing her their seed to awaken her fertility—and her pleasure. In astrology Taurus is linked to the planet Venus. This connection tells us that despite the all-male appearance of patriarchal religion, it derives its life and reality from the Empress.

We see in this picture three generations of men. The grandfather fills most of the picture. To his right, entering the picture from outside, appears the father, in profile. At bottom, outside the border, but looking in, we see the back of a boy's head. He wears a skullcap. The three are in a room with a window overhead, and a window to the left. Haindl based this structure on his own studio, a converted four-hundred-year-old barn, where the top room is used for group ceremony and meditations.

Despite the dominance of the faces, they really occupy only the right half (or two-thirds) of the picture. The right side signifies the dominance of thought and intellect in the male tradition. However, they look toward a light which shines in the upper quarter of the card. This light symbolizes God, always a lord of light in the patriarchal tradition, whether Jewish, Christian, Islamic, Hindu or Buddhist. The light appears on the left, in the darkness, to indicate the unknowable truth of the divine. This sense, that God is beyond human comprehension, beyond the physical universe, forms one of the glories of Judaism. The light shines on a key below, which seems to hand in the air above the pages of an old book. The light also shines on the R Rune, and partly illuminates the three faces.

Traditionally, the Hierophant card shows a priest or a pope, sitting on a throne, with two disciples at his feet. The keys of the kingdom appear crossed, in the shape of an X, at the throne's bottom. The Haindl Tarot uses three figures, but a family rather than a strict hierarchy, emphasizing the idea of tradition as something passed through generations, rather than a formal Church. We see a single key, but with three prongs. The image of the crossed keys remains in the crossed thumbs of the old man as he raises his hands in prayer. This subtle image, another example of the economy of symbolism, indicates that idea of union, or joining together. By replacing St. Peter's keys it indicates as well that simple prayer can join us to God. Finally, it suggests the emphasis on community rather than hierarchy.

The cast of the faces, the skullcap and, more subtly, the book all indicate Judaism. Hermann Haindl changed the card from a specifically Christian image to a specifically Jewish one for several reasons. For one thing, as a German who served in World War II, he wished to honor the people so horribly persecuted by his own nation. We saw in the Introduction how similar thoughts led him to join the Runes to the Hebrew letters. He also chose Judaism for his card of tradition because he saw this card as representing the positive values of patriarchal religion; and Judaism, the "father" of both Christianity and Islam (but distinct from both of them), represents, in European history, the essential image of patriarchy.

The Emperor symbolized the arrogance of male religion. The Hierophant remains unbalanced, for we see no women; indeed, orthodox Judaism makes no place for women in its rituals (though women create the home). Nevertheless, the card shows a gentler image, one devoted to learning and prayer. The world thinks of Jewish culture as somehow dedicated to suffering. In fact, Judaism at its best gives us an image of life. Legend tells us that when the Romans besieged Jerusalem the chief rabbi had his disciples declare him dead so they could smuggle him out of the city in a coffin. Many cultures (including, perhaps, present-day Israel, which celebrates the mass suicide at Masada) would consider such an escape cowardly. But the rabbi knew that if he died his school would die with him. Death, however heroic, would have served no purpose. He needed to live in order to teach.

The book, and the keys before it, symbolize the Torah, the five books of Moses and the "key" to Jewish culture. The Taurean symbolism also suggests Moses, for a mistake in translating the Bible caused Christians to believe that Moses, and by extension all Jews, had horns, an idea shown in Michelangelo's statue of Moses. The Torah represents both the idea of a written tradition and a God-given law of human ethics, as summarized in the Ten Commandments. The book also symbolizes human culture and knowledge, for writing enables us to pass these things from one generation to the next. At the same time, there is a shadow side to written law, for it can become too rigid, separated from people's immediate experience, and especially from nature. The law becomes absolute.

We see this, perhaps, in the hard straight lines of the windows, and the fact that the windows show only the sky and not the land. A completely male tradition, following a written law, loses its connection to the Earth. Notice also that the line of sight, from the eye in profile, through the two eyes of the grandfather, to the light, to the crossbeams, follows the Emperor's line of power, from lower right to upper left. At the same time, the fact that the windows form several lines rather than one (like the rod of the Emperor) suggests the subtleties of Jewish thought, where even fundamentalists emphasize discussion and analysis.

We see in the picture three figures. Unlike the Christian trinity, with its Holy Ghost, they are all human, a symbol of Judaism's emphasis on ethics over mysticism. In the Bible, and in the rabbinic tradition, we read of people (such as Abraham) who argue with God, or even put God on trial, on behalf of suffering humanity. The ages of the three, boy, adult, old man, suggest a male version of the triple Goddess, maiden, mother, crone. But there is no suggestion here of a link to the Moon or the Earth.

The boy appears outside the border, looking in. Though circumcision binds an infant Jewish boy to his heritage, he does not actually become a member of the community until his bar mitzvah. Bar mitzvah, in which the thirteen-year-old stands before the Torah and reads from the Scriptures, forms an initiation ceremony. Unlike native peoples' initiation ceremonies in such places as Australia or Africa, it does not involve physical tests or fearful encounters with spirits. It simply requires learning. Until recently (and still among orthodox Jews) it applied only to boys.

The three prongs of the keys also symbolize the sacred trinity. Each prong contains a hole and a piece pointing out, symbols of female and male sexuality. While Jewish tradition honors sex (calling on Jews to make love on the Sabbath), it also pictures God as entirely male and at the same time lacking a body. Therefore, the idea of divine sexuality becomes an esoteric secret, hidden from ordinary people and presented only in symbols. The Zohar, the basic text of Kabbalah, examines the phrase from Genesis, "Male and female, He created them," and says that the term "male and female" refers to "He." In other words, God is both male and female. This idea, however, does not appear in ordinary Jewish teaching. The Hebrew language does not even contain a word for "goddess."

And yet the Goddess, the Empress, remains—in the variations on the number three, in the sexual symbolism of the key, in the image of the bull, who not only "belongs" to the Empress, but to the High Priestess as well, for the horns suggest the Moon's curved sickle. When Moses denounced the worship of the golden calf he was denouncing the worship of the Goddess. And when he removed the golden calf and gave his people the Torah, he was substituting a religion of (male) law and knowledge for a religion of (female) nature.

Even the Hierophant's number, five, brings us back to the Goddess. We can break it down in two ways, one male, the other female. Five is 1 + 4, that is, the Magician and the Emperor. More commonly, however, we think of five as 3 + 2, the High Priestess and the Empress. Five is the sacred number of Wicca, or "witchcraft," the form of Goddess worship that has survived the patriarchal centuries and has reemerged in our own time.

Witches take as their most sacred symbol the pentacle, the five-pointed star. If you cut an apple in half through the middle instead of from top to bottom, you will discover a pentacle in each half. When Adam accepted the apple from Eve he was accepting the rule of the Empress—the greatest crime for the patriarchal Hebrews. The pentacle represents humanity as well. If you stand with your head up, your legs apart, and your arms out to the side, your body will form a pentacle. Therefore, the pentacle, the number five, connects God to human beings. And the idea of a human relationship to divinity—through teachings, through the passage of tradition from one generation to the next—forms the deepest value of the Hierophant.

DIVINATORY MEANINGS

Several ideas relate to the Hierophant, and any of these may come up in a reading. They draw from three connected ideas: tradition, community and teachings. Tradition permeates a great deal of ordinary behavior: the way we dress, the holidays we celebrate, the ways men and women or parents and children relate to each other. The Hierophant can show a time in a person's life when traditional patterns strongly influence the person. This influence may be helpful—support in a crisis, or problematic—preventing the person from acting independently. Very often, the Hierophant signifies conformity, acting from society's expectations rather than your own desires.

Connected to tradition, the card shows the influence of institutions. These may be religious, as for instance, the Church influencing a Catholic on such issues as birth control or divorce. More generally, the card can refer to society and its institutions, not just religions. These may include organizations, such as universities or government bureaucracies, or it may signify social institutions, particularly marriage. In contrast with the Lovers, the next card, the Hierophant indicates the stability and structure in a marriage. This may still form a positive image. If a couple have been together a long time the Hierophant may show that they have created a life that gives them support and a framework for their actions. In connection with marriage the Hierophant can refer to any solemn commitment.

The Hierophant signifies community, either the influence of society as a whole, or a smaller group. This influence may help or hinder the person. Does the person feel the community supports him or her? Or do the community's attitudes limit the person's choices?

In the Hierophant as teachings we find the same dichotomy. The card signifies the value of knowledge and education. It may refer to a specific religious teaching, sometimes of an occult order. It refers, however, to the doctrines, and without the High Priestess it can lose the inner meanings that give those doctrines their value.

REVERSED

The reversed card may intensify the problems—or it may show the person going in the opposite direction. The reversed Hierophant may emphasize social pressure. It may show a marriage or a long-term relationship that has lost the passion that inspired it. It may indicate doctrines and ideas that have lost their meaning.

More commonly, the reversed Hierophant shows the person rejecting such things. It may indicate refusing to continue in an empty relationship. This does not necessarily mean leaving. It might show the person insisting on changes, or bringing up long-buried problems.

More generally the Hierophant can indicate a person who is unorthodox, original. Sometimes this leads to gullibility, for without some fixed standard by which to measure new ideas the person may accept anything new, as long as it appears fresh and exciting.

Which of these possibilities actually apply? To decide you must look at the other cards. When you have worked with the cards for some time you will discover that intuition will help you choose the correct meanings. Remember, too, that several meanings may apply at the same time.

VI

THE LOVERS

THE LOVERS IS card 6. On the Kabbalistic Tree of Life the sixth Sephirah (circle of God's light) bears the name Tifiret, which means beauty. Tefirit is the circle of love, and it occupies the central position on the Tree, in effect holding all the other attributes together.

The Hebrew letter is Zain, which means "Sword." This may seem an unlikely image for love, but it becomes clearer when we remember that most traditional versions of this card show a young man choosing between two women. Because a sword cuts through things and separates them into parts it symbolizes the mental act of discrimination, that is, carefully distinguishing between one thing and another. Such discrimination is necessary for a proper choice between any two possibilities. At the same time, love and sexuality are the areas in our lives where we cannot choose solely on an intellectual basis. We need instead to follow our desires.

A sword, like the nail of the previous card, is a phallic image. We should realize that in earlier times most of the esoteric paths were created by men. Sexuality, therefore, was seen as a masculine question. Even in those esoteric practices involving sexual rites, the women sometimes served as a means to awaken and transform the man. This blindness to the sexuality of women came from patriarchal society in general. Sexuality leads to independence—this is one of the mysteries expressed in the card. Therefore, just as the Emperor has denied women creative and spiritual power, so he also denies that women are sexual creatures apart from men. In some societies, such as Victorian England, people believed that women endured sex for the sake of their husband's needs. In many places in the world today people remove a young girl's clitoris, usually making this a ritual. Some people think only Moslems follow such practices. However, Aristotle, the fountain of European rationalism, described sexual pleasure for women as "abominable" and prescribed clitorodectomy as a remedy.

The Lovers

In modern times this attitude is changing. Once again women are recognizing themselves as sexual. It is not a coincidence that the Goddess has begun to return. For it is one of the central meanings of the Lovers that sexuality leads to spiritual awakening. The Empress, after all, means pleasure as well as Goddess. In the famous Rider Tarot of A. E. Waite and Pamela Smith the card of the Lovers changed from a young man making a choice to a mature man and woman standing together. The Haindl Tarot follows this modern tradition, in which the two join together as equal partners.

In connection with Zain, Haindl originally painted a sword pointing at the cup. He then changed it to a spear. In the Haindl Tarot a spear represents the element of Fire, while the cup stands for Water. Fire and Water are the primary symbols for male and female. We will see in a moment that the six-pointed star consists of a "fire triangle" and a "water triangle." The idea of joining the two opposing elements relates both to alchemy and to Tantra, the ancient practices in India for awakening the kundalini through sexual yoga. The star, the spear and cup, and in fact, the man and woman, all connect this card to trump 14, Alchemy. Both cards deal with Fire and Water joining together.

The Rune for the card is Ken, or K. The name means "torch," another masculine symbol, and one directly related to the image here of a spear with a fiery tip. Descriptions of Ken often give "lust" as a key word. They stress, however, that lust does not mean something sinful or destructive, but rather a positive drive leading to reproduction and creativity. Now, the creation of babies is a very obvious result of sexual desire. But other kinds of creative acts also derive from lust. Freud described art as sublimation, a channeling of sexuality. Jung saw it as a transformation, the same energy changed into a genuinely new form. In some ways, both Freud and Jung gave a modern expression to a very ancient knowledge. The meanings for Ken refer to Fire as a creative force of its own. The hearth cooks the food and heats the home, while the forge allows people to create tools and objects of beauty from the materials of nature.

The shape of the Rune shows a single branch separating into two. The first organisms on our planet were single-celled organisms which reproduced by splitting into two parts exactly like the original. Thus the Rune echoes the origins of life. But it also shows the change from such simple forms into species of two sexes. The Rune shows that splitting into male and female but it implies as well the re-union through sex.

The occult tradition sees the mystery of sexes as a model for the universe. The cosmos existed originally as a spiritual whole. Then came the "descent" into material form, and with it the splitting up of existence into opposite poles, found in male and female sexuality, but also in such phenomena as light and dark, and the positive and negative of electro-magnetism. Such traditions as alchemy, Tantra, Kabbalah and magic seek to bring the two poles back together.

The form of the Rune connects to Earth mysteries. A forked tree figures in the Native American sweat lodge ceremony. This ceremony purifies the body for the coming ritual. We can also recognize Ken as the shape of a diviner's dowsing rod. People think of such rods as gimmicks for finding water, or telling fortunes. Fundamentally, however, they focus a person's natural sensitivity to the energy patterns of the Earth.

The astrological sign for trump 6 is Gemini, the twins. Gemini is often described as mental, seemingly the opposite of the sensual card. However, it also means duality and therefore reflects the same idea as the Rune. Some astrologers see Gemini as two-sided—physical desire contrasted with spirituality. The glyph at first appears phallic. However, it depicts two pillars, a classic symbol of the vagina. In traditional Tarots the High Priestess sits between two pillars, an image of the female gateway, but also of the gateway to truth. Therefore, Gemini relates to the High Priestess, the primary female card, and to the element of Water. But—Mercury rules Gemini, and Mercury is the planet of the Magician, primary male card (usually shown holding a phallic wand) and the element of Fire. Gemini combines the two poles.

The element for the Lovers is neither Fire nor Water, but Air, the element of mind. Of course, Earth is present as well, for even today we describe sex as "earthy" or even "dirty." Our sexuality connects us to the rest of nature. We will see in a moment how the imagery in the card suggests the ancient idea of the Earth itself as a sexual being.

The Lovers is one of the most complex cards, for it deals in several fundamental issues, including the nature of spiritual reality. And yet, because it does deal in reality, the picture is simple. We can look at it as organized in terms of distance, but also as vertical columns. For distance, we begin with the two trees, for they stand outside the border, rooted in the reality of the Earth. Behind them we find the woman and man crossing their arms behind the cup. Along the ground behind the people, the land swells. Behind (and above) that is a darkness, a barrier between the Earth and the sky. In the sky itself we see the spear in front, and behind that the goat and the rose within the star. Notice that while the trees are solid, the people, especially their legs, are very slightly transparent, while the rose is faint, and the goat merges with the sky.

Vertically we see three columns. The left consists of the tree, the woman and the goat. The right is formed from the tree, the man and the rose, while the swell of ground, the spear and the cup form the middle. These columns mirror the Kabbalistic Tree of Life.

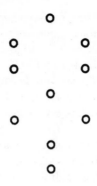

The right and left columns on the Tree represent the two poles of existence, while the middle column expresses the harmony that holds the two together.

The Runic theme of two coming together into one permeates the card. We see two trees and two people, with two symbols above them. There are also two symbols in the center, but these two join together. As we saw in the Magician these two symbols, the spear and cup, belong to the rituals of the Holy Grail. The cup, in fact, is the Grail itself. Haindl has painted it very simply, to show that the spiritual qualities of love are not apart from ordinary experience. The Grail symbolizes love itself, divine, emotional, sexual.

The trees refer us to the Garden of Eden, with its Tree of Life and Tree of Knowledge. Eden is Paradise (a word in Hebrew meaning "garden"). Many people believe that Adam and Eve did not discover sex until they'd eaten the forbidden fruit. However, if we follow the Jewish tradition on this point the commentaries state explicitly that they were sexual; the fall made them ashamed of sex, and so isolated from each other and from God. The card, therefore, returns us to a vision of sexual love without shame, or hostility between the partners, a vision of sex as a way back to God.

We should recognize at this point that the card does not refer only to heterosexuals, or even only to couples. In many cultures people practiced sexual rites in groups, sometimes all men or all women, sometimes mixed. The imagery of the card, derived from the Biblical tradition, shows a man and woman. The card does deal in issues concerning male and female and the way they relate to each other. Nevertheless, the basic theme of the Lovers—love—applies to all people.

The trees also suggest a particular story out of Greek myth. Zeus and several of the Gods disguise themselves as human in order to visit an elderly married couple. Though the people have very little, they open their homes to the strangers. As a reward for their hospitality Zeus transforms them into trees, so that they will remain together forever. As well as teaching a moral lesson on the value of generosity, the myth gives us an image of humanity and nature joined together.

The swell of ground between the man and woman represents the Earth as female. We will see this image more explicitly in the Hanged Man. Around the world people have expressed the idea of the Earth as Mother, the Sky as Father. This is not just an abstract idea. In our tradition we tend to think of religious matters as "theological," that is, intellectual and apart from ordinary life. Others have not made such a separation. To see the Earth and Sky as sexual joins our individual acts of love to the patterns of life to nature. For people in less technological times, spring brought a yearly demonstration of this unity. As their own desires reawoke after the winter, so did everything around them, the animals in heat, the Earth pregnant with buds and leaves. In the picture the trees appear the same height as the people, a sign of harmony between humanity and nature. We see this theme also in the way the colors of the land merge with the colors of the people's bodies. Partly transparent, they join with the Earth. The transparency also gives a lightness, the "walking on air" sensation of people in love.

The man and woman are the same height, suggesting equality. The woman appears slightly larger, an indication of the importance of the female in love and in nature. In contrast to the Emperor, the man stands quietly, with a graceful, almost feminine quality. The woman's hair is elaborate, decorated. In many species, such as the peacock (see Justice and Death), colorful males compete for the females. In some human cultures the men will paint and groom themselves, but in most the practice goes to the women. Here, the woman's hair resembles the pitted rock found on many cards, a sign of the ancientness of human sexual traditions.

In the ground we see the earthiness of love. In the people we see the emotional and personal levels. Above them, in the unicorn and rose, we find the mystical qualities. The images become more and more transparent. The ground and the trees are solid. The people are both physical and ethereal. Sexuality is the most bodily and the most emotional of human experiences. The unicorn and rose not only merge with the sky, but the unicorn is a head without a body, while the rose gleams within the star, a purely mental form.

With its phallic horn the unicorn symbolizes maleness. Modern paintings usually depict unicorns as horses with a horn. Some older images showed a goat, as we see here. The goat, too, symbolizes male sexuality, or rather a kind of sexuality we usually think of as male: a driving force, controlling the person. We will see this theme developed more fully in the Devil, trump 15 (1 + 5 = 6).

The rose symbolizes the softer, more subtle sexuality we tend to associate with women. In the card of the Sun we will see how the rose traditionally signifies the female. In our time people give each other roses to celebrate romance. The color of blood, roses represent suffering as well as love. People suffer from sex. We become obsessed, or we feel rejected, or the body aches with desire. More deeply, we suffer because lovers die or love itself dies.

The rose is natural, voluptuous, sensual. The star is austere, an idea. The leaves at the six points bring the two together. In the same way the human mind is both emotional and philosophical.

The six-pointed star is an ancient image. Most people today think of it as a symbol of Judaism. This idea, based on a tradition that says King David displayed it on his shield, is actually a modern one. In Europe the symbol goes back to the "seal of Solomon," a magical/alchemical symbol taken from the Arabs. We also find the star in India, especially Tantra. In the Haindl Tarot it suggests the Rune of the Mother, Hagall.

The two triangles signify male and female, Fire and Water, as cosmic forces. If we look closely at the card we see that the upward triangle is gold, the downward one, blue. Though they have become abstract they may have derived from the body. A downward triangle depicts female public hair, while an upward one suggests an erect phallus. The star, in other words, depicts intercourse.

Tantric and Gnostic rites use intercourse as a means to awaken cosmic understanding. Through arousal linked to meditation, the sexual energy of the body—the kundalini—awakens, rises up the spine, and becomes transformed. There is a difference here from the Pagan practice of sexual pleasure linking humans to the cycles of nature. In Tantra the person seeks to go beyond nature. The male avoids orgasm, for that would release the raised-up energy and let it sink down again.

The Gnostics joined some of these ideas to Christian myth. They described Jehovah, the jealous God of Genesis, as a false God, who created the material universe to imprison spirit in gross matter. They saw the serpent as the hero, for by leading the woman to the Tree of Knowledge—Gnosis—it led her to potential liberation.

Modern scholarship in archaeology and comparative religion gives us another radical reinterpretation of the Eden story. Merlin Stone and Joseph Campbell have each pointed out an older version of the story. Here there is no angry Lord who expels people from a long-ago garden for eating an apple. Instead we find a Lady—the Great Mother—who brings initiates into her ever-present, ever-continuing garden of paradise by *giving* them her magic apples.

How did the story get turned around? Both Stone and Campbell hypothesize that the patriarchal Hebrews (the young Emperor) sought to discredit the old religion of the Goddess (the Empress). They banished her initiation ceremony and then turned it on its head, transforming the Goddess into a disobedient wife. The serpent became the chief villain because in Canaan, as in so many other places, the old religion honored the serpent as the Goddess's most sacred animal. In the ancient pictures showing the Goddess giving fruit from her tree of everlasting life, snakes wind round her arms and the tree itself.

In discussing these various issues of sexual politics and spiritual reality, the Holy Grail and pagan rituals, Gnostic myth and ordinary love, we may get the impression that all we need to do is follow the old practices and we will achieve enlightenment, not to mention immortality. But of course the path of divine awareness is not so open. If it were, we would hardly need such images as the Tarot to point the way. Something in us prevents us from opening up our minds and lives to the great truths described in myth and religion. The Gnostics described spirit as imprisoned in matter. In the Haindl Tarot we see a dark barrier separating the Earth and the heavens. The barrier symbolizes our difficulty in transcending our weaknesses: ignorance, fear, isolation, the inability to love or completely give ourselves to someone else or even to our own joy. And yet, despite recognizing these things the Tarot remains optimistic. Just as the feet of the man and woman blend into the ground, so their heads—like the Grail—reach above the barrier. The Grail symbolizes both a path of initiation and the divine love that makes such paths possible. Its presence on the card of the Lovers indicates that human love, expressed in sexuality, can indeed raise us above our weaknesses.

So there are various themes in this complex card. We can summarize them as three levels, united in the bodies of the two people.

1. Human love. This is the theme that most reflects our ordinary experience. The card gives us a vision of people in love. Their arms are crossed and they hold the symbol of their joy. They walk on air, they stand strong and voluptuous at the same time. In contrast with the older ideas of adolescence or lust, this modern image shows the value of love and desire in people's lives.

2. Spiritual rites. With its references to Tantra, to Gnosticism, to alchemy, the Tarot brings in the fundamental esoteric idea of sexuality overcoming the barriers between matter and spirit. Sex is the activity that most roots us in our bodies, that most takes us out of our distractions, our feelings of isolation from other people and from the world itself. Because of this power sexual love can lead us to spiritual awakening.

3. The sexuality of nature. Through sexual love we can bring back something of the archaic sense of the whole world as alive, renewing and fulfilling itself through desire. If we recognize that the Gods are sexual, if, like modern witches, we worship a Goddess or God who will say, "All acts of love and pleasure are my rituals," then we will recognize as well that our desires join us to the rest of existence.

Through all these things runs one powerful idea. Sex and spirituality are not opposed to each other, but in fact form two expressions of the same reality. Most people will acknowledge the vital role sexuality plays in our lives. Even if choice or circumstance makes us inactive sexually, that energy feeds our activities. Sex is basic to us. So is spiritual yearning. The Tarot does not see God as something vague and unknown, outside the world. It views God/Goddess as filling all existence, including ourselves. Therefore, when we understand our own being, and the laws of nature, our own actions, especially love, will bring us to God.

DIVINATORY MEANINGS

The card of the Lovers may simply indicate the importance of love in a person's life. More often it refers to a specific relationship.

This relationship is likely to be an important one for the person. Usually the card indicates support from a lover. (I am using the term "lover" to apply to any romantic relationship, including marriage.) The two people have created something valuable between them. Through the relationship they have found or will find understanding, joy, perhaps courage that neither would have had alone. Together the two hold the Grail. The cup symbolizes their love for each other and the meaning it has given to their lives.

The position of the card in a reading may be especially important with the Lovers. If it appears as the first, or the central, card, then it says that the reading concerns a relationship. If it appears in a position such as Hopes and Fears in the Celtic Cross, it says that the person desires such a relationship—or fears it, for we should realize that people often fear the commitment depicted in the card. The card does not mean giving up your sense of yourself. It does call for a genuine openness to someone else. In Hopes and Fears the Lovers may refer to a specific person. The subject of the reading has met someone and desires a relationship. Or, a relationship has begun and the subject hopes it will become an important one.

If the card appears in a position showing Past Experience, it does not necessarily mean a relationship has ended. Very often it signifies that such a relationship has figured prominently in the person's life. Whether the relationship continues or is ending should show in the other cards.

If the card appears in a position showing other people, it usually signifies support from a lover. Sometimes the Lovers may come up in a position showing the relationship's importance, while the position of Others shows someone either hostile or simply withdrawn (such as the Hermit). This suggests that the partner may need to be alone for awhile.

There is a way the Lovers can indicate the person alone, rather than in a relationship. The Tarot, like other esoteric traditions, uses male and female to signify different states of awareness. The man symbolizes reason, logic, determination and action. The woman represents emotion, intuition, sensitivity, and in the Haindl Tarot, creativity. Neither figure in the picture holds up the cup alone. They hold it together, just as they both look at it. The card teaches the lesson that we need to harmonize our "male" and "female" aspects. This is the same message that we found in the Rune. In a reading, therefore, it signifies the person blending these various qualities. We should recognize, however, that the card more often means a romantic relationship.

REVERSED

The Lovers may signify a relationship coming to an end. More often, it indicates trouble in a relationship. The people are quarreling, or closed to each other. As to whether this occurred in the past, or is happening now, or will likely happen at some future time, the position and the other cards should give an indication.

In a position such as Basis in the Celtic Cross, the reversed card may indicate a lack of love in a person's life. Other cards would show the effect of this lack. They may bring out insecurities or loneliness. As an example, let us say the central card is the Magician reversed, and the Basis is the Lovers reversed. The Magician would say that the person feels weak and finds it hard to take action in life. We would then expect two possible meanings for the reversed Lovers. The first would be that the Magician problem is immediate, caused by trouble with a lover. The other would describe it as more long-term, coming from loneliness. Both meanings might apply at once. Difficulties with a lover, or rejection, might bring up deeper problems.

If we think of the card as a diagram of a personality in harmony, then reversed indicates a loss of balance. The person has become overly logical, or overly emotional. The person acts without an inner sense of what is right, or else feels so strongly about everything he or she finds it impossible to act at all. The other cards would make it clear in which direction the person has gone. The reader can then help the person see the need to restore harmony by bringing in the missing qualities.

VII

THE CHARIOT

THE NUMBER SEVEN traditionally means "Victory," or "Triumph." As 3 + 4 it hints at a unity of the Empress and the Emperor. The Hebrew letter for trump 7 is Cheth, which means "Fence," especially a fence enclosing a field. The image suggests cultivation, the human mind taming nature. But just as a fence implies the safe area it encloses, so it also implies the world beyond the fence. In earlier times, with so much of nature wild, towns literally existed within fences—walls protecting people from wild animals as well as human enemies. With the current human mastery over so much of nature, we tend to think of the whole world as safe, mapped out, understandable. But we still exist inside the fence. Existence remains vast and mysterious, even terrifying. For if something happens that strips away the fixed ideas of what we call "reality"—if for a moment we find ourselves outside the fence—then a fear rises up from somewhere so deep inside that except in such a moment, we are unaware of it.

The traditional Chariot usually symbolizes the fence of civilization, "controlling intelligence" as some commentaries call it. As number seven, the card represents a victory of human will over the ordinary problems of life. It remains, then, for later cards, such as the Moon, to once again go beyond the known areas.

The Haindl Tarot retains the idea of will, but carries it further, showing the confrontation of willpower with fear. The self—the figure in the boat—rides on the surging sea of life, driven by the primal beast, experienced as just over the shoulder, just out of sight. And yet, the figure remains calm, unshaken.

For the Rune we find Hagall, H, the "Hailstone," the pattern of the universe. This again takes us beyond the usual theme of civilization, while keeping the idea of the Chariot as the ability to bring a sense of order to the chaos of life. Hagall also links the Chariot to the Empress and the Wheel of Fortune. Hagall is similar to the German word *heilig*, or holy. If we look at the Runes on the Devil and

73

The Chariot

the Tower, we will see that Hagall joins the two of them. Since those Runes mean "Man" and "Woman," Hagall is actually androgynous. As the primal pattern, it returns to the state before male and female became split. The shape also unites above and below, Heaven and Earth.

As the H-Rune, Hagall also connects the card personally to Hermann Haindl, who lives in Hauptstrasse, in the town of Hofheim. We will see in a moment that he created this image as one of the statements of his own life. Hermann Haindl was born on 9–30–27. Each of these numbers connects to 3, the Empress (9 is 3×3, 30 is a form of 3, 27 is $3 \times 3 \times 3$). The numbers reduced add up to 21, the Universe (and Hermann's house number!), which of course also reduces to 3. Also, $3 + 4$ (the four letter H's in the artist's name and address) $= 7$, the number of the card and the Rune Hagall.

The astrological sign is Cancer, whose symbol is the crab. The connections to the sea of the unconscious become more emphasized in the Haindl version of the card, where the Chariot rides the waves. The crab's hard shell protects the vulnerable inside, in the same way that the Charioteer is protected by his psychic fence. Cancer is ruled by the Moon. We see here a lunar crescent below Hagall. Many of the themes developed in this trump usually do not emerge in other Tarot decks until the Moon.

The element is Water, symbolizing life and the unconscious. Many versions of this card show a Roman chariot standing on the edge of a river bank, often without wheels. The gentle river shows the Chariot's mastery over his emotions. The lack of wheels indicates the solidness of his success in life. The Haindl Tarot changes all this. The image becomes more powerful, yet more disturbing at the same time.

Of all the trumps the Chariot stands out as the card that most evokes myth. It exists in a visionary world of its own imagination, reaching deeply into mystery and power. We see a boat with wheels, rushing through a rough sea. The boat is red, the color of energy. A red glow surrounds the figure standing in the boat. The boat carries huge blocks of stone, pitted witih holes to indicate great age. They help give the picture an archaic quality, a sense of experience older than civilization. The stone appears in blocks, like the blocks used in creating the pyramids (esoteric versions of the Chariot often show a pair of sphinxes instead of horses). Like the symbol of the fence, and like the pyramids themselves, the carved stones represent human mastery over nature. And yet, we get no sense here that the person has conquered nature. The courageous mind—and the card is an emblem of courage—faces the world in all its power, seeking mastery over the self rather than the environment.

The bottom of the stones appears to melt, turning into waves as the boat rushes forward. This unites the two "female" elements, Earth and Water. We see a similar hint in the boat's wheels, as if it travels on dirt as well as the sea. Many mythologies tell us how land emerged originally out of the ocean. The Bible describes how God separated the waters to create the world.

Above the stone stands a human being. Traditionally the Charioteer is a man (though in some very early decks we see a woman), and the card signifies masculine willpower. Though the card

represents his own experience Haindl wished to stress that the qualities shown here applied to women as well. Therefore, he deliberately made the figure androgynous. While working with this card I
showed it to several women friends and asked for their reactions.
Each of them assumed the figure was female.

Despite the mad rush of the boat, and the fire surrounding the
human, the figure stands unshaken, arms out to indicate openness
to life. Above and behind the human appears the giant head of a
mythical beast, a mixture of boar and wolf. It rushes forward from
a great distance, its mouth open like a black hole. We see the hint
of a second pair of eyes below the main pair. The lower left eye,
however, is the head of the Charioteer. A violet glow surrounds the
boar's head. Violet belongs to the crown chakra, the most developed
level of consciousness (see also Justice, and especially the Hanged
Man). We might think of it as the color furthest away from the dark
beast. However, if we truly confront our deepest fears and instincts
we may discover them as a source of the energy which can become
transformed into spirituality. The crown is the seventh chakra.
Seven signifies spiritual victory.

On the right-hand side, below Hagall, at the level of the top of
the animal's head, we see a crescent Moon. If we look closer we can
see the whole circle described by the Moon, with a star in the dark
center. This image, repeated from the Magician, recalls the famous
yin-yang symbol, ☯, showing the constant interchange between
light and darkness, action and stillness. In most Tarot decks the
Charioteer holds together two horses or sphinxes, one black, one
white.

Hermann Haindl has described the Chariot as *his* card. It
describes his sense of being "hunted by time," a phrase he used
when we talked about the picture. This means mortality, for having
reached the age of sixty, Haindl works with an urgency to make his
statement to the world. Therefore, we see speed in the card, the
boat rushing forward, carried by the sea, symbol of emotion, of life
and therefore, the constant presence of death. In Walt Whitman's
great poem, *Out of the Cradle, Endlessly Rocking,* the young poet
asks the sea to whisper "the word final, superior to all." The waves
answer with the "low and delicious word death."

Deep in our minds we all carry the knowledge that we may die
at any moment. Most of us, for most of our lives, banish this awareness, acting as if we will live forever. As we grow older the aware-

ness pushes up at us, though we try not to think about it. Haindl confronted this knowledge very early in life. As a teenager with very little political or spiritual awareness, he entered the German army in World War II. He found himself in a Russian prisoner-of-war camp, where for several years he never knew if he would live from one day to the next. Four times his captors forced him to dig his own grave; each time they might have carried out the threat.

Haindl does not recall this experience to show himself in any special light, and certainly not to excuse the Germans' own crimes in the war years and before. He only recognizes it as one of the sources of his knowledge. The figure in the boat, calm and unshaken, shows us the hope that we can master our fears, master our mortality, use these things as sources of energy and understanding.

The boat symbolizes this ability to overcome fear. Through boats, human beings have made the dangerous sea a road and a source of food. The seas retain their power, but boats enable people to use that power.

The stones, too, signify human achievement. According to most archaeologists the Egyptian pyramids were built as giant tombs. We might describe them as an attempt to deny death by making it both monumental and as much like life as possible. The Egyptians filled their tombs with possessions and even food, as if the dead person would continue a perfectly normal existence in the next world. In this card of the Chariot we see less of a denial. The charioteer does not hide from the sea but travels over it. (In Death we will look at the Egyptian idea of death as transportation.)

The beast emphasizes the card's mythic quality—not an actual animal, but something in us represented by the figure of an animal. It rushes forward like some long-buried terror rising to the surface in a moment of panic. It signifies our deepest fears, unnameable and wild, below the conscious mind and the safety of civilization. The mouth opens to remind us of the child's terror of darkness.

The beast appears behind the shoulder. In situations where archaic fears arise—say, walking alone in a dark wood—people often sense something just over the shoulder, just out of sight. When a shaman begins her or his perilous journeys to the land of the spirits, the teacher often warns against looking behind. Whatever you hear or feel behind you, the teacher might say, do not look over your shoulder. In the Orpheus legend, Orpheus travels to the land of the dead to bring back Eurydice. She may follow him, but only if he doesn't look back until they have reached the outside. Orpheus looks over his shoulder and loses Eurydice forever. The stories tell us that he looks because of impatience, or a fear that Eurydice hasn't come. But maybe he looks because *something* follows him, and it might not be Eurydice.

The beast may symbolize the shaman's confrontation with terror, but it also symbolizes mastery. For when the traveler completes the journey he or she will meet a guardian, a spirit being in the form of an animal. In the ancient tribal culture of Europe, every community counted on the protection of its totem.

The idea of archaic terror usually comes in the card of the Moon, number eighteen, and therefore one of the final triumphs. By bringing it up to number seven the Haindl Tarot stresses the necessity of recognizing fear and overcoming it. Traditionally, the Chariot triumphs over "daylight" challenges: building a career, finding a place in the world, creating a family. The Haindl Chariot speaks to us of a nighttime triumph: the human will confronting its deepest fears.

This theme of confrontation forms only half a truth. For the other half, a sense of unity with life taking us beyond fear, we look to the Hanged Man (where the theme of death returns). But the Chariot shows us something very real. To become a whole person, to master our lives, we need that shamanic victory.

DIVINATORY MEANINGS

The Chariot indicates first of all the importance of willpower in dealing with the problems shown in the reading. If it appears in the position of Self in the Celtic Cross, it says that the person has a strong will and this may help to bring about a satisfactory outcome. In a difficult situation it may show a will to continue. In fact, meditation with this card can increase the person's willpower. If several cards in the reading suggest weakness, but the Chariot appears in some key position, such as Possible Development, then it advises the person to approach the situation with optimism and determination.

Sometimes the Chariot may show a negative influence. The situation may require a more passive approach, allowing others to take the lead, or just experiencing events without trying to direct them. The surrounding cards should give an indication of whether the Chariot's particular qualities help or hinder the person.

The Haindl Chariot may refer to some deep fear driving the person. She or he may not even recognize the fear, but if the picture strikes a response then the person may wish to explore whether such a fear exists, perhaps discussing it with the reader. The card does more than push us to acknowledge fear. It tells us we can triumph over that fear. It tells us to seek a sense of calm openness, like the figure in the boat.

REVERSED

The reversed Chariot signifies a lack of will. It can refer to passivity or weakness. Sometimes, in a difficult situation, it means that the person lacks the will to continue. If so, the person faces a choice— either get out or find some way to turn the Chariot right side up, that is, overcome the reluctance. In other situations, depending on the cards, the reversed Chariot may recommend that we stop trying to dominate events and other people. Let things run their course. Finally, the reversed card may indicate our fears getting the best of us.

VIII

STRENGTH

Mastering others requires force;
mastering the self needs strength.
—Lao Tsu

IN MOST TRADITIONAL Tarot decks Strength is trump 11, and Justice
is 8. The famous esoteric society, the Order of the Golden Dawn,
switched the two cards because it believed the attribution of the
Hebrew letters worked better with Strength as 8 and Justice as 11.
The switch became well-known when A. E. Waite, a one-time member of the Golden Dawn, followed it in his own Tarot deck, the
extremely popular Rider deck, painted by Pamela Smith.

Today, while some Tarot decks follow Waite and the Golden
Dawn, many go back to the older system. The problem only becomes crucial for those people who wish to use the Tarot in a strict
system of Kabbalistic magic. If we look at the Tarot in terms of what
each card can teach us, then we are justified in seeing Strength and
Justice in *both* positions. As number eight, Strength begins a new
level. It comes after the victory of seven, the Chariot. In order to begin this new and deeper journey, we need inner strength. Strength
can be seen as a feminine counterpart to the masculine qualities of
the Chariot. As number eleven, Strength is the middle card of
trumps 1–21. This would make inner strength an essential quality
for the whole Tarot.

As number eight, Justice would represent the first step in going
beyond the ego. As eleven, it places the principle of Justice at the
center of a person's life. Clearly, both arrangements are valuable.
The two cards indeed have a great deal to do with each other. It
takes strength to accept the truth (Justice) about one's life. On the
other hand, discovering one's personal truth can become a great
source of strength.

Hermann Haindl followed the Golden Dawn system for several
reasons. First of all, he wished to keep the connection of Strength

Strength

with the Hebrew letter Teth, which means snake. The letter belongs to the number and not the card. In other words, the letters follow the fixed order of the alphabet. Teth therefore goes with trump 8, whatever that might be. Haindl wished it to be Strength.

Just as important was the number itself. Strength is a female card. In German the word *Starkte* is grammatically feminine. Strength signifies the power inherent in the female principle. We can describe Strength as the quality that gives the Empress its creative force. In the card of the Empress we described her as the Goddess Shakti. But we also saw that Shakti was energy. Strength is that energy.

Eight is a female number. Its figure, 8, mirrors the female body, with round breasts and hips, and a narrow waist. Moreover, a circle represents the full Moon, and also a dish or a cup, symbols of the womb (the Holy Grail is such a symbol). The numeral 8 doubles the circle. It shows the Moon connected to the Earth. And we have seen (in the High Priestess and the Empress) how the female principle lives in both these planets. In some esoteric traditions seven is a number of male magical power and eight of female. This is because the male body has seven openings, the female body eight.

Seen another way, the number 8 is androgynous, for the numeral shows the Fool's number, 0, twice. We can describe the Fool, the Nothing, as Ancient Mother of all, but only if we see that image as both male and female, the "Mother" as source, origin.

The Hebrew letter, as mentioned, is Teth, which means "Snake." We have already discussed this animal in the Empress. It will appear again in the Devil. Just as Strength is the higher octave of the Magician, so the Devil is the higher octave of Strength. We have discussed the "serpent-power" of the kundalini, and how the occultist seeks to raise it up. Strength signifies this power. It also signifies the ability to deal with the power once we have awakened it. In the picture the woman holds up the snake. We can also describe her as wrestling with it, getting it under control. Shakti energy is very great, and not to be treated lightly. The person needs strength to deal with it—not aggressive force but the strength of inner peace and belief. As card 8, Strength follows the Chariot. The Charioteer was a shaman confronting his deepest terrors and overcoming them. Strength comes out of this victory. In this card we again see a shaman. With her snake she performs a ritual under a waxing Moon.

Serpent-power is not simply an idea from India. We find it in Africa, in the Americas, in the Near East. Many scholars believe that Jehovah was a serpent-God of ancient Israel before becoming the unknowable creator. The two ideas might have coexisted. The Bible contains a curious passage in which God instructs Moses to create a brass structure of a serpent in the desert.

When we come to the Rune we find ourselves back in the eight/eleven question. The Rune shown here, Sigil, S, which means "Sun," is actually Rune number eleven, while the Rune for Justice, Nyd, is number eight. Just as Teth fits so well with Strength, so the two Runes, Sigil and Nyd, fit Strength and Justice. Therefore, we can say that Strength is eight with the Hebrew letter, but eleven with the Rune. This double approach borrows from the principle in quantum physics of complementarity, where an electron is either a particle or a wave, depending on the situation.

It may seem odd to describe Sigil as perfect for Strength. After all, we see the Moon in the picture and not the Sun. But Strength is actually a solar card. Just as the Sun gives life to the Earth, so the Shakti power burns with energy (see also the dragon fire in trump 21). The astrological sign for the card, Leo, is ruled by the Sun. As the higher octave of the Magician, Strength radiates—but also transforms—the Solar principle.

The astrological symbol is Leo, the lion. In many decks Strength shows a woman taming a lion with gentleness. The lion represents passion and desire, which the woman does not suppress, but learns to transform. As the sign of "fixed Fire" (each sign is fixed, mutable or cardinal) Leo symbolizes the eternal flame. This makes Leo a very strong, confident sign. If Leo does not transform that energy it can lead to conceit and a desire to dominate others. When raised up it becomes a source of divine inspiration.

The shape of the Leo sign resembles a snake. It also recalls the Egyptian Goddess Nut, who as the night sky, arches over the Earth (see the Mother of Swords). Finally, it suggests Ur, the Rune of the High Priestess. Leo is a sign of great confidence. The person with Strength is open, without modesty or shame. Just as Nut's naked body frames the sky, so the woman in the card stands strong and naked, not concerned to hide her vulva.

This is not arrogance. We see her kneeling down on one knee, a posture of natural humility. She is neither arrogant nor meek. Her strength, in fact, comes from her unity with the Earth and with her own divine energy. Conceit and shame are two sides of the same problem, a concern for outer appearances. The *self*-conscious person worries about her position in the world. Should she be proud or bow down? But the worry becomes forgotten when the person unites the self with nature.

This concern for true humility, as opposed to weakness, forms an important theme in the Haindl Tarot. We will see it again in the following card, the Hermit, and then in the great cards of reversal, the Hanged Man, the Star, and the Universe.

As mentioned above, the picture shows a shaman performing a ritual under the Moon. It takes place in a woodland by a pool of water. If we have discussed snakes as symbols, we should remember that when people recognize spiritual power all around them and in themselves, symbols become more than intellectual notions or pretty pictures. A living snake does not just *represent* the power of the Goddess, it *is* that power. And when we find that power in ourselves we discover an identity between ourselves and the serpent. Therefore, the shaman raises her own Strength as she lifts the snake from the pool. The pool is the unconscious, the hidden mysteries. By holding up the snake the shaman connects the Above and Below, the Sky and the Earth, the conscious and the unconscious, heaven and the underworld.

The woman's legs form the Ur-Rune. She holds the snake in something like the figure 8. However, the circles do not close. The snake does not bite its own tail. The image here is more of a spiral than a circle. This indicates the opening of new possibilities. When we find our own Strength, our lives open up. We see the world and ourselves in new ways. We will see this theme of the snake forming an open spiral in the Universe, the final trump. Here, the snake spirals upward, a symbol of personal evolution, personal power. In the Universe, the dragon spirals down, the power returning to the world.

The snake is green, the color of new life. The underside, however, is red, the color of the energy which allows that life to exist. We see the red at three important points—where the tail leaves the water, where the woman's hand holds it, and behind her body. Red suggests the salamander, the legendary lizard that lives in fire. The salamander symbolizes the divine flame.

The way the woman holds the snake recalls the ancient image of a snake wound around a stick. This is the sign of the healer, best known as the wand of Aesculapius, the Greek God of healers. Aesculapius was the son of Apollo, God of the Sun.

The snake looks to the left, the side of the unconscious. The woman looks right. It is the task of the shaman, of the human, to bring the power into consciousness. Discovery of it is the first step. The shaman is a healer. She or he does not travel to the Otherworld for pleasure. She does not raise the serpent just for herself. As a healer, she serves the community. This is part of what allows her to tap the energy without being overwhelmed. She does not do it for herself alone.

As a shaman, the woman in Strength is an aspect of the Magician. Strength, remember, is the Magician's higher octave. Trump 8, however, does not simply repeat trump 1. The second level complements the first. It shows the female pole of the Magician's primary male energy. We see this in the pictures and the themes, but also in the numbers. The figure 1 is as fundamentally male as the 8 is female.

In the Haindl Tarot, Strength is far more than the female version of the Magician. She is the source of the Magician's power, his Shakti. Through ritual magic, meditation, yoga, vision quest or other disciplines, the seeker connects him or herself to the fundamental life-energy of the universe. And so he becomes a magician, a shaman, able to travel between the worlds and perform rituals, heal, even transform the material world. But the magic does not lie in the person, not in our usual sense of "person" as something separate and distinct from the universe around it. If we think of a human being as a channel between Spirit and the physical world, we gain a better idea of how magic works. There is a Christian description of humans as "halfway between the angels and the beasts." Moralists see this as humans being subject both to noble purposes and base desires. We can also see this phrase as meaning that which connects the angels (sacred reality) with the beasts (physical reality). Now, most of us close ourselves off to that great power. We do this automatically, for our own protection. Without knowledge and a trained will (the Chariot) the energy would overwhelm us. The story of the *Sorcerer's Apprentice* is an allegory of this danger. The Magician, then, is a person who has opened up the energy and knows how to direct it. The energy itself, the Shakti, is Strength.

In the picture, the woman rests one foot firmly on the land, while the other touches the water. The end of the snake's tail remains in the pool. The woman keeps her connection to the unconscious. At the same time her position on the ground shows her commitment to action.

The woman has gray-white hair. She stands among old trees. As in many other cards we find symbols of great age, a reminder that the Tarot reaches back to ancient wisdom. The sacred traditions go back a long way. They remain true because they originate in the realities of nature. And yet, the woman is young, while fresh plants grow round the water. Because the ancient paths come from psychic reality, they never become worn-out. When we feel Strength in ourselves we become old and young at the same time.

DIVINATORY MEANINGS

In readings the Strength card focuses on the personal quality of inner strength. The card is one of love and gentleness. The person deals with life and specific situations in a positive way. She or he is firm without being aggressive. She can do this because of a positive attitude toward herself. She is at ease with herself, and therefore with the world around her. Many of the positive qualities of Leo apply as well to Strength.

We should realize a difference between the sign and the Tarot card. If someone is born under Leo, the properties of that sign stay throughout the person's life. The way it shows up will change over the years but the basic quality remains. A Tarot reading describes a moment. As a number of people have pointed out, the Tarot is a "book of changes," like the *I Ching*. It shows the way life constantly moves out of one state and into another. It shows the way circumstances change, and the way people either help or resist the changes. Therefore, Strength does not describe a person in any absolute way. It says that at this time the person is strong, confident, able to give love to others and the world. If the card appears in some long-term position, such as Basis in the Celtic Cross, it suggests that Strength is fairly basic to the person at this stage of life. If it shows up in a more transitory place, such as Near Future, it advises the person to use the strength while it lasts.

Strength can mean a taming of your inner passions. If the person has been struggling with some problem, especially such things as anger, or depression, or perhaps an obsession or addiction of some kind, Strength indicates overcoming it and finding peace. Strength shows the ability to continue and not be overwhelmed. Thus, it would go very well alongside the Chariot, which indicates the will to continue. Together, the two cards might say that the person finds strength by making a firm decision.

All these positive qualities become possible when we discover we are not cut off from the universe, with only our own limited reserves of energy to carry us through life. As a card of advice, Strength tells us to give up the ego focus on "my strength, my power." Instead, we need to open ourselves to the energy all around us. This meaning becomes emphasized with the Hanged Man or the Star or the Ace of Cups.

REVERSED

When Strength is reversed, the person feels blocked from her power. She feels weak, overwhelmed, with very limited resources. Outside situations or her own feelings become too much for her. The other cards should give an idea of whether the problem is temporary or long-term. Either way, the person needs first to recognize the weakness and then begin a program of restoration. If the card indicates a health problem, then diet and rest may help. If the person is overwhelmed by emotional problems, then she needs to step back from them, to recognize her limits and not feel guilty.

Strength reversed shows a person cut off from that unlimited energy source described in the card. The person needs to have more confidence in life. Meditation, or tai chi, or some form of relaxation, may help restore the person.

Sometimes we feel weak because we want to feel weak. If people find themselves with responsibilities they do not want, weakness can seem like an excuse. The reader should pay special attention to this possibility if Strength reversed appears in the position Hopes and Fears. The fear of weakness can mask the desire for it. If this seems the case, the person needs to ask, "What would I get from being weak? Would it give me privileges, or let me make demands on people?" And finally, "Can I allow myself to ask for things out of strength rather than weakness?"

IX

THE HERMIT

A s number nine, or 3 × 3, the Hermit relates to the Empress, and indeed we see the Mother Rune, Hagall, within the lantern. Nine is a lunar number, a sacred number of Wicca (witchcraft). If we think of solar qualities as action and being busy in the world, and lunar as withdrawn, contemplative, then we see that the Hermit does indeed belong to the Moon. And nine forms the higher octave of two, the High Priestess. Just as Strength added the female pole to the Magician, so the Hermit adds the masculine qualities of intellectual teachings to the deep instincts of the High Priestess. The High Priestess contains all knowledge, but at a level that cannot be expressed in rational terms. The Hermit shows the beginning of an awareness that can bring the High Priestess's inner wisdom into the light of consciousness. Traditionally the Hermit depicts a wise teacher who has withdrawn from society to gain wisdom, but who now holds up the light of knowledge for the guidance of others.

The Hebrew letter, Yod, means "Hand." The Hermit's hand carries the light and the staff. The hand (more precisely the thumb) separates us from other animals, allowing us to hold tools and thereby create culture. Many of our human tools have gone to subjugate and now destroy nature. But the Hermit's tools work for harmony and spiritual guidance. Yod also forms the first letter of God's four-letter name in Hebrew (spelled in English YHVH). It symbolizes the beginning of wisdom, and God's healing grace. Healing and wisdom therefore come to us through meditation with this card's warm and joyous image.

The Rune, Is, or I, means "ice." A difficult Rune, it traditionally represents inertia, a cooling-off. In terms of the Hermit, however, these become positive qualities. Having withdrawn from the outside, the Hermit does not need to go anywhere or do anything. And the lunar qualities include coolness, compared to the hot action of the Sun. Is also means the self, I, in English. In German the word light, *licht*, contains "ich," the same as "I" in English. The Hermit

The Hermit

does not seek to submerge his sense of self in nature. On the contrary, he leaves society to discover the true "I." The ninth Rune also suggests the numeral 1, that is, unity, focused will, the Magician. In Goethe's *Faust,* the "alphabet of the witches" tells us that nine is one. The Rune also resembles the Hermit's stick. The stick, however, curves down, a symbol of humility. The straight Rune also suggests the human spine, and therefore the kundalini, which rises up the spine to the head.

The astrological symbol is Virgo, the virgin and an aspect of both the Moon and the High Priestess. Again it suggests withdrawal, for the Virgin does not mean only sexual innocence, but a conscious choice to avoid sexual involvement. While Virgo belongs to the new Moon, some recent Tarot decks have connected this card to the old Moon by changing the Hermit to the "Crone." The crone is a wise woman, a teacher and a healer. Being beyond childbearing she has returned to a "virginal" state. Because of her experience she signifies a higher level of consciousness, the same concept we saw in the number nine as a higher octave of two.

Like the Chariot, this card derives from Hermann Haindl's own experience. Some time ago he visited Glastonbury Tor, one of England's major spiritual centers, a place seen by many as Avalon, the entrance to the "fairy world," which is to say the mythic realm of the Goddess. While there, he saw a vision of light around the mountain, despite heavy clouds. In this card he transmitted that vision, not literally, but what it meant to him. Interestingly, British pagans teach that the physical tor at Glastonbury only embodies a more ancient tower, a pillar of light, visible to those initiated into the mysteries (see Alchemy and Aeon).

The owls filling the picture derive from another experience. Many Native Americans consider owls as carriers of dreams. Now, in the Tarot dreams relate to the Moon, and therefore the Hermit. We can, in fact, view the Hermit as an interpreter of dreams, and his wisdom as the understanding that comes from knowing the ways in which the unconscious expresses itself. While in America, Haindl received an eagle feather (the high-flying eagle symbolizes the soaring spirit), with owl feathers attached for powerful dreams. The person who gave him the feathers did not prepare them himself, but got them from a medicine woman. Knowing nothing of Hermann Haindl, the healer added special medicine because she sensed that the person who would receive it needed healing from some deep pain. Hearing this, Haindl identified the pain as the physical and psychic suffering he'd undergone in the war.

The picture shows a man standing on a mountaintop surrounded by birds. A large owl spreads its wings above his head, reminding us of the swan on the card of the Fool. As we have noted before, birds symbolize the spirit. In mythology they act as messengers between the gods and humanity. The hero who learns "the language of the birds" has achieved the power of prophecy, wisdom denied to ordinary perceptions. In European folklore owls bear a double symbolism. On the one hand, they bring wisdom, an image current today in children's books and Disney cartoons. On the other hand, people sometimes considered owls as servants of the Devil, witches' "familiars," like black cats. The fear of owls comes from the fact that they hunt at night, and so embody humans' fear of darkness. The Hermit holds up his lantern, bringing light to the owls and the dark clouds. Human wisdom can enlighten nature. It exposes the dark fears of superstition. True wisdom, however, will not throw away all mythology and spiritual teachings. Instead, it will light the way through the maze of beliefs to the core of mystery and truth.

As well as birds, gnomes appear around the Hermit. They seem to emerge from the rock; the rock itself contains just the suggestion of a face, as if in an earlier stage of emergence. The gnomes symbolize elemental spirit forces alive in nature. Many cultures have recognized all of nature as a living being, filled with spirit, with no hard difference between organic and inorganic. We can also view the gnomes as symbolizing earlier stages of human evolution, when people had not separated themselves from nature. Through the creation of culture and individuality we have achieved that necessary separation. The task now is to find harmony. This does not mean merging back into the rock. It simply means creating a relation to our world that is respectful and not destructive.

The curved stick in the Hermit's right hand symbolizes this relationship. The stick carries several associations. As a shepherd's crook it indicates humanity's responsibility to nurture and protect the world around us the way a shepherd protects his flock. As a bishop's staff, it reminds us that the Hermit may separate from society to gain wisdom, but ultimately he must return as a teacher. A stick with a hook on the end also figures in the Native American Sun Dance, a yearly ritual involving several Native American nations. Hermann and Erica Haindl have had the privilege of observing this ceremony a number of times. The Sun Dance cannot begin until the dancers have found a curved stick similar to the one the Hermit is holding.

The stick rises in a straight line and then turns down again. This tells us that we gain wisdom, even mastery over our lives, yet ultimately return to the Earth. Our religious teachings tell us "ashes to ashes, dust to dust." But is this such a terrifying idea, to come out of nature and return to nature? The stick also says something about humanity's relation to divinity. The curve indicates true humility, the knowledge that we will die. But if we accept that, we can then worhsip God joyously, opening our arms, like the Hermit, to the divine presence in all existence.

As well as the shepherd's crook the card carries two other images of human culture, the lantern and the ornate eye in the triangle on the left of the card. The lantern symbolizes human knowledge and the teachings that transmit that knowledge from one generation to the next. When I discussed the eye with Hermann Haindl and his wife, Erica Haindl, Erica said that as something man-made, it seemed almost out of place in this card emphasizing nature. Hermann described it as the eye of God watching over the world. Erica pointed out that it showed a man-made image of God's eye.

An eye inside a triangle forms a traditional image of God. We saw a similar form over the Empress. Americans may recall the occult image on the back of the dollar bill: an eye inside a pyramid. These things do represent human conceptions of God. As a teacher, the Hermit works with such images. True images, however, take us within the outer form to the spiritual reality that inspired it.

Real-life hermits have often withdrawn from human society for just this purpose—to reach beyond cultural ideas for a personal connection to God. In India we find the ancient tradition of yoga; in medieval Europe we find accounts of hermits in woods and deserts, mountaintops and caves.

The card carries a certain mythic quality, suitable for a bringer and interpreter of dreams. Beside the mysterious gnomes we find the bright light around the Hermit's head. Elliptical rather than round, it cannot come from any heavenly body. Instead, it matches the light from the lantern. We can call it the light of wisdom, or divine grace. The lantern shines with a small part of this light. We see rainbows around both, but the one above shines more brightly. The image of the rainbow will return, more powerfully, in the Hanged Man.

We have assumed that the Hermit stands on a peak. This accords with the idea that human beings go "up" to enlightenment. We talk of "rising" to a "higher" truth. In much religious symbolism the ground equals physical limitation, the sky equals spiritual release. But we can also look at the Hermit as standing in a cave, with the light above as daylight shining through a hole in the roof. Real-life hermits often retreat to caves. And remember that humans once performed their rituals and painted their magnificent art deep in caves, such as the Lascaux Caves in France. To go down into a cave means to re-enter the womb of the Mother. To leave the daylight and enter the dark requires the ego to give up its sense of separateness from the world. In the cave we become part of the whole.

Therefore, we can look at our Hermit in two ways. We can see him going "up," for wisdom, enlightenment, and service as a teacher. And we can see him going "down," into unity with the Empress and her eternal rhythms of life.

DIVINATORY MEANINGS

The Hermit signals a withdrawal from outside interests, for some private purpose. Usually this will not mean anything so drastic as climbing a mountain or living in a cave. Most of us could not do such things even if we wanted to. The Hermit means a psychological withdrawal, paying more attention to yourself, or to some "higher" spiritual purpose. The idea of lack of involvement connects the Hermit to the High Priestess. But the Hermit calls for more mental activity. Instead of sitting in silence the Hermit works on him or herself.

As a teacher, the Hermit will eventually return to others. For now, however, he needs time for himself. Sometimes, though not so commonly, the Hermit may indicate an actual teacher or some other wise figure, such as a therapist. This meaning might come in if the card appears in a position representing other people. In Hopes and Fears it may show a desire for a teacher. More likely, it will refer to a desire to be left alone.

As a figure who has followed his own path and acquired wisdom, the Hermit symbolizes self-reliance, the ability to do things on your own without leaning on others. It can also mean self-creation, developing your personality, gaining wisdom, learning more about yourself, bringing out abilities and talents. If the subject relates to the image of the Hermit with a fear of loneliness, then the reader might help him or her to see the positive side of being alone.

Because of the owls, and the mysterious quality of this version of the Hermit, the card can indicate powerful dreams. It may suggest that you interpret your dreams, thinking about what they mean, exploring them with your imagination, seeing what emotions they arouse.

REVERSED

The Hermit reversed means, first of all, involvement with others. The card may act as a recommendation, saying this is not the time to withdraw. See people, get the advice or assistance of friends. Do things with other people.

In Hopes and Fears the reversed card may indicate a fear of loneliness, or a belief in your own weakness that makes you think you cannot accomplish anything on your own.

With the Haindl Tarot the reversed Hermit may mean disturbing dreams. This meaning, however, will not come in as often as the simpler ones. Tarot readers should be careful of following any interpretation (for themselves as well as for others) that implies psychic disturbance.

The Hermit shows an old man, the quintessential symbol of the adult. Right side up, therefore, the card may indicate maturity. Reversed, it may refer to a desire not to grow up, like Peter Pan, wanting to play instead of following the Hermit's path to wisdom.

X

THE WHEEL OF FORTUNE

THE NUMBER TEN ends a sequence of numbers and begins a new sequence. Therefore, the tenth trump shows a turning wheel. The image implies a confrontation with life, for a wheel has long symbolized fate, sometimes up, sometimes down, always changing, bringing us unexpected experiences.

The Hebrew letter for the Wheel of Fortune, Kaph, means "Palm." Palmistry has always ranked high among humans' attempts to gain some knowledge of their destiny. Hermann Haindl did not know the Hebrew letter when he painted an open hand at the center of the picture.

The Rune, Jara or Ger, J, means "year." The other great theme found in the turning wheel is that of the year, the essential cycle of birth (spring), flowering (summer), withering (autumn) and death (winter), followed once more by birth. People have seen the wheel of the year as an indication that all life follows such a pattern, rebirth comes after death and new creation arises out of destruction. The shape shows a diamond for the four seasons with a single line indicating the unity of life. The shape also describes the four directions or "quarters" of the world. The line is the center, or the vertical axis of the world, in mythology a great tree or a mountain. Another version of the name is Ar, which suggests the German word *adler*, in English, "eagle." In Norse myth an eagle flies at the top of the World Tree (see the Universe, trump 21). The high-flying eagle symbolizes looking over one's whole life as if from above. We will see this idea developed further in the following trump, Justice.

According to astrology, the Earth follows a 24,000-year cycle, with each 2,000 years in a particular sign of the zodiac. This is not a theory but a fact of astronomy expressed in astrological terms. Any good book on astrology will explain it in detail. When people talk of the "Age of Aquarius" they refer to the fact that the 2,000 years of Pisces have almost ended, and the period of Aquarius is beginning.

The Wheel of Fortune

Many people see the 24,000-year "Great Year" as a cycle of harmony and destruction. For the first 12,000 years, as the Wheel turns upward, life expands, becomes joyous, creative. As the Wheel turns down, disharmony comes in, ending in times of violence, confusion and suffering. We have come to the final stage of this cycle, the age of destruction. Certainly the last centuries have displayed a panorama of war, genocide, death factories and now environmental collapse. But if we have reached the final stage we can also hope that the cycle is ending.

We still face terrible dangers. We still see violence and hatred throughout the world. And yet, the last years have brought signs of hope as well. The concern for nature, the push toward disarmament, the liberation movements, the condemnation of racism and war, the reawakening of sacred traditions among such people as

Native Americans, the return of the Goddess into human consciousness—these all point to a turn of the Wheel.

Whether such events signal a real change in the world we cannot know at this point. The concept of the turning Wheel includes the mystery of time as well as its cycles. As mortal beings we cannot know the outcome of events until they happen. When we do Tarot readings, we often cannot see the real meaning within situations until they work themselves out. So we must wait, and struggle for good outcomes to our world's dangers. But we can hope as well.

The planet for trump 10 is Jupiter. As the largest planet, Jupiter represents expansion and prosperity, positive ideas for the constant turning of the Year. The card contains another divinity, Fortuna, Roman Goddess of luck. And behind her (according to Tarot writer Barbara Walker) stands the more ancient figure of Vortumna, She Who Turns the Year. The element is Fire, the energy of life which keeps the Wheel turning.

The picture shows the Wheel set against a field of stars symbolizing the cosmos. Outside the Wheel we see three faces. Below, looking upward, we see the Mother, the Earth. At the upper left appears a man, the Sky Father, Zeus (Jupiter), the Father of the gods. Lightning—Zeus's energizing power—flashes before him. At the upper right we see a child, androgynous, like the Fool. The child symbolizes humanity. The face is old, withered, representing our ancestors. We are children, and like children we must always learn everything over again with each turn of the Wheel, each new generation. But we are old as well, like an old soul going through yet another incarnation. For the child symbolizes each individual human as well as all humanity, and the woman and man represent our own mothers and fathers, as well as Gaia, the Earth, and Zeus, the Sky.

The Wheel has six spokes. The Buddhist "Wheel of Being," a symbol of the universe, has six spokes, as does a wheel held by a Celtic statue of a God who also carries thunderbolts, making him a figure of Jupiter. Here, the spokes form the Rune Hagall, linking it to the Empress. When we lay out the trumps in rows of seven, the Wheel comes below the Empress, as the higher octave. The spokes all go through the transparent hand. A drop of light emerges in the center of the palm, at the meeting point of the spokes.

Each of the six sections of the Wheel contains an image. From lower right and moving counter-clockwise, we see mushrooms, a snake, a unicorn, an eye, a dinosaur and a stain. Outside the Wheel cosmic bubbles appear, dark blue below, gold above.

The Wheel of Fortune was the first card Haindl painted when he began his work on the Tarot. Perhaps he did so in tribute to "the turn of the wheel" that gave him the time for such a large project. The mushrooms resemble the very first painting Haindl did as a child, inspired by children's books, with their pictures of the fairy world. In Germany, mushrooms symbolize luck, a fitting image for the card. But the "fairies" actually form a debased version of the pre-Christian deities. And part of worshipping those deities may have involved eating hallucinogenic "magic mushrooms."

The snake symbolizes the deeper truth within the world of the fairies. The snake links the halfway card to the final trump, the Universe, with its serpent (and to the Empress, Strength and the Devil). In many decks the Wheel and the World (the Universe) bear a strong resemblance, for achieving the final triumph means to know the eternal truth within the center of the turning Wheel. A snake often appears on traditional versions of the Wheel, usually pointing down, to symbolize death. In the Haindl Tarot the snake winds upward, signifying rebirth.

The unicorn is another childlike image. Compare it to the unicorn of the Lovers or the Moon. In our culture we have taken powerful symbols and reduced them to nursery cartoons. Still, the white unicorn symbolizes purity and sincerity. It also signifies the Spirit leaping beyond the Wheel.

The eye in the next section of the Wheel is old, indicating time. The Wheel turns, creating the passage of time in a person's life. But the soul and the world are ancient, traveling through many cycles. The eye also foreshadows both the following card, Justice, with its peacock "eyes," and trump 20, with its eye behind the cloud. The eye demands that we look at fate, not simply accept it. In discussing this card, Haindl told of a story he had read that the entire human being once stood open to the universe. Now only the eyes remain willing to take in the outside. And for most of us the third eye, the center of spiritual perception, remains closed.

The dinosaur, another cartoonlike image, reflects the unicorn. But the dinosaur is a fantasy of a creature that really existed. It symbolizes all those things lost in the turning of time. They become pictures in our minds.

In the final section we see only a dark stain, symbol, perhaps, of mortality, or just of the *messiness* of life. Drops of dirty, oiled water drip down on the left, and up the right, indicating a counter-clockwise turn, the direction of liberation (when we turn a screw clockwise to attach something, and counter-clockwise to detach it, we actually follow a very old esoteric tradition).

The face above, the Father, stares with great intensity, even giving off lightning. He represents the active approach to life, concerned with power and involvement. Below, the Mother looks up from the dark with a dreamy quiet, simply watching the Wheel turn. Christianity teaches us to prepare for a future existence. Buddhism instructs us how to remove ourselves from the Wheel of karma. But daily life and nature do exist, even if ultimately a dream. The revival of Paganism has celebrated the physical and the ordinary, with festivals following the seasons, and rituals to bring happiness for oneself and others. The Tarot, through such cards as Justice and the Hanged Man (the following two trumps), suggests that we can release ourselves from karma without detaching ourselves from the world. Freedom involves self-knowledge and choice, but not necessarily removal.

The stars around the Mother give a sense of distance, of age. They remind us of fate, for astrology arises from the human desire to discover our destiny from the patterns of the universe. In a way, we reduce the stars to our level when we see them only in terms of astrology, or of constellations modeled on human mythology. In the stars above the face we see no patterns, no constellations.

The center of a Wheel does not turn. Therefore, say the mystics, focus on the center of life, and not the constant change. In the center of the card we see the hand. Originally Haindl painted a drop of blood, like the stigmata of Christ, or the wounded swan. Blood suggests accepting life despite its suffering. In Italy, however, Hermann and Erica Haindl performed a ritual of raising their hands to the Sun, letting in the light, as if the palms had opened like the third eye (see the open arms of the Hermit and the Hanged Man). And so, the blood became light, assuring us we will receive joy if we open ourselves to life.

Though palmistry, and astrology, may suggest a pre-ordained

fate, the modern approach to both these arts—and the Tarot—
emphasizes free will. The potential events shown in our palms or
our horoscopes only "collapse" into reality (as the physicists say)
when we act, or fail to act, in a particular way. The open hand implies accepting what life brings you. But it also means taking hold
of your life, not denying it or running from it, but using it. A woman
I know suffered grreatly as a child due to sexual attacks. For many
years she tried to ignore what had happened. As a result, she found
herself fearful, depressed, unable to work. Finally, she decided not
only to confront her experience, but to do something with it. Now
she runs a center and a counseling service to help other women who
suffered in their own childhoods, and she feels joyous and strong.

We need to take more than our personal destiny in our hands.
The fate of the Earth depends on us. We need to make sure the
Wheel turns round, giving life a chance.

DIVINATORY MEANINGS

The Wheel of Fortune indicates a change of circumstance, or
some unexpected event. The wheel of the person's life turns, either
for better or for worse, and she or he needs to deal with the new situation. The other cards may give some advice on the best approach.

If Court cards appear,* or other cards indicating a powerful person (such as the Empress or Emperor), they may signify that the
change comes largely from someone else's action. We should take
care with such an interpretation. For one thing, such literalism can
cause people to anxiously examine all their relations. Also, we need
to remember that Court cards, like the other cards that can be used
to refer to a person, may refer to the subject of the reading.

The imagery of the traditional Wheel of Fortune has always
implied a certain powerlessness. The picture here, of the hand rising
through the Wheel, suggests taking hold of our lives. In its deepest
meaning, the Wheel of Fortune in a reading can refer to a person
grabbing hold of his or her own fate. If the cards, or the person's
own sense of self say the person has been drifting, then the Wheel
says now is the time to take what life has given you—and use it.

---

*See Volume II.

REVERSED

The reversed card may suggest that the Wheel does not turn. Whatever situations exist now will likely remain for a time. More often, however, the reversed Wheel shows a difficulty in adjusting to changes that have occurred.

The medieval image of the Wheel of Fortune (source of the Tarot card) showed a powerful king crushed by turning fate. Because of this some commentators describe the Wheel right side up as a disastrous turn of events, and the reversed Wheel as beneficial. In practice, I have found it more useful to look at the question of acceptance. Right side up, the person tends to adjust. Reversed, he or she resists. The open hand clenches into a fist.

Readers often find the Wheel of Fortune a hard card to interpret. For one thing, since a Tarot reading reaches forward in time as well as back, it may refer to a change that has not yet occurred. Also, it shows actions and events coming from outside the person. Most cards depict the subject of the reading—his or her behavior, desires, background, actions, etc. But the Wheel of Fortune reaches beyond the person to events created by others or simply life itself.

XI

JUSTICE

THE NUMBER ELEVEN implies a union of the Magician and the High Priestess, for 1 + 1 = 2. Trump 11 bears the Hebrew letter Lamed, which means "Ox-goad" or whip. Spiritual Justice goads us into development. When we realize that we must suffer the consequences of our actions we become more conscious of what we do. We learn to take responsibility for our lives, and this leads to directing our lives in ways that will benefit us, and the world.

The Rune Nyd, N, means "Necessity." Spiritual Justice does not deal in moral issues. Events do not happen because they should, but because they must, as the consequences of our own actions and the conditions of life. Necessity, therefore, refers to the working out of situations in the only way possible. It also indicates situations or circumstances we cannot control or change. Such things as sickness (in ourselves or in others), death and social upheavals form necessities, in that we must learn to deal with them in the best way possible.

This does not imply a limit to free will or argue that humans lack the power to control their own lives. Part of the challenge of life—and this trump—lies in facing difficulties. As we shall see, the meaning of Justice rests in the scales, the balance of inner and outer, necessity and free will.

The shape of the Rune resembles a sword. In traditional Tarots Justice carries a sword as well as a set of scales. The sword represents the ability to reason and make choices. It also indicates action, for Justice does not only mean self-knowledge, it also demands that we act on that knowledge.

The astrological sign for Justice is Libra, often depicted as balanced scales. The element, Air, signifies thought; to discover the inner truth of our lives we need to think, to analyze. Some time ago it became fashionable to believe that people think too much, that we need to trust our feelings. The Tarot teaches us that thought and emotion do not oppose each other. A true analysis of any situation

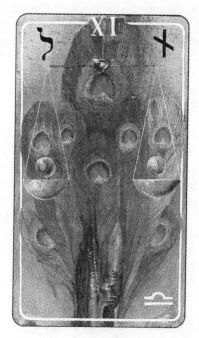

Justice

will base itself on an honest recognition of feelings. It will not stop there, however, but will examine these feelings and the events surrounding them. We need to avoid intellectual games, but not intellect.

In the Haindl Tarot, Justice occupies the eleventh position, a change, as we saw with Strength, from the older tradition. If we take the Fool as separate from the other trumps, then Justice appears in the exact middle of the Major Arcana, with ten cards before it and ten after. Justice indicates coming to terms with our lives so that everything comes into balance. By understanding our past experiences we free ourselves to create a new future. Justice requires contemplation on one side, but action on the other, for the future requires that we make choices.

The scales also balance the interactions between ourselves and the world. On one side we need to recognize outside influences on our lives: other people such as parents, lovers, children, teachers, but also the things implied in the Rune of Necessity: natural occurrences, social conditions, political events and so on. On the other side we balance the scales with our own actions and choices.

It may seem extreme to place the whole world on one side and ourselves on the other. And yet, how else can we understand what has formed us up to the present moment? Justice tells us to take responsibility for everything that happens to us. Balancing the world and yourself leads to liberation. To take an extreme case, people who suffer sexual abuse as children often feel guilty, believing that they have somehow caused their trouble. Or else they may try never to think about it, and as a result find it hard to create sexual lives as adults. Many people who deal with these problems stress that the person needs to recognize that she or he did not cause the event; the other person caused it. Nevertheless, it happened. It formed part of the person's world. The child, and later the adult, needs to balance these two fundamental facts.

Everything in the Haindl picture of Justice suggests this theme of balance. We actually see two separate images of balance, the scales in the foreground, and the peacock feathers behind them. The scales form an abstract image, hanging from some invisible holder, unchanging, with the cosmic balls suspended above the pans. This signifies that Justice always exists in the universe as a perfect principle. Ultimately, the cosmos and every being in it are in balance. On the other hand, the feathers exist in a much more precarious balance. At the moment they appear symmetrical, with two large feathers in the middle, and the same number and arrangement of feathers on either side. But a breath of wind would disrupt them. In the world of ordinary experience Justice often seems remote. Droughts occur in one part of the world, floods in another. People suffer terrible oppression, as in the Nazi camps, or under apartheid. Invaders destroy entire cultures and peoples, as in the conquest of the Americas. On the individual level, good people die of painful diseases, while people selfish or cruel may live to a healthy old age.

And yet, something in us believes that Justice exists. Therefore, we see the two images: the unchanging abstraction and the fragile reality. This duality becomes something else we need to balance.

We can look more closely at the two images. The scales hang from a downward-pointing Water triangle. In its center we see a ball.

If we look closely we can see silver on one side, gold on the other. The sphere forms a kind of yin-yang symbol, like the Moon and star on the Chariot. This reminds us that the whole idea of duality, so basic to everything in the card, is a fiction, for life changes constantly, with all its aspects moving in and out of each other. Such a realization gives more meaning to the idea of a perfect moment, when life becomes suspended, and we can see clearly the past and the future, the outside world and ourselves, *as if* balanced on separate scales.

The scales themselves hang from wires whose shapes form upward-pointing Fire triangles. The triangles imply the six-pointed star. We see the star more clearly in the arrangement of the feathers. Because we see the triangles combined in the feathers but separated in the scales, we understand again that in nature everything mingles. In the abstract vision we find the possibility, even the necessity, of seeing the elements as isolated forces for the purpose of understanding.

The idea of duality continues in the two scales. The one on the left, silver, indicates the Moon (the yin, or High Priestess principle), while the gold scale, on the right, symbolizes the Sun (yang, or Magician). Above each scale floats a ball, transparent to symbolize clarity, and freedom from attachment. We need to see through the outer circumstances of our lives to the inner meaning and the causes of events. Justice carries the faculty of *clear sight*. In order to see our lives we may have to step back from them. This idea of detachment gives a new meaning to the idea of Justice as a special moment. We would not wish to live our lives in a state of standing back. Such an approach becomes as unbalanced as never thinking about our lives at all.

If clear sight implies a cool analysis, that, too, is only half a truth, one side of the scales. The peacock feathers each contain an eye, and in fact, one peacock eye appears above each of the two balls. They represent "seeing" our emotions. If we confront our feelings honestly we often can trace them back to the truth of our experiences. The Tarot writer Mary Greer has described how we can use the Tarot for this purpose, following our feelings back to our own truth.

The scales hang from silver wires suspended from a silver cross bar. The wires and bar are spiraled, symbolizing evolution. To achieve the clarity of Justice does not simply leave us who we are but raises us to a higher level. And the teachings of many cultures tell us that true spiritual Justice requires many lifetimes.

The feathers come from the peacock, a symbol in India for reincarnation and karma (see Death for the Christian symbolism of the peacock). We have looked at Justice primarily as an assessment of this life. Full understanding demands that we balance all experience, including past lives. Ultimately, perfect Justice sees the entire history of the universe in any single moment. Buddhist doctrine teaches that Gautama achieved enlightenment, and therefore liberation, when he remembered—when he saw clearly—every instant of all his past lives.

We have looked at the arrangement of the feathers as a six-pointed star. They also appear, more or less, in three vertical columns, symbolizing the various aspects of life brought together through the principle of Justice. We saw in the Lovers how the Kabbalistic Tree of Life forms three columns. The outer columns symbolize opposing forces in the universe—contraction and expansion, harshness and mercy. By balancing the two sides, the middle pillar keeps the cosmos from pulling apart.

There are eight feathers. The number reminds us of the traditional position for the card. Moving it to 11 does not wipe out all its past associations. We can still view Justice as the higher harmonic of the Magician. Eight $= 4 \times 2$, that is, the outer laws and powers of the Emperor transformed by the inner truth of the High Priestess. If we think of the Major Arcana as three rows of seven, then Justice—as 11—comes directly below the Emperor. In other words, it occupies the fourth position in the second row. Even as 11, therefore, the card is 4×2. The 8–11 duality for Justice is a kind of false issue. Actually, the card occupies both places.

Though the feathers display many colors, violet and indigo predominate. The colors of the two highest chakras, they indicate the evolutionary quality of Justice. These two chakras are the crown, for spiritual openness, and the third eye, for awakened understanding.

Instead of emerging from the body of a peacock, the feathers appear rooted in a tree trunk. On either side we see the top of a stone, hinting at the mass of the Earth. This suggests that spirit does not exist apart from nature. At the same time the tree trunk and the rock provide a dark contrast with the bright colors of the feathers and the transparent balls. We even see a cavelike hole in the tree. These things remind us of the barrier on the card of the Lovers, separating our physical knowledge of the world from spiritual truth. The fact that we can only see the top of the stones tells us that so much of the universe remains hidden from us. If Justice means complete knowledge of the self, most of us live our lives in ignorance.

The picture, however, gives us hope of transcending that ignorance. The tree trunk and the two stones lie behind the white border. The feathers, however, overlap the border. Through dedication to spiritual practices, and a willingness to see the truth, we can achieve that perfect moment.

DIVINATORY MEANINGS

The meanings for Justice focus primarily on the idea of awareness. When we receive Justice in a reading it calls us to examine our lives, to weigh things in balance. This may refer to an overall assessment, in other words, to consider what we have done with our lives up to this point, what choices face us in the future. More immediately, it may call for a review of some particular situation. A relationship is going badly. Upset, one of the people reads the cards and gets Justice. This suggests looking at the history of the relationship —who did what, how the people acted in particular situations and crises, what emotional baggage they carried with them from past relationships. All this has to be balanced against the choices facing them for the future.

This may sound cool, distant. As we have seen, Justice sometimes requires a step backward. But an honest assessment means emotional honesty as well. Experience your feelings about the situation as openly as possible. This will help you discover what they actually are. Try to keep some awareness of what you and the other people involved are doing. For instance, if someone does something that makes you angry, be aware of the way he or she has provoked you and why. But be aware also of the way you have chosen anger as a response, and might have chosen something else. Through such assessments we move toward freedom. Instead of acting entirely through conditioned responses, instead of believing we have no choice, we learn through Justice to exercise our free will.

If Justice appears with Swords cards, especially the Ace, it emphasizes the faculty of analysis. The Ace of Swords is the sword of truth, cutting through illusions. We then weigh and analyze what we discover, being as honest with ourselves as possible. Justice, as a therapist friend of mine says, is "a hard one."

Because the picture emphasizes balance, the Haindl version of Justice calls for us to take a balanced view of the situation, not going to one extreme or the other. This is true especailly when it appears with Alchemy. But the image is more than a recommendation. Through meditation the picture can help us achieve that balance, making a situation, or life in general, more manageable as we free ourselves from emotional extremes.

In some situations the simple title of the card may count for more than the picture. Justice, in other words, can mean a fair outcome. Obviously, this becomes especially important in legal matters.

REVERSED

Justice reversed shows the qualities of the card blocked or denied. The person does not try to balance or analyze. He or she may insist, "It's unfair, I don't deserve this," or alternately, "It's all my fault." Both are distortions; both avoid looking at what really has happened.

Reversed Justice warns the person against acting out of habit. Stop and think about what you are doing and why. What do you really want? Can the situation give it to you? What do you need to do to make it happen?

The reversed card warns against imbalance. Or, it may say that you are acting unfairly. If it appears in some position referring to other people, it may describe their behavior as unfair or extreme.

If Justice reversed appears in a position showing your Hopes and Fears it may indicate a fear of being mistreated. But it also may show a hope of avoiding that kind of honest evaluation shown in the card right side up.

XII

THE HANGED MAN

THE NUMBER TWELVE joins together the male and female polarities. As 12 it consists of 1, the Magician, and 2, the High Priestess. Twelve = 3 × 4, the Empress times the Emperor. Also, 12 is the reverse of 21, the final trump; reversal forms one of the basic images of the Hanged Man. In many traditional Tarot decks, the dancing woman on the world (trump 21) strikes the same pose, only right side up—like an upside-down Hanged Man. In the Fool's journey to wisdom, the Hanged Man signifies the fundamental stage of sacrifice and reversal. He sacrifices the Emperor's desire to dominate the Earth, and he reverses his previous beliefs. The Hanged Man gives up what other people find important: success, power, pride, the ego's sense of being unique and special and separate from the rest of the universe. He gains understanding, peace, union with the Earth, the joy of life.

The Hebrew letter means "Seas," and by extension, the element of Water. Water is indeed the element indicated by the border, while the planet, Neptune, gets its name from the Roman God of the Sea. We do not see water in the picture, though the rainbow implies it. Nor do we see it in most traditional images of the Hanged Man, though a few modern decks show him suspended over the sea, or a pool. Yet water, as a symbol of dissolution, lies deep in the card's meaning. The ego dissolves itself; the separation from life dissolves.

The Fool has that watery sense of unity with all things. The Fool knows that he or she is "no-thing," no fixed pattern of behavior. But we cannot stay innocent, and so we build up a personality, an outward form that enables us to manage our daily lives. In the Chariot we saw the power of that personality—the focused will, the mastery of fear, the ability to confront mortality. There we saw the self riding on the sea of the unconscious, protected by the boat of intellect and will. In the Hanged Man, however, the self surrenders to the unconscious. In place of separation we find unity; in place of primal fear we find peace. If water forms such an important theme why do

The Hanged Man

we find a mountain instead of the sea? The answer is that the surrender becomes possible when we join with the Earth. We can give up the illusion of controlling the world because we know that we belong to all life.

The Rune is T, Tyr, or Tewaz. Most often known as a war God, Tyr was also seen as God of law. Both these things become reversed in the Hanged Man. The aggressive impulse gives way to unity. The laws of nature replace human laws. (Notice how the body forms the international peace symbol, also seen as the Rune for the Tower.) We saw, in the Emperor and the Hierophant, how codes of law can become isolated from natural rhythms. Here we return to those rhythms. The word *Tewaz* connects linguistically to Zeus, the Sky God of the Greeks. In the Hanged Man, the Sky and the Earth become united. Tyr also represented spiritual discipline. The Hanged Man literally sacrifices himself. This theme expands in the card's "true" divinity, Odin. The shape of the Rune resembles the spear which wounds Odin (and Christ) on the World Tree. It also resembles the World Tree itself.

We have already discussed the card's element, Water. Astrologers see Neptune as a planet of inspiration, spiritual light emerging from the dark waters of the unconscious. Odin achieved the Runes by sacrificing himself in the dark well at the base of the World Tree. In the *Elder Edda* (English translation by Paul Taylor and W. H. Auden), Odin says,

> Wounded I hung on a wind-swept gallows
> For nine long nights
> Pierced by a spear, pledged to Odin
> Offered, myself to myself
>
> I looked down: with a loud cry
> I took up the Runes; from that tree I fell.

In a sense all the previous cards have led up to the Hanged Man. The importance of the masculine recognizing the feminine, of humanity returning to the Earth, of a life based on harmony with Nature, all these themes come to fruition in this magnificent image. Haindl has said he could not have painted this picture in this way as a young man. He would have resisted more the idea of surrender. But surrender does not mean resignation, and certainly not defeat. In his sixties, Haindl feels he has learned a basic lesson—the way for humanity, and for the individual, lies in connection, not separation.

Turn the picture around. Notice how the figure seems to fly, like the resurrected Christ ascending to the heavens. In the Church of the Holy Sepulchre, in Jerusalem, the painting of Christ over the tomb exactly mirrors the World Dancer in the traditional version of trump 21. We have already noted how that figure mirrors the Hanged Man. The outstretched arms of the Haindl Hanged Man teach a similar lesson to the open arms of the Hermit. True surrender brings ecstasy and power. He does not submit to a jealous divinity demanding obedience, but to life.

This card forms the second part of a trilogy: the Chariot, the Hanged Man, the Star: 7, 12, 17. As the middle point the Hanged Man is separated from each of the others by the number five, a symbol, as we have seen, of spiritual teachings (the Hierophant), and the Goddess (the pentacle). The Chariot signifies mastery over life. With its imagery of power and totem animals, the Chariot suggested shamanism. Here in the Hanged Man we see Odin, often described as the archetypal shaman. Yet here, Odin—the young god who strode away from the tree—returns to Erda, the Earth. And in the Star, we see this Erda, or Gaia, renewing herself. If only these three cards remained, the Haindl Tarot still would make its statement.

The picture organizes itself around a vertical axis and three receding levels of distance. The axis consists of the Hanged Man himself, with the branch and Venus symbol above him, and the Earth mounds below. The arms stretch out but also downward, matching the curve of the hill. The rainbow, too, matches this curve. At the same time, the line of the trees behind the hill joins with the upward slope on the left to form a diagonal line, rooted on the left and climbing to the right—the Empress direction of harmony.

The Hanged Man's hair seems to merge into the ground, like the roots of a tree. He not only hangs suspended from a branch, but has become the tree himself. We have already compared this Odin/Zeus with the young version in the Emperor. There, the Sky God denied his Earth origin by leaving the tree that mirrored his body. Here he returns, allowing his body to mirror a tree. The imagery also recalls the Magician's dark treelike shadow. That conflict—between consciousness and unity with nature—becomes resolved here, by the Hanged Man's deliberate giving of himself. A stigmata of light appears in the right hand—the side of consciousness—while the left hand remains dark.

The three levels begin in the front with the Hanged Man, the branch and the hill. Behind them we see the two mounds on either side of the hill, and the line of trees. And behind that, in the sky, we see the Moon, and the birds, and the rainbow. The rainbow, however, goes through all levels, coloring the trees and the man, though not the hill. The rainbow derives from a trip Hermann and Erica Haindl made in Ireland. Rainbows there appear in sharp definitions of color. Seeing this, Haindl realized that the order of the colors exactly matches the chakras. In the yogic system, each of the seven chakras radiates a particular color, from red at the root, the base of the spine, to violet for the crown of the head. The order of these colors matches the rainbow—but only when the body is reversed, as in the Hanged Man, or in the yoga posture of standing on one's head.

The landscape forms the body of the Goddess lying on her back. The two side mounds become her breasts, the central hill her pregnant belly, with the bushes at the bottom even suggesting pubic hair. To some, this may seem obscene, or even blasphemous. We have all grown up in a culture based on a transcendent God, detached from the world. This God, declaring His jealousy, forbids the making of any images. How then could we see the land as an image? But in other cultures people have done exactly this. In such places as Crete, or Malta, temples were built to align with some natural image of a female body. Twin mountains became holy as the Goddess's breasts. Caves became sites of rituals because they form an entrance to Her womb. At Silbury, England, prehistoric people built an entire hill to represent the Goddess's pregnant belly. For if the Earth is the Mother, a living being, shouldn't we expect to see Her actual form? And shouldn't that form mark Her places of sacred power?

In the trump we do not see Erda's head. In place of it we find Odin. He hangs from a symbol of the Empress. On one side shines a crescent Moon, signifying the High Priestess, Goddess of mystery. On the other appear Odin's twin ravens, Hugin and Munin (Thought and Memory). According to myth these birds flew about the world, returning with news to their master. But ravens signify death. Black, they ead dead meat. And so, the news they bring is not simply gossip, but information of the "other world." Some historians believe that Odinism (or Asatru, the worship of the Aesir) derived from an older shamanic tradition. And the shamans could heal the living because they traveled in the land of the dead. Odin and the birds look ahead to the next card, Death.

The black ravens match the black "pubic hair" at the bottom, uniting Earth and Sky. Odin, the Sky God, gives himself to the Earth. The Lakota, remember, see black as the color of inspiration, for like Neptune's water it represents the darkness that gives way to light. There are three realms, really, linked to the triple Goddess: the Sky (the Virgin), the Earth (the Mother) and the Underworld (the Crone). In the patriarchal traditions the Sky and the Underworld (Death) belonged to male deities, but the Earth remained female. Even under monotheism we refer to "Mother Nature." In Odin's submission the three become one.

The myth describes Odin as voluntarily sacrificing himself. Pierced with his own spear he hangs on the tree. Though we may think of this as "obviously" referring to Christ, most historians accept that Odin's sacrifice predates the introduction of Christianity to Germany and Scandinavia.

We can also see certain connections between the Runes and Tarot in this story. Odin does not hang upside down, but otherwise he matches the twelfth trump. In the *Edda* Odin describes a twelfth Rune:

> I know a twelfth; if a tree bear
> A man hanged in a halter
> I can carve and stain strong Runes
> That will cause the corpse to speak
> Reply to whatever I ask.

Artists and storytellers often portray Odin as a wandering magician, wearing a floppy hat with a brim that curves down over one eye. This resembles the traditional image of the Tarot Magician, a conjuror who wears a hat with a brim curved to form the infinity sign, ∞.

As the Emperor, Odin strode away from nature and from history. Now he returns, but the way back includes suffering. In the myth not only does he hang in pain from his wound, but he must sacrifice an eye to Mimir, the God of the well of wisdom. He has looked outward; to reach inner wisdom he literally must put out an eye.

The Haindl Hanged Man shows no such agony, only a peaceful reversal. But we have already seen an image of suffering in the wounded swan of the Fool. And the old man on this card, so different from the young, arrogant Emperor, symbolizes humanity's ancientness, which includes its history of pain, stupidity and destruction, as well as its wisdom.

In the patriarchal tradition of Scandinavia Odin sacrifices himself to *himself*. The male God recognizes no outside power. The Haindl Tarot reverses this. Odin gives himself to Erda. In returning to the Earth, he shows us humanity finding its way back to harmony with the natural world. He does not become an innocent child-Fool. Instead, he comes as a seeker of truth. The World Tree, in Scandinavian *Yggdrasil*, does not only hold the physical planet, called Middle Earth in Scandinavian cosmology. It holds the nine worlds, reaching from Asgard, the home of the Gods, to Helheim, the world of the dead. The "ecology" of the Hanged Man recognizes that as spiritual beings we live in all these worlds, not just the middle, but Above and Below.

DIVINATORY MEANINGS

The meanings for the Hanged Man emphasize the idea of attachment. We become so certain of the basic realities in our lives that nothing can shake us. This may mean an attachment to nature, or to a moral principle, or some important purpose in life. It can also indicate a deep spiritual awareness.

The image of the tree suggests an attachment to something greater than day-to-day problems. If a person feels blown about by outside influences, then meditation with the Hanged Man can often have an anchoring effect. Imagine your body literally on a tree, one whose roots sink deep into the Earth, and whose branches reach into the stars. However weak you may feel as an individual, attachment to this tree makes you unshakeable. As part of the meditation you might try standing on one leg, with the arms out. The point of this meditation is to gain a sense of yourself as part of something greater. This does not mean sacrificing your individuality. The Hanged Man remains himself. In my own experience I have found the Hanged Man a great help during times when I've felt myself weak or overly influenced by people or situations. If the Hanged Man comes up in a reading, it tells you to seek such an attachment, or that such a feeling already exists, giving you confidence and peace.

The Hanged Man signifies independence. It shows a person not subject to social pressure, or to fashionable ideas or to manipulation. It tells you not to battle against other people's opinions or demands on you. Recognize that they can do what they like, they cannot shake you. The card advises you to recognize your own strength.

With the Fool the Hanged Man advises action. With various other cards, such as the High Priestess, it might indicate stillness, waiting for the proper moment. Again, this waiting may require ignoring other people's demands to do something, make a decision.

Some people emphasize a more negative view of the Hanged Man. They describe it as a "hang-up," a delay of some kind, or else a psychological block. Or else they emphasize the idea of sacrifice.

What do you need to give up to achieve your goals? Do you need to sacrifice something real, such as a job that demands too much time and energy? Or do you need to give up some stubborn attitude that stops you from dealing with a changed situation? This last meaning might become emphasized if the card appears with the Wheel of Fortune. Still, in practice I have found it best to emphasize the idea of attachment.

REVERSED

The reversed Hanged Man indicates someone overly influenced by outside ideas. It may refer to a particular person or people making demands on the subject of the reading. Or it may stress a pressure to conform. Let us say you wish to do something unorthodox or scandalous. The Hanged Man reversed will suggest that you are hesitating because of social attitudes. Maybe you worry what people will say. Or you fear looking silly. Remember that the reversed card will show the man standing upright—in other words, normal. Turning the card right side up means reversing yourself.

If the card means sacrificing something to get past your hang-ups, then reversed will suggest holding on. Look at your life and see if there is anything you do not want to give up. If you are reading for someone else ask her or him to examine this possibility.

In its most general sense the Hanged Man reversed will depict a person who does not see any purpose in life beyond his or her immediate situation. If the person feels cut off, or weak, the card says to look for that deeper meaning. In terms of the picture, the time has come to return to the Tree.

XIII

DEATH

Ever since Tarot cards became numbered, Death has been card 13. Our culture sees this number as fearsome and therefore suitable for a disturbing card. But what exactly gives thirteen its reputation? In an earlier book I suggested a number of reasons: thirteen "ruins" the perfection of twelve, a number seen around the world as sacred. Judas Iscariot was the thirteenth man at the Last Supper. But there is another reason for the stigma on thirteen. The lunar calendar contains thirteen months (the words "month" and "menstruation" derive from Moon). The lunar calendar belongs to women, and to the Triple Goddess of the Moon, the great enemy in patriarchal religion. When the "Emperor" replaced the old months with a solar calendar, arbitrarily divided into twelve unequal months, he did so partly as a means of taking power away from women. But the physical facts remain, and so do the spiritual truths created by those facts.

The Hebrew letter is Nun. Some commentators give the meaning as "eagle, snake, scorpion"—animals associated with transformation, and therefore death. A more traditional view defines Nun as "fish." In connection with fish spawning, Nun also means "to sprout, to grow," in other words, new life. Many people take this idea—the link of new life with death—as a reassurance that death does not mean the end of everything, but only a prelude to a new existence, either in the "next world" or reincarnated into a new body. The card of Death, however, teaches a deeper lesson than, "Don't worry, death doesn't really matter." Death is necessary for new life. Without the old growth dying and decomposing into the soil through fall and winter, the new buds could not sprout in the spring. Without death, nothing could change. In society, death allows for new growth to take over, with new ideas, new energy, new hope and idealism.

The Rune, Ba or Beorc, B, means "Birch Goddess." However,

Death

the aspect that comes in most strongly here, in connection with
Death, is the "terrible Mother." So far, we have seen the first two
faces of the Goddess, in the High Priestess—the Virgin, and the
Empress—the Mother. This Rune brings us the Crone. The
monthly "death" of the Moon joined with the lessons of othe seasons to teach our ancestors of death's necessity.

According to historians, worship of the Birch Goddess in ancient
Germany involved human sacrifice, possibly of the king identified
with the old year. Around the world, in fact, we find evidence of
sacrifice in connection with Goddess worship, based on the belief
that just as the Earth required dead vegetable matter for fertilizer,
so the Goddess of the land demanded blood to fertilize new life.

In recent years feminist writers have reinterpreted this practice.
They suggest that originally women "offered" their menstrual blood
to the Earth, thereby joining the lunar cycles to the land. When the

men seized religion they turned this around. They depicted the Mother as monstrous and bloodthirsty. They declared menstruation unclean. According to Joseph Campbell, Zoroaster taught that all evil in the universe originated with menstruation. The Bible instructs women to ritually cleanse themselves after their periods. To this day superstitious Jews believe that a single drop of menstrual blood will kill a plant. Though they banished women from spiritual practices, the patriarchal conquerors kept the idea of blood offerings to make the crops grow. They substituted ritual killings for the women's natural flow.

Much of this interpretation remains theoretical. We should also remember that in earlier times, death was an everyday part of people's lives, and to see the Goddess only as a figure of birth and not of death is as distorted as the contemporary American practice of putting makeup on corpses so they will look "normal" during the funeral. Still, whatever the origins of human sacrifice, few people today would wish to return to it. What we need is some way to recognize the reality and importance of death, without letting this awareness overwhelm us.

The Rune also means "barque," or boat, and bier. The bier on which a corpse lay often was seen as a boat, while the Vikings sometimes used burning boats as funeral barges. In many cultures people have depicted the dead souls journeying to the next world in boats, either across a river, or out to sea. The Greeks believed that Charon (seen in the card as the figure standing in the boat) ferried souls to Hades. The Egyptians described death as a passage over water, and sometimes buried their kings in actual boats. In Egyptian myth, when the gods condemn Set for killing his brother Osiris, they transform Set into a boat to carry Osiris to the underworld.

The image of a boat belongs to birth as well as death. The baby's cradle originally symbolized a boat. A German saying describes life as "from the cradle to the bier." Another spelling of the Rune is Bar, which suggests the German word *gebar*, giving birth, just as birth is close to birch. The sea represents formlessness, dissolution, mystery. We come out of mystery and we return to it. Despite the many reassurances of the world's mythologies, no one really knows the origins of an individual soul as it takes form in a body. Nor does anyone know what happens after death. We arrive out of the sea of nothingness into our mothers' wombs. The fetus grows, becomes a body, the body ages and dies and so we return.

The astrological sign for Death is Scorpio. Because the scorpion's sting kills, the sign carries an association with death. Scorpio also rules the sex organs. Again, we see the link between death and generation. But this connection says something else as well. For Scorpio also signifies sexual magnetisim, often dark and destructive. This hints that death fascinates us with an almost sexual power. Many people find themselves drawn to destruction, or to a sexual obsession that effectively destroys their freedom. Freud came to believe that Thanatos (desire for death) ruled the psyche alongside Eros (desire for life). American weapons designers commonly describe new systems for mass slaughter as "sexy," while for some people such horrors as Auschwitz hold a terrible fascination. Part of the challenge of the thirteenth trump lies in recognizing the reality of death while at the same time committing ourselves to life.

Most signs in the zodiac display a single image, such as the bull for Taurus. For Scorpio, esoteric astrology assigns, beside the scorpion, an eagle and a phoenix. This recognizes that spiritual energy and sexual energy are the same. We have already encountered this idea in the Lovers. Here, we should notice that Death is the harmonic of trump 6, and that the fear of death can lead to a fear of sex. In Shakespeare's time and after, people in England referred to orgasm as "dying" or "the little death." In sex, we surrender ourselves. If the ego wishes to barricade itself against the fear of death, any surrender feels like a threat. But we can "overcome" death best by accepting it.

The element for Death is Water. In a certain sense, however, all the elements belong to death. Some writers on religion theorize that the four elements originated in the four ways of handling dead bodies. Water means burial at sea. Fire means cremation. Air refers to ritually offering the body to carrion birds (still practiced in Tibet), while Earth means burial.

In this picture of Death we see more an accumulation of images than a single composition. Deliberate distortions of perspective make it difficult to view the card in a unified or serene way. For instance, the tree branch appears in the background. Yet the leaf that falls from it appears in the front, blocking the sickle. The size of the bird would indicate closeness to us, particularly in relation to the sickle, which appears quite small. Yet the skeleton hand rises up in front of the bird's beak.

Despite this distortion we do get a sense of receding distance. With each layer we see more of a whole. First comes the arm of the skeleton, then the bird's head, then the entire figure of the ferryman. But if we can see all of Charon we cannot see any details, only a shrouded figure in a black boat. When we look at a single death we see a hard reality. When we try to view death as a whole we find a mystery.

When we examine the different levels in the picture we discover the material world. The trees and grass signify plants, the bones represent minerals, the birds the animal world, and the ferryman the human. The fact that a mythological figure represents humanity suggests that, unlike the rest of nature, we exist in several worlds at once—the physical, the imaginal and the spiritual. We should also remember that long before the guide became a figure of story, people depended on shamans, living members of the community, to lead them into the next world.

Let us look at the symbols one by one. The tree branch recalls the Hanged Man. The joyous surrender of that card allows us to accept death without fear. A dead leaf falls from the tree, but new leaves are already growing.

The sickle belongs to the traditional symbology of trump 13. Most versions of this card show a skeleton cutting down heads, usually crowned, as well as hands and feet, all growing out of the ground. The image came from a medieval lesson in moral democracy, that is, even kings and queens must die. Haindl, however, did not intend the sickle as something ominous, but rather a suggestion that at the end of our lives we harvest what we have grown. One reason for recognizing the presence of death in the world is to remind us to do something with our lives. People who survive serious illness or accidents often think of the rest of their lives as a second chance for them to do the things they postponed or didn't dare.

The shape of the sickle, a crescent Moon, brings us back to the Goddess. Sickles are among humanity's oldest tools. When archaeologists found prehistoric versions of the sickle they assumed the things were weapons, used by male warriors. When they examined them and found glutinous vegetable traces, they recognized that the instruments were harvest tools, used by women and therefore shaped like the Moon (we can wonder if the archaeologists also recognized some truths about their own imaginations).

The connection of a skeleton with death is as obvious as it is traditional. However, most people do not know the importance of the skeleton in the shamanic traditions. When a person dies, the flesh decays very quickly but the skeleton remains, seemingly forever. Therefore, the skeleton signifies eternity, or the part of the self that cannot die. For the shamans, this is not an intellectual idea. Young shamans undergo severe hallucinatory initiations. Very often, these involve attacks by spirits who flay the shaman's body, boil it alive, even chop it up, all to take away the outer flesh and reduce the initiate to a skeleton. The bones then "grow" a new body, stronger, with magic powers, able to heal others. Having survived this terrible death and rebirth, the shaman can travel safely between the dead and the living.

The peacock dominates the card. Its connection with Justice reminds us of the traditional idea that we carry our unbalanced karma with us when we die, and that this karma propels us into a new life which will give us a chance to balance the scales. The link also reminds us to view death in a balanced but honest way. The color of the bird's neck resembles the colors produced when we mix oil and water. Death brings together different energies: the destruction of the old with the birth of the new.

The peacock's eye occupies the center of the card. Its form and colors recall the eye in the triangle above the Empress. It signifies looking at the truth in regard to death.

Early Christianity saw the peacock as a symbol of Christ's resurrection. People believed that the peacock did not decay when it died. When the peacock molts, it loses its beautiful plumage, only to have it grow back again.

Other cultures have depicted the soul as a bird. The Egyptians described three spiritual aspects of a person, two of which were birds. The third, ka, meant life force, that which animates the body. According to Mircea Eliade, ka did not take a special form. The ba, however (same word as the Rune), indicated the soul, that is, the essence of a person. The Egyptians saw it as a bird. The other bird, the akh, symbolized the divine potential of a person. The term akh means "shining, glorious" and when a person dies, he or she can become an akhu, or "divine being." Originally, Eliade writes, the texts spoke only of the Pharaoh having a ba or becoming an akhu. In later papyruses we find this idea extended to all Egyptians.

So far, we have looked at the card as signifying the importance of death in nature and in our own lives. But Death carries another meaning, one having nothing to do with physical death. In fact, when we get this card in readings this other meaning is the one that most applies. Death refers to giving something up, letting something die to make room in our lives for new possibilities. Very often people cling to old habits or patterns long after these have ended their usefulness, or even their reality. A girl suffers in childhood from rejection. She builds up defenses against this pain by not letting people get close to her. As an adult she finds friends and lovers, and the old patterns no longer serve any purpose. The ego is often very conservative, always preferring to hold on to what it knows. A break with old habits feels like dying. And so it is. For just as physical death makes room for new people, so a psychological death makes room for new possibilities.

Some people who know of this idea look at the image of Death in a very positive way. And ultimately it is a very positive experience. But we should avoid letting this knowledge mask the real power of Death. "Death-of-the-old-self," people say comfortably. But this is not always comfortable. People in therapy sometimes understand their destructive patterns of behavior quite early. They may recognize that nothing stops them from letting go of those useless patterns. And yet, it may take years before they will let that old self die.

To face either psychological or physical death with ease we need first of all the Hanged Man sense of a connection to all life. If we overcome our separation from the rest of the world then our individual existence no longer counts for everything. In psychological terms, if we recognize life all around us we will not cling too tightly to the past. We also need the Fool, for the courage to accept Death and see what comes next. This eagerness for change represents one of the Fool's great qualities. And what a Foolish thing to do, to give up what you know for an uncertain future.

DIVINATORY MEANINGS

The card of Death in a reading very rarely refers to anything to do with physical death and never at all to the cliché of the Tarot reader saying, "You've only got six months to live." We can understand why filmmakers and thriller writers, if they use the Tarot in a story, almost invariably show Death. Unfortunately, this usage helps to frighten people when they see the card in their own readings. To be fair, the name alone would frighten most people. Be assured. Death in your reading does not predict fatal disease or an impending plane crash.

Before discussing its ordinary meaning, let us look at the way it can refer to physical death. This occurs in situations where the fact of death figures prominently in the person's life. A relative has just died; the card of Death may signify the importance of that event. A person has a phobia about dying. The card may indicate this fear—not death itself but the fear of it. Death, therefore, may show the importance of death in a person's life at that moment—but only when this importance is obvious and clearly defined.

Most often in a reading, Death means that psychological letting-go. It indicates that some pattern or phase of a person's life has ended and the person must allow it to die. This may feel painful, particularly if it means something special, such as the end of a relationship, but the "death" ultimately will benefit the person. Energy becomes freed. New opportunities open up. This meaning becomes enhanced in combination with such cards as Aeon, the Ace of Wands or the Ace of Cups,* the Magician, and so on.

REVERSED

When Death is reversed, the person is resisting some necessary change. He or she clings to old patterns of behavior, or old situations that are no longer valid. The person's life may already have changed, but he or she does not want to recognize this. Death reversed can indicate stagnation or inertia. New opportunities are waiting for the person, but until Death is accepted, the person will find it hard to recognize possibilities, let alone take action on them.

Reversed Death may indicate the pain of giving something up. The reading gives the person a chance to look at the pain and try to deal with it. The reader can help by discussing it with the person, exploring what specific resistance the card might indicate. If other cards emphasize the idea of new life, the reader can help the person see this.

---

*See Volume II.

XIV

ALCHEMY (TEMPERANCE)

As card 14, Alchemy, or Temperance to give it its traditional name, constitutes the second of the three victories. The Fool, in his/her journey through the Major Arcana, has examined his/her life in Justice, joined with nature in the Hanged Man and faced the reality of Death. In Alchemy the opposing energies of life—light and dark, active and receptive, male and female—come together. One of the great traditions for achieving this unity is alchemy, and so the card gets its new name and much of its symbolism.

The Hebrew letter is Samekh, which means "Tent-peg." Since Hebrew derives from a time and place when people lived in tents, "tent-peg" today would imply the foundation of a house. The practical side of the trump—the advice to avoid extremes, to walk the middle path—forms a solid foundation for our daily lives.

The name Alchemy for this card comes from Aleister Crowley. In his own description Crowley refers to Samekh as the "elixir" or "philosopher's stone" of the alchemists. We saw in the Magician how Wolfram von Eschenbach described the Grail as a stone. He also identified it with the philosopher's stone. The alchemists sought to turn "base," or common, metals into gold (commodities traders still use the terms "base" and "precious" metals). To this end they performed various physical experiments with different substances. Studies by Carl Jung and others have shown that the alchemists sought a psychological transformation, using metals as symbols for themselves. In other words, "base" represented ordinary human existence, plagued by sickness, "base" desires and other weaknesses. Through finding the philosopher's stone—the occult secrets of life—they would transmute themselves into gold—enlightened beings, with direct knowledge of God. This is very like the quest of the Tarot. In traditional Tarot decks, the last trump, the World, often shows a hermaphrodite, symbolizing the unity of the two principles shown before as a man and a woman. The image of a hermaphrodite derives directly from alchemy, which sometimes

Alchemy

depicted its perfected human as half man, half woman. In the Haindl Tarot we see the same idea in the faces on either side of the diagonal.

The Rune Laguz, L, means "Water." As the formless sea it contains the potential for life. Symbolically it precedes Hagall, for Hagall, as an ice crystal, must solidify out of water (though Hagall melts back into water). Laguz also means "psychic" because of the connection of psychic powers with the unconscious. Some commentators describe Laguz as a Rune of initiation. We can think of alchemy as a medieval form of the ancient initiation mysteries found around the world. Laguz also means "love and polarity," the themes we saw in the Lovers. The Rune is said to bind the poles together, bringing man and woman together. These themes apply to the trump Alchemy, for love becomes the "elixir" that unites the opposite poles.

The astrological sign for trump 14 is Sagittarius, the archer. Here again we see the theme of duality, for the dividing line in the glyph, the cross, separates the "lower" human qualities from the "higher." One basic meaning of the term "polarity" refers to humans experiencing two urges, one creative, the other destructive. An arrow can symbolize both. As a weapon it brings destruction, but as an image it represents the intellect speeding straight to the truth. The alchemists believed in lower and higher qualities. They talked of burning away the lower, or evil, part of the body in order to release the higher. Alchemical art includes pictures of the seeker sitting in a giant cauldron.

The astrological element is Fire, derived from that alchemical idea of burning off the weak mortal form to free the immortal self. But the alchemists also saw polarity as a matter of Fire and Water, and sought to bring them together. The six-pointed star and the hermaphrodite both signified such a unity. In the card we find the two elements in the border (Fire) and the Rune (Water).

At first, the picture on the card appears very complex. The many details may seem almost forbidding. Actually, the picture is one of the simplest. A diagonal line rises from bottom left to upper right, the direction of harmony. In the Hanged Man a similar diagonal arose from the curve of the hill and the line of trees—in other words, nature. This line, however, is straight, with the objects on either side symbolic. This gives a mental quality to the card. The driving straightness of the line, like the arrow of Sagittarius, creates a sense of power and purpose.

When I first visited Hermann and Erica Haindl's home, we sat in their garden and went through the cards, discussing the symbolism and the impressions generated by the pictures. As the day wore on, the sun moved across the courtyard. At the moment we came to Alchemy, removing the painting that stood in front of it, the sunlight shone on only half of the canvas, leaving the other half in shadow. The dividing line lay precisely on the diagonal.

The diagonal line does not actually bisect the picture. At the bottom the line begins a centimeter in from the corner. This gives the left side—the Empress—a slight advantage over the right. Also, the lack of perfection takes us away from total abstraction to something closer to nature.

The diagonal divides the card between blue and red, Water and Fire. The arrow, lower right, forms a primary Fire symbol, for Sagittarius is a Fire sign. The interlocking circles, upper left, signify water. The design comes from the covering of a well at Glastonbury

Tor in England. We have previously encountered Glastonbury, the physical site of mythological Avalon. In Christian times the myth developed that St. Joseph of Arimathea landed at Glastonbury when he brought the Holy Grail to England.

The Grail actually apepars in the picture, twice. A red one shines in the blue half, a blue in the red, producing an interchange of energy. The two cups come from the traditional image of the card as Temperance, which shows an angel pouring water from one cup to another. Thus we come to the idea of mixing elements together. The term "alchemy" suggests something very complicated, but we can think of the card as learning to blend qualities that normally we might think of as separate: work and play, intellect and emotions, masculine and feminine, and so on.

Alchemy also means measurement, which is to say science, for all scientific experiment depends on accurate measurement. The two equal cups are symbols of measurement. So is the line precisely drawn to separate the two parts of the picture.

The circles give the left side a quality of spirituality. On the right we see a circle containing the Sun and Moon. The red Sun changes into the silver-blue Moon, an image of the material world moving between day and night. The background on the red side is pitted rock, a symbol of age. On the blue side (the left) we see ageless light, again a quality of spirit. Traditionally, esotericists have thought of the left side as dark, the enemy of light and spirit. "Black" magic is sometimes called "the left-hand path." But the left is also the female side. A Babylonian poem says, "Let my Goddess stand at my left hand! Let my God stand at my right hand!" And in India the term *left-hand path* means "the way of the Goddess." Throughout the Haindl Tarot we have seen the polarity reversed. Both the High Priestess and the Empress are cards of light.

On both sides, but especially the left, the light shines through the objects, giving them a foggy quality. Remember the Gnostic idea of the light being "trapped" in matter. Alchemy seeks to liberate the light by transforming the physical body. This is a very old idea, much older, in fact, than alchemy itself. The alchemist in the giant cauldron is a descendant of the shaman boiled alive by spirits. And so we see the aged rock. But transformation is also fresh, for it does not just describe an idea, but an experience. Alchemy tells us to transform our lives, to change our behavior so that we can liberate the light contained within us. The great Kabbalist Isaac

Luria taught this liberation as the moral responsibility of every human.

The Sun/Moon represents changing nature; the group of images diagonally opposite show spiritual perfection. The various circles and swirls combine gold and silver, the spiritual "Sun" and "Moon" of alchemy. In some traditional versions of Temperance the angel pours water between gold and silver cups. We also see gold and silver in the objects below the circle: seven silver grapes, a square formed of gold fruit, and a five-leafed flower made of gold and silver. In the circles themselves we see blue on the left and violet on the right. Violet, remember, is the color of the crown chakra. But the violet is muddied, with the top half obscured by a dark cloud. The picture suggests—like the Magician, with the dark lumpy face rising from his forehead—that we can never escape our bodies. The devil face inhabits the cloud. The devil signifies sexual life energy. When we deny this, or see it as base or evil, then the energy becomes distorted, tempting us away from the spiritual light to a path of darkness.

On the other side of the diagonal from the devil we find her reflection: the angel. The Tarot has always linked these two, by making the angel of Temperance trump 14 and the Devil 15. The Haindl Tarot makes the connection explicit. The angel here symbolizes that "higher" self sought by the alchemists. To achieve such perfection, some people try to banish all sexual desire, all "evil" temptation.

The devil here appears as a woman, just as the angel seems to be a man. With their fear of women (and their own sexuality) medieval theologians described angels—like God—as masculine, yet without bodies.

The devil and the angel do not look at each other. And yet, red eyes shine within the blue face of the devil, blue eyes in the angel. The true alchemist, who seeks to unite rather than separate the different sides of his (or her) own being, will seek to overcome ideas of good and evil, male and female. And so we find images in alchemical art of the crowned hermaphrodite, or the "alchemical marriage." And in Kabbalist literature we find the description of God as androgynous.

Below the angel and devil we find another pair, a clown and a skull. The clown, or fool, signifies life, the skull, death, and these two do look at each other. Their faces, in fact, join together, unlike the two above, who do not touch the diagonal. If we look closely we see that the skull slightly crosses the line. Both the clown and the skull are androgynous. Both mingle the two sides of the card in their symbolism. The clown's blue face shows spots of red makeup. In the clown's hair we see an upward-pointing Fire triangle, in the skull's headdress, a Water triangle. The clown's white hat displays six silver bells, a reminder of the Fool with the six bells, but also of the Lovers. Death wears a bride's headdress. As we learned in the previous card, death and life are bound together, "married" in nature. The alchemist must recognize this fact in order to begin the "Great Work" of unification.

DIVINATORY MEANINGS

Alchemy encompasses very large themes, not least the theories and practices of alchemy itself. For ordinary people, who are not alchemists but wish to find messages for themselves when the card appears in readings we can look to the ideas of *measurement* and *combination*.

Measurement is an activity that requires great care. Therefore, it suggests caution. Trump 14 tells us to move carefully, to think before we act, to examine the situation before we commit ourselves or make decisions. The idea of measurement means to think about what will happen rather than acting from intuition, like the Fool.

In English, the image of "measuring your steps" means moderation. Traditionally, Temperance in a reading urges the person to avoid extremes, particularly going from one extreme to another. If you feel very positive about something, be careful you do not allow some setback or rejection to turn your enthusiasm into its mirror-image of dejection. An example: someone is engaged in a project at work. Excited, he thinks of it as the best thing ever done in his field. Halfway through he shows it to his boss, who reacts negatively. Immediately he becomes depressed, believes his project is terrible and finds it hard to continue. Alchemy warns against such extreme shifts. Going too far in a positive direction can result in a swing to the negative.

Some people dislike Alchemy (or Temperance). They find it boring, and think of moderation as sacrificing the highs in order to avoid the lows. But Alchemy means more than a balancing act or a compromise. Trump 14 signifies a victory, not a stalemate. Alchemy actually means taking control of your life. It means to act on your conscious choices rather than follow moods of optimism or despair. People find moderation boring when they do not want to accept responsibility for what happens to them. They want life, or other people, to push them along.

The theme of combination comes from the two cups. It tells us to bring together the different elements in our lives. If a person feels torn between two opposing sides in a situation, Alchemy suggests the possibility of bringing the two together. Some people think of their whole lives as divided. A person may act very differently at work than at home. Alchemy suggests combining these different aspects.

REVERSED

Alchemy reversed in a reading means going to extremes. Sometimes, especially in combination with the Fool or other cards suggesting spontaneity, reverse Alchemy can be a recommendation. Avoid caution and hesitation, it says. Do not try to know everything in advance, because you cannot. Act now.

More commonly, Alchemy reversed warns against excessive behavior. This warning becomes stronger among cards that show collapse, or distress or some kind of defeat. Be careful, it says. You might need to conserve your energy, or take a more cautious approach, either to the situation, or to the other people. In its strongest form, the reversed card indicates a person out of control. He or she may need to work at getting Alchemy right side up.

XV

THE DEVIL

THE DEVIL is trump 15. And 1 + 5 = 6, the Lovers, one of several clues that the card deals, in part, with sexuality. The one and the five also show links to the Magician and the Hierophant. Like the Magician and Strength, the card starts a new cycle. It takes us into dark areas of ourselves, unexplored up to this point. The Hierophant signified religious and moral teachings. These teachings lay out a path for us to follow in order to lead good lives. The path is a safe one, for it comes from tradition. Many generations have followed it before us. The Devil shows a more dangerous path, that of the "dark side" of hidden desires.

This dark exploration links the card to the previous trump, Alchemy. The alchemists described a process known as "nigredo," a word derived from blackness. It involved the breaking down of the base substance in order to purify it. In psychology, a breaking-down often occurs from the acting out of long-repressed desires, especially sexual desires. The released energy opens up new possibilities in the person's life. The danger of this process is that unless the person is stable to begin with, the nigredo can lead to an actual breakdown. The card of Alchemy signifies, among other things, stability. And so, the victory of card 14 precedes the explorations of 15.

Traditionally the Devil has *not* signified exploration of the self, but rather various forms of oppression. Foremost among these is the idea of illusion. If the Tarot as a whole represents truth, then it makes sense that a card of "evil" would represent illusion.

The Hebrew letter is Ayin, which means "Eye." Some people interpret this to mean superficiality, that is, looking at the outer appearances of things rather than the inner truth. Traditionally the most important of the senses is sight (we speak of understanding as "seeing"). Sight represents all the physical senses. This leads to the idea of materialism, the doctrine that nothing exists beyond what we can physically perceive and measure. But the eye can be fooled,

The Devil

as any artist knows. Materialism is considered the Devil's chief illusion.

The senses imply sensuality. If a culture treats the body and nature as evil, the opposite of spirituality, then an animal approach to life means sinfulness. Now, certainly some people become slaves to the devil of sensual gratification. Most people at some time in their lives have been sexually or romantically obsessed with someone. A few people live their whole lives this way, moving from one obsession to another. Other forms of unbalanced sensuality include gluttony and some types of drug and alcohol addiction. Therefore, the Devil carries among its meanings, 1, illusions, especially materialism; and, 2, desire for gratification of desires over all other considerations.

These various meanings derive from the idea of Ayin/Eye as physical sight. But the Haindl Tarot shows the third eye, seat of revelation. This implies our first idea, that the path of sensuality can lead to a spiritual awakening. Tantric yoga and Gnosticism are among the esoteric traditions that have used sexual rites to awaken the kundalini. We have already looked at this idea in connection with the Lovers, and we have seen in the Empress how the snake symbolizes the kundalini itself.

Ayin hints at a connection of this card to the Fool. This is because Ayin, like Aleph, is a silent letter, a carrier for vowel sounds. Silence implies secrets, and therefore esoteric doctrines and practices. Those who perform sexual rites have usually done so in secret, due to the tendency of society to view their practices as orgies. The Christian Church has interpreted pagan sexual magic as Devil worship (though some early Christians also performed sexual rites). This still occurs today, when the Church and ordinary people confuse Wicca with Satanism, when the two things have nothing to do with each other. We should, of course, recognize that people do sometimes use esoteric practices as excuses for sexual license. While preaching the path to enlightenment they actually fall prey to the illusions of total gratification.

On the individual level, the Devil/Ayin's silence can suggest secret desires. These may be sexual desires, but they also may be desires for a different life, or for more passion in a life that outwardly may appear dull. Often we do not know our own desires. Habit and fear and social conditioning hide them from our conscious awareness. In order to reach the total awareness shown in the later trumps we need to explore the dark areas of ourselves. The Devil raises up—and so transforms—hidden passions.

The Rune for trump 15, Eolh, carries further the issue of the Devil and paganism. The Rune means Elk, another version of the Horned God we discussed with the Emperor. When the Church gained power in Europe, it condemned all the doctrines of the old religions as evil. It also took the old gods and distorted them into demons and monsters. The Horned God became a variation of Satan. This tied in with a similar action taken in Rome. One of the ancient Gods of nature was Pan, depicted as a goat dancing upright, like a human, while blowing music on his pipes. This music supposedly inspired his followers to abandon all social restraints and let loose their secret desires. The Church gave Pan a new name—Satan, the evil one. To this day most people think of the Devil as a half-man, half-goat, and in fact most Tarot cards of the Devil show a picture of Pan.

The Rune also means "man." If we project all unpleasant desires, fears, and obsessions onto supernatural beings we never learn to handle them in our lives. To transform that energy—we see a dark hole at the bottom of the picture and a crystal at the top—we need to accept it as human, as part of ourselves. This applies to entire cultures. When the Nazis scapegoated the Jews and other minorities, they projected all their own fears and violence onto groups they saw as alien. The projection allowed them to exercise that violence in the most extreme form.

Traditionally, Eolh means protection, especially from enemies. According to some historians, people in old Germany protected themselves from the evil eye (Ayin again) by holding up three fingers. Other commentators claim that when the Church forced Paganism to become a secret religion, worshippers of the Horned God would raise three fingers as a secret sign (secrets again) of recognition. In a similar situation early Christians used to signal each other by tracing the sign of the fish in the dirt (the birth of Christ began the age of Pisces).

An experience I had several years ago ties together the Rune and the goat in a remarkable way. Around the time I began my own interest in the Runes I went on a holiday to Madeira, where my friend and I planned to hike in the mountains. Following the old tradition I carved the Rune Eolh on the inside of my belt and on a curved stick I found in the woods. On the first day, everywhere we walked I encountered Eolh. At one point, I found two twigs that had fallen, one on top of another, in the shape of the Rune. Another time, I saw what looked like Eolh markings on a stone. When I picked it up, I discovered that the markings were delicate lines of dust that had fallen exactly in that form.

Two days later we went on a walk that took us over the tops of the highest mountains on the island. On the way back, a mist covered the path so that we could not see more than a few meters ahead. We lost our way and found ourselves going in the wrong direction. Fighting off panic ("panic" derives from Pan) we headed back, not sure any more where we were heading on a steep and now slippery path, with sheer drops on either side. Just as we became scared we had again gone the wrong way, a goat came out of the mist and began walking up the path in front of us. When we stopped for breath the goat stopped. When we started again so did the goat, leading us back. Just as we spotted the small building that marked the end of the path, the goat bounded back into the mist. Within seconds, it was gone.

The astrological sign for the Devil is Capricorn, the goat. People sometimes link this sign with a strong sexual appetite. In English, an older man who chases women is called "an old goat." At the same time, Christ was born under the sign of Capricorn. The Devil and the Messiah are more linked than people realize. The element is Earth—the material universe.

The picture is another example of receding levels. In the forefront we see a snake, coiled in a backward S. Just behind it rises the goat. Behind both of them we find a rock wall. At the bottom of the wall we see a hole. Further up, holes in the stone show a blue background. Hermann Haindl comments that this blue is not the sky.

The picture is also organized around a diagonal line in the direction of agitation, from lower right to upper left. This line does not show as obviously as on some other cards. It runs from the snake in the corner, along the head of the goat, and up to the crystal. The crystal, which transforms the aggressive instinct of the Devil, breaks the diagonal line.

The Devil's third eye links it to the Empress, as do its three horns (the third appears to emerge from the crystal). The third eye is not in the middle, as with humans, but above, forming a Fire triangle, symbol of spirit and transforming energy. The eye looks out from a stone diadem set with jewels. The three horns contain three, four and seven curls, signifying the combination of the Empress and the Emperor producing the victorious will of the Chariot. The curls turn upward, the direction of matter evolving to a spiritual awareness of itself.

The goat's hair, on the other hand, curls down, a return to the physical. Among many peoples, hair represents a person's power, either sexual or spiritual. In the Bible story of Samson we read that God commanded him not to cut his hair. The abstention was a mark of his dedication to God's service. However, some modern readers have interpreted Delilah's cutting of Samson's hair as an allegory of castration. In our picture, all the curls—the horns, the hair and the snake—symbolize the kundalini, which uncoils and rises up the spine to the head.

We have looked, in the Empress, at the universal symbolism of the snake, its connections with Goddesses, its androgynous symbolism, its image of rebirth through shedding of its skin. Because of its poison the snake also signifies evil; because it slithers unseen, it suggests cunning. But some snake venom can also produce visionary experience, like peyote. Therefore, the snake carries these complex meanings, suitable for the Devil.

In the picture, the snake's teeth shine. Forbidden desire, especially sexual desire, attracts at the same time that it can destroy. But the gleaming teeth also imply light, a theme developed in the third eye and in the crystal. We also see traces of yellow light around the mouth of the goat. This is the paradox of the Devil. Desire can destroy, but it also can liberate. The name Lucifer means "bringer of light." In their reversal of Biblical mythology the Gnostics described Lucifer as the hero and Jehovah as the villain.

The snake and goat meet in the center of the card with the snake before the goat. We do not see clearly whether or not the snake actually bites the goat, but the picture recalls the Fool touching the wound in the breast of the swan. The Christian idea of Original Sin says that that physical world (the goat) is infected by Adam and Eve's sin (the snake). The world of matter, and particularly human beings, is flawed with evil, especially sexual evil, for sexual generation is what passes Original Sin from parents to children. This is why the myth describes Christ's mother as a virgin. Because of this flaw, Christianity teaches, all our efforts come to nothing until we join ourselves to Christ, who was conceived without sex.

Now, the Tarot recognizes the evil in the world. In the twentieth century we have seen too much of it to cling to some sweet idea of life as perfect. And the Tarot recognizes the danger of simply following our desires. On the most ordinary level, we have all known people who seem to fall apart whenever they become involved sexually with someone. And yet, the Tarot rejects the idea that we can save ourselves only by referring to a higher authority. The Tarot is not anti-religious. But it insists that salvation comes through the body as well as the mind. And it tells us that we need to recognize the "evil" in ourselves as well as the good.

This does not mean doing whatever you want, to anyone at any time. Anyone who thinks the esoteric path gives them an excuse to act out their "dark side" has fallen into the illusion of the Devil. The Tarot only says that we need to acknowledge all our qualities, explore all aspects of ourselves. But we need to do this with the goal of transforming the energy. Experience of hidden thoughts and desires serves no purpose if it leads to destructive action, or to horror at discovering something terrible about our secret feelings.

The card of the Devil shows a journey. It begins in the dark hole, the home of the snake. It travels along the snake, symbol of the unconscious, to the goat, symbol of the body and the physical world. But it ends in the pure light of the crystal.

DIVINATORY MEANINGS

Traditionally, the Devil in Tarot readings has indicated oppressive situations, often bad relationships. The card has also carried the meaning of illusions, the most important one being that the situation is hopeless, that the person has no options. The Haindl Tarot emphasizes more the ideas of temptation and sensuality. The Devil says that the person is encountering something exciting, but possibly dangerous, or at least forbidden. This may be seen as an opportunity to do something. If the Devil comes up in a reading dealing with a new relationship, this indicates the relationship may be very exciting but difficult, possibly damaging. The difficulties may come from emotional problems between the people. They may also come from the relationship stirring up long-dormant feelings or desires in the person. Sometimes a person will go along for years vaguely unhappy or dissatisfied, but not sure why. Then something happens —a new lover, perhaps—and all the passions awaken. If the person is not prepared to deal with these passions they can lead to distress or instability.

In most readings the Devil will not mean anything so drastic. But it may refer to some sort of temptation. If the Devil seems to refer to another person—for instance, if it appears in a position such as Influence of Others—then it describes that person as attractive but possibly dangerous.

As sensuality, the Devil may refer to a time in a person's life when physical gratification becomes important. This may mean sex, or a more general need for pleasure.

If we wish to follow the spiritual path shown in the Devil, this involves exploring our darker feelings, the things we usually suppress. On a mundane level, the bored person may find that some wild action opens up whole new areas of life. Only, the Devil says, take care. Things may be stirring deep down, and the person might not know her or his own feelings.

REVERSED

Traditionally, the Devil reversed has meant releasing yourself from an oppressive situation. It has meant seeing past illusions, especially illusions of helplessness. If, however, the Haindl Tarot means primarily temptation, then the reversed card will indicate resisting temptation. It may show the person turning down some offer or opportunity.

The reversed Devil says that this is not a time for sensuality. Some kind of mental activity may be more important, or hard work or putting others ahead of your own pleasure. If, for example, a person faces a choice between taking care of a sick relative or going away for a holiday, then the Devil reversed would indicate the likelihood that the person will stay. Another example: if the Devil reversed comes up for a student facing exams, it reminds him or her to study instead of going out for a good time.

The reversed card may indicate a fear of one's own desires. It may show the person trying to suppress something, because acting would open up too many buried emotions. At one time people automatically assumed they should reject the Devil in themselves. Any "evil" temptations had to be suppressed. More recently, people have come to believe that we should *never* suppress desire. We will become unfulfilled, or frustrated, or neurotic. Neither position can really serve us in our lives. The Tarot can help us understand the possibilities, and dangers, in any situation. The decision remains with us.

XVI

THE TOWER

THE TOWER IS trump 16. Sixteen is 1 + 6 = 7, the Chariot. That card showed the power of the human will to gain mastery over the dangerous forces of nature (as well as its own fears). In the Tower we see the dangers of the human will completely unchecked, dominating nature with a kind of insanity that can lead to humanity's own destruction. The chariot was driven by time and mortality. The Tower is built on pride.

The Hebrew letter, Peh, means "Mouth," and by extension, speech, communication. In this case, the implication is ironic. The Tower of Babel symbolizes lack of communication, language as a means of separating people rather than bringing them together. There is, however, an esoteric side to the Tower, in which the lightning bolt represents revelation, rather than destruction. Illusions become destroyed by sudden knowledge of the truth. "Speech" in this sense means God communicating directly with humanity. Instead of Babel, we have the Biblical account of Pentecost, in which the Spirit descended into a group of worshippers and they all began "speaking in tongues," that is, in many different languages, just as in the story of Babel. In the story of Pentecost, however, everyone understood what the others said. The barriers had broken down.

The Rune is Yr, or Irr. In German, *irren* means "to be wrong." The English is *err*, almost the same. The Rune, like the card, tells us we have followed an *irrweg*, a wrong path.

If the Rune of the Devil means Man, then this Rune means Woman. The energy of the card, however, is primarily masculine, with the phallic tower and the astrological glyph for Mars, a symbol as well of the male sex. We can look at the Rune simply as a reverse of the Devil. The Devil traditionally symbolizes oppression. The tower can mean a violent release of repressed energy. If a bad situation goes on for a long time, the pressure can build to an explosion. Psychologically, this can be an outburst of rage. Politically, this can

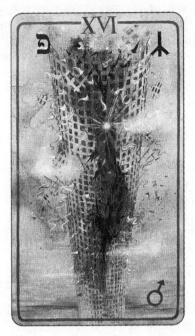

The Tower

mean revolution. Ecologically, it refers to disasters brought on by years of abusing nature.

The Rune carries a very special meaning. It forms the symbol of the international peace movement. Since the Tower card suggests the arms race as well as technology gone crazy, the Rune implies an opposition to the Tower. In this sense, the meaning of "Woman" applies very well—not just because a higher percentage of people in the peace movement are women, but because the Rune evokes the values of peace, values which are traditionally associated with women. People who march against nuclear weapons are often called irrational, idealistic, cowardly—and unmanly. We have seen this Rune before, in the body of the Hanged Man as he returns his consciousness to the Mother.

The astrological planet, Mars, is named for the God of war and aggression. Mars is exalted in Capricorn, another link between the

Tower and the Devil. Mars carries a destructive quality; it is said to break down structures and traditions. In the picture we see a structure literally being broken open. The Tower itself symbolizes the destruction of tradition. In many societies the introduction of modern technology has brought a break with ancient customs, often leaving people rootless and confused. It also leads to ruined land, when traditional farming gives way to such things as chemical fertilizers.

As noted above, the symbol for Mars also signifies man, just as the Venus symbol means both love and woman. At one time people viewed war and conquest as men's most noble activities, and many still glorify the military. Yet ordinary people, and not just soldiers, have always suffered in war; for women, rape is a common wartime occurrence.

The Tower's element is—of course—Fire.

Trump 16 is one of the simplest in the Major Arcana, maybe because of the urgency of its message. We see a curved tower, like a skyscraper, with both its base and its roof outside the picture. Flags of many nations fly from its windows. An explosion has struck the tower. We cannot tell whether it explodes from inside, because of something out of control, or whether lightning strikes it. The explosion exposes a darkness inside, as well as fire and clouds of smoke. At the bottom the sun rises, while behind the clouds and the tower we see blue skies.

The Tower symbolizes an arrogant technology that constantly desires more and bigger monuments to its conquest of nature. Skyscrapers in particular represent this attitude, for they separate humanity from the Earth. For Hermann Haindl, as for many people, skyscrapers epitomize the desire of our civilization to divorce itself from nature, to pretend that we exist apart from the plants and animals that feed us. In many skyscrapers people cannot open the windows. Skyscrapers also disrupt the weather, creating wind tunnels.

For those, like Hermann Haindl, who follow a religious path linked to the Earth as Mother, the phallic shape of skyscrapers (and missiles) is no accident. In places where people have sought harmony with nature they have tended to build structures close to the ground, sometimes curved or round, imitating the shape of a woman.

The Tower symbolizes more than literal skyscrapers. It refers, for instance, to problems of atomic energy, with the explosion a depiction of the terrible accident at Chernobyl. That disaster caused the long-term poisoning of groundwater throughout Europe, and precluded eating certain foods for fear of radioactivity. The Tower also represents the space program, for Haindl, and many others, another example of humanity's desire to break away from the Earth. The explosion may refer to the space shuttle Challenger, or to plans to turn space into a military playground.

Illusions of separateness lead to a break with reality. For what do we think we will breathe if there are no rain forests and only poisonous waters? What kind of life would promoters of the arms race lead in a nuclear winter?

Inside the Tower we see darkness and fire. In the High Priestess, darkness meant mystery, wholeness, the origins of life. Here it means fear, and the aspects of ourselves we keep hidden. The fire—points of yellow light at the end of columns of red—looks like the clawed fingers of some monster ripping open the Tower from within. In the Devil we discussed the idea of exploring secret desires. These included the desire for destruction, our own as well as others. In the Tower we see the dangers of not recognizing the darkness inside us. Technology gives us more and more power. We often lack the self-knowledge to use it wisely.

The picture shows a modern image of the Tower of Babel. People desire to communicate with each other but cannot. This comes from barriers of language and culture, but also from arrogance. We all want to speak, and not to listen. People fly flags from their windows, announcing themselves to the world. But in the curved tower everyone looks out. No one can see anyone else. In an overcrowded world people remain isolated.

In the story of Pentecost we find the opposite of isolation. People all understand each other. This happens through a divine flash. Revelation overwhelms all our limited views of the world. It overwhelms rationality by giving us direct knowledge of a truth normally hidden from us. It is not for nothing that the card occupies the same place in the final row of seven cards as the High Priestess in the first row. Spiritual experience allows human beings to know their own irrationality, but in a creative life-giving way. Ecstasy opens something inside us, leading to harmony and love. But if we try to deny that something, if we try to see ourselves as completely rational, then the darkness becomes fearful, and the power inside us becomes a devil, clawing its way out.

However grim the card looks, the Tarot remains optimistic. The sunrise, the blue sky behind the clouds, these suggest hope. They lead us to the next card, the Star, in which Gaia, the Earth Mother, renews the power of life.

DIVINATORY MEANINGS

The meanings for the Tower in Tarot readings usually emphasize some kind of upheaval or explosion. It can refer to arguments or disturbing events, especially if they occur suddenly. Sometimes the Tower indicates the collapse of some plan or existing situation, especially when this collapse comes from internal pressure. If the Tower should appear with the Wheel of Fortune (especially with the Tower as Outcome), the two cards might indicate some difficult turn of events.

The Haindl version of the Tower may refer to some kind of long-standing activity or particular approach to a situation. The person has been stubbornly continuing in the same path despite clear signs of danger. If he or she continues, then some kind of explosion or other disaster is likely to result.

In all these things the Tower acts as a warning. The pressure is building up. The person must find a way to let it out before the Tower explodes. In a relationship this may require exposing long-standing problems that the people have tried to ignore. If the Tower refers to some dangerous course of action, then the person needs to find a way out. Often the cards will at least hint at an alternative. When the Tower appears, it is wise to look at the other cards carefully. People have a natural tendency to freeze at the sight of some card they find fearful. This is one reason why many people have trouble reading their own cards.

If the Tower refers to some event that has already happened, we need to look at what we can do now to make the best of the situation. The Tower may have a liberating effect. Unpleasant to experience, it may release people from oppressive situations, or else open up new opportunities. If two people have stopped communicating, then the Tower may let loose long-buried emotions or grievances.

Though the Haindl Tower does not stress the esoteric side of the trump we should consider those possibilities in readings. Usually these will not deal with spiritual enlightenment, but rather some sudden discovery of revelation. This may come in the form of news or messages. It may be an event which allows the person to see things in a new way. Or the person simply may experience a flash of understanding. The Tower implies seeing things in a more complete way.

If cards of renewal follow the Tower then the experience has cleared away blocks, either between people, or just within the person alone. If cards of analysis, such as Justice, follow the Tower, then the person needs to examine the experience. If Death or other cards of letting go follow the Tower, then the person might need to recognize that the old situation has ended and not try to cling to it.

REVERSED

With the reversed Tower the upheavals and storms become less severe. The experience is similar, but milder, with less of a disruption to the person's life. The Tower right side up sweeps away old patterns of behavior, old structures in a relationship or in a person's life. The structures might be in work or family as well as in romance. Reversed, the structures will experience a shaking-up, but major changes are not likely to occur. And because things do not change, the Tower reversed can sometimes indicate repression. People try to protect themselves from anger. Instead of letting the Tower expose problems, or clear away rigidity, they hold in their emotions.

If the other cards show that the difficult time passes and the person finds harmony or more creative energy, then the Tower reversed was likely a minor disturbance. But if the other cards show some difficult or painful condition continuing, then the person might need to bring things into the open.

XVII

THE STAR

T STAR IS card 17, and seventeen reduces to eight, the number of Strength in the Haindl Tarot. The two cards have much in common. The openness of Strength, the belief in the future, these qualities fill the higher trump.

The Hebrew letter for the Star is Tzaddi, which means "Fishhook." The image suggests a fish drawn from the sea. Now, just as the sea represents the unformed energy of the unconscious, so a fish symbolizes that energy taking shape. A fishhook symbolizes the mind entering the mysteries of the High Priestess and bringing forth ideas, concepts, artistic beauty.

The Rune is Eh, or E. Literally, this means "Horse," an animal considered holy by Indo-Europeans from India to Scandinavia. The Rune was often seen as Sleipnir, the horse Odin rode on his travels between the worlds. Thus, Eh is a Rune integrating the different levels of existence.

Notice that the Rune reverses the Rune for Justice, Necessity. Necessity showed the principle of contraction, or harshness, in universal law. Here we see the principle of expansion, of joy and new growth. Eh is a Rune of trust and loyalty. It calls us to believe in the Earth and the hope of renewal. "Eherne" means eternal.

The astrological sign for the Star is Aquarius, one of the four fixed points of the zodiac. Aquarius means "water-carrier"; the symbol for it derives from the Egyptian hieroglyph for water. With all this, we would expect the element for Aquarius, and therefore for the card, to be Water. In fact, as the white border shows, the element is Air. We can understand this if we look again at the symbol, which shows waves—that is, wind stirring up water. This indicates thought bringing out ideas from the deeps of the unconscious. Aquarius is the sign of visionaries, teachers and inventors. Aquarius is also the sign of the new age, the coming two thousand years. Aquarius, therefore, fits very well with the card of renewal.

Like the Tower, the Star is one of the simplest pictures in the

The Star

Haindl Tarot. And that very simplicity helps make it one of the strongest statements in the deck. Actually, the Tower and the Star belong together. For while the Tower shows the dangers facing our planet, the Star gives us belief that somehow we will return to the basic principles of respect for nature, and that this return will allow the Earth to cleanse itself.

The picture shows a woman at the bottom of a bare rocky hill where a stream of water splashes into a pool. She is washing her hair, a simple human act, yet the gesture of bowing her head becomes an act of unity with the Earth. The woman's hair blends into the water, recalling both the High Priestess, whose hair becomes a rain of light, and the Hanged Man, whose hair grows into the hillside like roots. We can see the rock through the woman's hair. At the bottom of the cascade of hair, and up near the scalp, there's a suggestion of red, as if the woman washes out blood from a wound. (This interpretation of a wound is mine, rather than something indicated by Haindl.) We see this red in the water, though only a trace mingled with brown, as if the wound is old and only needs cleansing. Like the High Priestess's river, the water is dark, impenetrable. At bottom right, however, we see bright colors, recalling the peacock from Justice and Death. Though we only see the pool, it may lead to a river and the river to the sea, for the water appears to flow.

The rock is old and pitted, especially at bottom right. We do not see any flowers here or grass or trees, but only the Earth's oldest forms: water and rock. The holes in the rock merge with the holes in the woman's dress, as bare as the hill. The dress suggests age, because of the ragged hem, but also because it displays no decoration or individual style. It simply protects the woman.

The diagonal of the hill, and of the woman's back, goes in the direction of agitation, opposite to the Hanged Man. Yet the picture creates a wonderful sense of calm. This happens because of its simplicity, and because of the woman's humble gesture of bending over to clean her hair. The picture takes the forceful energy of the diagonal and reverses it, just as the woman subtly reverses her body.

Above her shines a cluster of stars, seven small ones, and one large double star. The total is nine, the number of the Hermit; or, if we count the double as one, the total is eight, the number of Strength. In the ring of seven small stars we see subtle suggestions of rainbow colors. We know from the Hanged Man that these colors also radiate from the chakras, a connection between the heavens and individual human beings. The big double star in the middle is one star on top of the other. Instead of two triangles producing six points, we have two pentacles producing ten points. The pentacle, remember, is the Goddess's star. It also represents the human body. With the point up, the head—place of reason—dominates. When it points down, the genitals—place of passion—dominate. Here we see both combined, though the right-side-up pentacle appears in front. A white light shines from the center. The seven small stars suggest the Chariot; the ten points suggest the Wheel of Fortune. Together they make seventeen, the Star. Hermann Haindl did not make this connection consciously when he made the design.

The Tower gave us a picture of human pride leading to disaster. In the Star we see a picture of humility. Humility does not mean believing ourselves inferior or weak. It does not mean lowering ourselves before a church or ruling class. Such "humility," as Haindl says, only feeds someone else's pride. Instead, we simply need to recognize ourselves as part of nature. The woman in the picture does not bow her head to some authority, either secular or spiritual. She bends forward to join herself to the water. In German, the word for humility, *demut*, means courage to God.

We saw above how the water flows beyond the picture, to a river or the sea. Aquarius is a sign of unity among peoples. As we move toward a New Age, we find the separate streams of humanity coming together. We can see this in the world communications network, in the concern for human rights in different countries, in various campaigns to ease suffering or end hunger. In religion, our time has seen something virtually unknown in human history—a drawing on many different cultures to form a new awareness, based not on doctrines, but on people's experiences of God.

The picture recalls the Hanged Man. There, however, the picture suggested esoteric rituals as well as a renewal of values. Here the gesture is a part of everyday life. Some people become involved in esoteric work because they find it glamorous and mysterious. The idea of occult secrets sets them apart from the rest of society. While the esoteric path does teach us things unknown to most people, it also stresses the need to bring the understanding into the ordinary world. The Hanged Man separates himself, like Odin, for a mystery of initiation. But he still needs to integrate this mystery into his life.

Earlier we saw that the Chariot, the Hanged Man and the Star form a kind of trilogy. The Chariot exists in a mythic, or shamanic world. The Hanged Man is closer to nature, but with highly mythic overtones. In the Star we find one of the most naturalistic images in the whole deck. And yet, the Star gives us a picture of mystical unity at the most basic level. For many religions, cleaning yourself forms the first step to unity with God. Christians become baptized to cleanse them of original sin and to become a new person. Jews go to the ritual baths, while Hindus bathe in the Ganges, and Moslems clean themselves five times a day, before prayers. In occult rituals, the seeker often washes and then puts on white robes.

The Chariot showed an androgynous figure mastering the dangers and terrors of life. The Hanged Man showed a male figure —Odin, emblem of patriarchy—giving up his arrogant sense of separation from nature. To do this required a reversal of consciousness, symbolized by Odin literally hanging himself upside down. The Star, however, shows a kind of consciousness that doesn't need such extreme measures. She bends down to wash her hair, and so becomes part of stone and water. With the star in the sky giving us fire and air, we find all four elements, not as in the mystic Grail emblems of the Magician, but in nature, in daily life.

The picture shows nature in its oldest forms. The woman, too, wears an old dress, with no design to signify culture. She is Gaia, the Mother of Life, in German, Erda, the Earth, the Ur-Mother, origin of all things. In Greek myth Gaia is the first divinity, mother of Ouranos (Uranus), the sky, who fathered Chronos (Saturn), time, who fathered Zeus, the ruler of the Olympian Gods. In the Star we return to Gaia, past all the fathers to our first mother, the Earth.

Besides the idea of unity with nature, the bareness and simplicity of the card take us back to life's origins. They give us a sense of beginning over. The Star gives us the courage to hope. Our world will cleanse itself. Even if we suffer a Towerlike disaster, life will continue.

Nor should we think of the Tower as inevitable. In recent years people have talked of great horrors necessary before the New Age can begin. We hear prophecies of war, of continents sinking, of two-thirds of humanity dying. People sometimes seem excited by these prospects, as if disaster would answer the pessimism or just the boredom of modern life. (On this question, see also Aeon.) The Tarot, however, teaches free will. If a reading shows a person heading for some great mistake it allows for a change of direction. The same applies to our world. The Star does not just follow the Tower; it shows an alternative. We can change our ways. We just need the humility to bend down, to wash the world clean of violence and destruction.

DIVINATORY MEANINGS

The meanings for the Star are as direct as the picture. They speak of optimism, hope, openness. They say that the person either has these qualities or can have them. Sometimes the Star comes after a period of troubles or a Towerlike upheaval in the person's life. Obviously, this aspect becomes stronger if the Tower (or some of the Swords cards*) actually appear in the reading.

---

*See Volume II.

The Star is a card of renewal. The person has a chance to start over in some long-standing situation. Or a new beginning becomes possible. The Star may require that the person go back to basic principles. If the person feels that life has become over-complicated, then the card says to discover what really matters. What does she or he actually want? What basic approach has worked in the past? Can it work again? Has the person cluttered his or her life with unimportant commitments, or with desires that only seem important? Has a relationship gotten bogged down in too many minor arguments, too much, "I did this, you did that"? The Star says to find the most basic elements, the bare rock of reality and the flowing water of feeling. Notice that these recommendations go in a different direction than, say, Justice. That card called for a careful examination of history. The Star goes back before all the history to find the basics. Both cards are valid but at different times. One reason to do readings is to get a sense of what approach to take in a given situation.

This return to basics involves a cleansing. If the person has suffered or feels wounded in some way, he or she may want to look for a way to wash away the pain. For some people, this may mean a ritual, done alone or with friends. For others, it will mean finding good things in their lives, especially things that give them a sense of simplicity and hope. The appearance of the Star means renewal. We need to allow ourselves to experience it.

The Star means humility. It says to avoid acting out of pride, or arrogance, towards others. Humility does not require the attitude, "I don't matter. What happens to me isn't important." Instead, it tells us to recognize ourselves as part of something greater. This is the underlying basis of the optimism of the card. We can believe more in a future that does not depend entirely on our own efforts. When we see the Star, we know that life is on our side.

REVERSED

The qualities of the Star become blocked when it comes up reversed. The person fears for the future, and finds it difficult to express action, particularly love. He or she may feel isolated. The Star reversed can indicate tension or anxiety.

The person has lost track of the basic issues in his or her life. In a specific situation the person has become too involved with details, especially if the reading deals with work. If it deals with relationships, the person may be focusing too much on history, especially resentment. The Star advises letting go of such things; reversed, it shows the person finding that difficult.

If the person feels repressed or cut off from life, the reversed Star may indicate some old pain that needs exposure in order to clean the wound or allow renewal to emerge. In some readings this can reach back to childhood. In others it will refer to some recent event. In reading for someone else the reader may want to discuss the possibilities.

Ultimately, whether right side up or reversed, the Star means hope. Because of its powerful and simple image, the card works well in meditation. Allow the picture to move you, to open up your emotions so that you experience yourself flowing into the Earth. In Germany I had the opportunity to lead a guided fantasy with the Star and the Hanged Man. We saw ourselves climbing the World Tree, with our roots deep in the rock, and the stars above us among the leaves and branches. When we looked down from our high place we saw Gaia, the old woman washing her hair. Through that action we allowed renewal and hope to enter our world and our own lives.

XVIII

THE MOON

THE NUMBER FOR the Moon card is 18, which reduces to nine, the Hermit, seen as a lunar card. Because 18 is also 2 × 9, it connects the Moon to the High Priestess, the third lunar trump. We can also form it as 3 × 6, relating the card to the Empress, the triple Moon Goddess, and the Lovers, a connection we see in the unicorn. Finally, 18 is 1 and 8, the Magician and Strength. The Moon is a realm of magic, where we need strength to make the passage back to the light of the rational world.

The Hebrew letter is Kaph, which means "Back of the head." The following card, the Sun, bears the letter Resh, which means "Head," so that Kaph is literally in back of it. Traditionally seen as the site of reason, the head symbolizes the rational, the known, the clear and logical. The back, therefore, signifies the irrational, that which remains hidden, dark, mysterious. Even in a mirror we cannot see the back of our own head. The Moon's power opens up parts of ourselves normally kept hidden, at least from our conscious self-image. Paul Foster Case, in his writing on the Moon, points out that the back of the head contains the oldest parts of the brain, the cerebellum and the medulla oblongata. These areas reach back in evolution to something more primitive. Case remarks that the medulla remains awake when the rest of the brain sleeps. In many traditional Tarot decks only the Moon card shows no human figures (in the Haindl Tarot there are six cards in which no humans appear: Justice, the Devil, the Tower, the Moon, the Sun, and the Universe).

The Rune, Othal, or O, means "Property." The meaning connects to the idea of a sacred enclosure. As a mystic card, the Moon takes us into a sacred reality beyond ordinary perceptions. At least one commentator on the Runes, Michael Howard, describes Othal as a sacred grove of trees, where people became initiated into spiritual mysteries. We saw such a place in Strength, where the woman performed her ritual under the Moon.

The Moon

Zoltan Szabo describes Othal as the Holy Grail. It symbolizes happiness through divine protection, and was sometimes worked into the wood below the roof of a house. At the same time, Othal, or Odil, is one of the Runes belonging to Odin. Now, the Grail, as we have seen, is female, while Odin is the Father of the Gods. Haindl suggests that the Rune originally signified the unity of the creative force as Mother and Father. Over a long period the patriarchal Aesir drove out the Goddess and claimed the Rune solely for Odin. But, as Hermann Haindl says, the time has come for a correction. We see the image of that correction in the Hanged Man.

The astrological sign is Pisces, associated with dreams and psychic experience. In astrology, the Moon rules Cancer, whose symbol is a crab. Following a Tarot tradition, Haindl has changed this to a lobster. Both the crab and the lobster belong to a lower level of evolution. Usually we think of these kinds of animals as alien to us. And they are alien, at least to the rational, human, cerebral cortex. But the medulla brings us closer to that experience of scuttling along at the bottom of the sea of the unconscious. The lobster, therefore, symbolizes the Moon bringing up deep fears and anxieties, the same sort of feelings mastered by the willpower of the Chariot, whose sign was the Crab. The Charioteer did not turn around to look at them. He kept them, in other words, at the back of his head. In the Moon we allow them to emerge.

The lobster's claws can reach up out of the water and grab hold of something with an unbreakable grip. A powerful dream will sometimes grab hold of us that way. And the Moon is the card of dreams, especially the very deep ones that grip us with a physical force. The Moon is also the card of myth (symbolized by the unicorn). Like dreams, myths are truest when they touch us at some level beyond rational explanation.

The element is Water, the river flowing through the card.

Like other cards, the Moon is organized both vertically and in terms of distance. At the bottom we see the lobster, then above that the unicorn, and above the unicorn, the Moon itself. There is a slight diagonal from lower right to upper left, for the lobster lies slightly to the right of the unicorn and the unicorn slightly to the right of the Moon. We find a more pronounced diagonal in the horn, rising straight into the upper right corner (like the line in Alchemy) from the vertical axis of the unicorn's body.

In terms of distance, we see the lobster in the foreground. It actually floats in the air above the water, a surrealistic touch. In contrast, Hermann has painted the unicorn, a creature out of myth, with realistic detail. Beyond the lobster, we see the cliffs and the river, similar to the river in both the High Priestess and in Aeon, trump 20. The water appears as a stream until we notice that the size of the lobster puts the river at a great distance. The land becomes large cliffs, softer and more realistic than those on the High Priestess card. We can see waves on the water, a sign of activity in the unconscious. Because of the waves, we get a sense of seeing individual details and the whole landscape at the same time. Bubbles rise from the water to float beside the unicorn.

Beyond the river we see the unicorn, rising up like a stone tower, or a column of dirt pulled up by a tornado. Beyond the unicorn we find the air, with the Moon, and below it, to the unicorn's left, an apparently lifeless plant. Both the lobster and the unicorn have rough pitted bodies, indicating ancientness in the Haindl Tarot. The unicorn's body almost crumbles into the air.

The air itself seems hard and rough, like the inner wall of a cavern. We find the same suggestion as with the Hermit; what appears outdoors may be inside a cavern, or under the surface of the Earth. For the Moon resembles a hole, a way out from the sensual lunar world into the realm of truth. Rings of light surround the Moon.

In Plato's dialogue *The Phaedo*, Socrates says that while we think we live on the world's surface, actually we live under it. His detailed description of the outside world as a place of perfection shows that he does not intend this as a scientific account but rather as a metaphor for a powerful human perception: our everyday world prevents us from experiencing a greater world, one within us as well as the one outside. This is the world of the mystic, where God fills the universe, and every particle connects us to all the rest in a great web of meaning and beauty.

In a famous passage Plato describes humanity as living in a cave, staring at the wall. When we think we see reality, we only see shadows of the true world outside. Going further back in Greek culture, we find an interesting detail about Hermes, the Greek God of thought and the patron of the Tarot Magician. The myths describe him as born in a cave, from a sky nymph named Maia. Now, this name sounds similar to Indian Maya, which refers to the "illusion" of reality. The physical world is seen as false by Indian philosophy, which seeks to free itself by discovering the truth beyond the world. Greek Maia, in fact, means "old woman," a figure, as we have just seen in the Star, of the Goddess. But the word *maia* also means something else—a large crab.

Medieval European cosmology referred to the physical world as "sub-lunar," below the Moon. The universe, they believed, consisted of concentric spheres, with the Earth in the center, and heaven as the outermost shell. The lunar sphere surrounds the Earth, so that if a human consciousness could ascend through the layers to God, it would first pass through the realm of the Moon. In the Haindl Tarot we find ourselves traveling in the Moon-land of myths, illusions and wonders. But the Moon itself opens to a higher realm, from which light pours down on the back of the unicorn.

We can look at this in another way. If we wish to reach the mystic sense of perfect knowledge, the way leads through the imagination, for the imagination gives shape to the unconscious. The Moon is the card of myth. The Hermit and the Chariot, cards with a strong lunar influence in the Haindl Tarot, both took place in mythic worlds. But this trump deals with myth itself. People have formed many definitions of myth. Most people think of it as a false story. A skeptic might say of Noah's Ark, "It never happened. It's only a myth." Or, "The British stiff upper lip is a myth. They're actually very emotional." But if we think of myth as a reflection of spirituality, we might better define myth as a *true* story. A mythic story or image (pictures and statues can serve as myths) gives us a sense of some truth we cannot express in ordinary terms. It leads us inward, to the unconscious, and outward, to spiritual awareness. "The myth is the penultimate truth," wrote Ananda Coomaramswamy. One step away from revelation.

But why should the Moon symbolize such things? Two reasons really—an idea and an experience. The idea comes from the fact that the Moon emits no light of its own, but only reflects the light of the Sun. In the daytime, under the Sun, we see things clearly. Therefore, the Sun signifies truth. Myth reflects truth in the way the Moon reflects the Sun.

The experience comes from the fact that the Moon shines at night, with just enough light to give objects a mysterious half-reality, but not enough to dispel the darkness. We all know, as well, the strange sensations and actions evoked by the full Moon. In earlier times (and in modern witchcraft) people sought the power of prophecy through rituals under the Moon. The police in big cities have learned to expect more violence and more bizarre behavior during the period of the full Moon. We should remember that the trump does not deal only in philosophy and theories. To do occult work (or shamanism) means, at some point, to enter that lunar realm of imagination and distortion.

The Haindl version of the card deals in these matters, but also stresses the mystic awareness that lies beyond the imagination. So we see the Moon opening to something greater, the light streaming down into our world, while the bubbles rise up, an exchange of energy. Aside from the lobster, the picture does not carry images of fear, such as the dog and wolf of traditional versions. In the High Priestess, the river of the unconscious flowed dark and menacing through steep cliffs. In the Chariot, the boat protected the Charioteer from the foaming waves. Here the water runs through a soft landscape. When we reach the higher levels of the Major Arcana, when we achieve the peace and openness of the Star, then we can enter that lunar world and discover fear transformed into beauty.

The Moon is primal, not social. Maybe the fears inspired by the Moon are common to all humanity, but we experience them personally, as deep in ourselves. And while the mystic understands the unity of all existence, she or he can never communicate this understanding except through inadequate symbols—such as myths, Tarot cards, paintings and stories.

The landscape represents peace. The lobster represents the fear. It floats in the air, like the kind of anxiety that doesn't belong to any rational cause. It comes from deep in the water—the unconscious— and rises into the air—conscious awareness. The image of a creature pulled out of its normal home suggests again the strangeness of this card. Under the influence of the Moon we find ourselves in extreme situations, peculiar mental states, cut off from ordinary experience. And yet, the experience is a true one. We make a mistake when we think of our day-to-day world as reality. The universe, and our own psyches, are much stranger than we realize.

The unicorn replaces the traditional dog and wolf. This shifts the card from wildness to imagination, for while wolves exist in the human mind (as symbols) as well as in nature, the unicorn springs entirely from fantasy. Both ideas give the Moon a prehistoric quality, for just as the animal side of our nature is older than culture (and always present) so the world's mythologies reach back to humanity's earliest confrontations with the mysteries of life. We see this theme of ancientness in the crumbling stone of the unicorn's body. In our urban society, the power of myth often seems to decay and almost vanish. Yet, like the unicorn, it remains.

Hermann Haindl has painted this unicorn "realistically," with more detail than those on the Lovers and the Wheel of Fortune. Our tendency to reduce mythology to nursery tales (editing out things disturbing or sexual) leads us to think of myth as vague and rosy. But myth is hard and real, dealing in the psychic facts of our existence, and based on natural laws. For decades, psychologists such as Carl Jung, philosophers such as Ernst Cassirer, and anthropologists such as Claude Levi-Strauss have attempted to discover those laws. They prove only that myth remains slippery, as impossible to define as the unconscious.

The unicorn is a sexual image, as we saw in the Lovers. This links dream and myth with the sexual-spiritual energy known in India as the kundalini. Researchers have found evidence suggesting that dreams are sexual—not necessarily in their meaning, but in their very nature. For instance, during the rapid eye movements connected with dream sleep periods, the body is sexually aroused. This is not the case in the rest of sleep. Sometimes when we wake up from dreams we experience a strong sexual current running through our bodies—like the river in the card of the Moon.

All this means that dreams, and by extension, more conscious creations such as stories and art, come from the basic life energy called in modern psychology, "libido." Dreams and myths are the shapes taken by the formless unconscious as it seeks to become known to us. Now, if dreams really are sexual, then myths are both sexual and spiritual at the same time. While myths describe the Gods, they often do so in erotic (and violent) terms. In myth we find the energy in the process of transformation. We see this movement symbolized in the unicorn's spiral horn. We see it as well in the hole created by the Moon. The Moon is the only thing in the card depicted as eternal, without the erosion shown in the animals and even the air. For when we pass through that hole we pass beyond the lunar sphere, beyond images and words to the ultimate, rather than penultimate, truth.

DIVINATORY MEANINGS

The Moon means a time in the person's life when the imagination is very active. The person may be filled with fantasies, strong dreams, daydreams. Hopes and fears may become exaggerated or swing back and forth. In general, during a Moon time the emotions become heightened. People feel things more intensely, they concern themselves more with feelings and less with external activities, such as work.

The person may wish to channel this imaginative power into creativity. The Moon for an artist means a surge of energy, but it may be chaotic, hard to direct. The Moon takes us back to the sources of creativity. It doesn't concern itself with such things as artistic discipline. The ideal combination for an artist might be the Moon and the Magician.

Usually with the Moon we need to allow ourselves to experience fantasies, strange feelings, even fear if the Moon brings that out in us. Yet the Moon does not have to be a fearsome experience. Think of the loveliness of the full Moon as it shines on a river. The Moon can have a calming effect, especially when we do not fight against its dreams and visions. The Chariot in a reading recommends mastery over the roaring waters of emotion or deep fears. In the Moon we go into the experiences instead of trying to conquer them. As a result, the sea becomes a river. The water is active in the Moon, with small waves on the surface, but it doesn't threaten. If the Moon and the Chariot both appear in a reading, the reader needs to look at the other cards to see their direction. Do they imply that the person has gone through a lunar time and now needs once more to exert some conscious control? Or, the opposite, has the person been trying too hard to master his or her emotions and needs to sink into them? Or can the two work together? An easier combination with the Moon would be the Hermit emphasizing the person's need to be alone and explore the lunar visions.

REVERSED

The reversed card may indicate that a Moon experience is passing and the time has come for the person to return to more "solar" activities, to become busy in the world again, to look at life in a more rational way. Other cards, such as the Sun or Justice or the Chariot, might reinforce this interpretation of the upside-down Moon. Remember that the Moon passes through phases, from new to full to old, and that this applies to people as well. In other words, Moon experiences will be stronger or weaker at different times in our lives.

Sometimes the Moon reversed may show that the conscious mind is blocking the unconscious. The person feels that lunar stirring of visions and emotions but fights it back. If the other cards indicate a successful outcome to the reading, then it is appropriate at the time for the person to suppress the lunar influence. Often, however, such an attempt to suppress dark emotions accentuates the fear or disturbance connected to the card. The Moon reversed may show a person who works hard, rushes around, goes out every night, or watches television until it's time to fall asleep—all of this to avoid letting out feelings, thoughts and images from the unconscious. Such a person needs to seek the Moon's calm aspect, to let the unicorn of vision rise up from the water.

XIX

THE SUN

THE SUN IS card 19, which reduces to ten, the Wheel of Fortune. We saw how that card represented the year. The year is a solar cycle, depending on the Earth's movement round the Sun. People used to think the Sun revolved around the Earth. Now that we know that the Earth moves, we can see the Sun as the unchanging energy source at the center of our lives. Because life cannot exist without light and warmth, people associate the Sun with God, seen as the ultimate source of life in the universe. Many cultures have seen the Sun as male and the Moon as female. The Moon goes through phases linked to menstruation, while the Sun is more constant, like males. There is also a more subtle idea, that of the womb as a dark place, like the Earth in winter, needing the semen—the Sun in spring—to awaken life. In some places people made the connection Sun-year-God-king, and in order to help the Sun return in Spring after its "death" in winter they would ritually kill the old king and choose a successor. Sometimes this did not occur every year, but only after a period of years, when people believed that the king (or priest) had lost his vital power. For while the Sun pours out light year after year, male vitality wears out. Sometimes the human God could stay alive as long as he could demonstrate his mystic potency. Some years ago I read that the Aztecs invented popcorn as a test of the High Priest. He would pop the corn over some ritual fire, and if all the kernels opened, then the power of the God still burned in him. But is some of the kernels stayed closed, the worshippers would cut his throat with their marvelous knives of volcanic glass.

Just as nineteen reduces to ten, so ten reduces to one, the archetypal male number. This gives the Sun a double meaning—the yearly cycle, and the life-giving power at its center. Interestingly, no other trump number reduces twice in this way.

The Hebrew letter for the Sun is Resh, the "Head." As the site of the brain the head represents rationality and intellect, qualities belonging as well to trump 1, the Magician. Our tradition of "right

162

The Sun

reason" sees the head as the dominant part of the body, even as a metaphor for other forms of dominace, such as "head of state." In a further connection with the Wheel of Fortune, the Hebrew term for New Year, Rosh Hashanah, means "head of the year." We consider it natural for the head, the rational mind, to direct our lives. If someone seems too emotional, we say sadly that the heart is "ruling" the head. The Tarot demonstrates, however, that true rationality does not consist in repressing feelings, desire or imagination. Only when we know all these aspects of ourselves can we begin to direct our lives. This is one reason why the Sun comes after the Moon.

The Rune, Gebo, or G, means "Gift." In the card it signifies the gift of life we receive from the Sun. We do not have to work for the Sun's light. The universe gives it to us, unending. Thus, the Sun symbolizes both God's power and God's love.

The Rune symbolizes religious ecstasy and magical power, in particular sex magic. We can see this in the two diagonal lines crossing in the middle. Going in opposite directions, they symbolize male and female. They also form two triangles, in this case meeting at the point instead of overlapping to form a star. The unicorn on the Moon and the rose on this card suggest that the two cards are linked. The Sun and the Moon are the two energies brought together by the man and woman of the Lovers.

The planet for the Sun card is the Sun. In astrology the Sun governs the head. It acts as the primary center of personality. Almost all people know their Sun sign, even if they consider astrology foolish. Though astrologers will look at a person's whole chart, they usually will give the Sun sign special attention. The glyph for the Sun, a circle with a dot in it, implies the esoteric idea of the Sun's light awakening the Earth's fertility. The dot represents the sperm quickening the egg in the womb (the egg is much larger than the sperm). The dot also signifies the mystery of God as unknowable. In Kabbalist teaching we learn how the divine light descends through the various Sephiroth. But if we can follow the light back we will find that it begins with a single point. Beyond that, God remains unknowable. Remember that both the circle and the dot signify zero.

The element for the Sun is Fire, both the physical warmth of the Sun and that divine flame of the Rune.

In most Tarot decks the Sun represents simplicity and clarity. At first glance the Haindl Sun also appears direct. However, Hermann Haindl found this card the most difficult to paint of all the trumps. We may think of it as naturalistic until we look again and see that the Sun itself is not a fiery ball but a labyrinth of spirals. The trees line up with an order never found in nature, while the rose, with its slightly wilted perfection, appears as dreamlike as anything found in the Moon. We have not returned to the ordinary world but have moved to another level of myth. The card shows an idea of nature, not nature itself. It shows us an image that is soft and without danger. But there are deeper things going on in this picture.

Like the Moon, the Sun is organized around a vertical axis, and also in terms of distance. Vertically we see the rose, then the trees, then the sky, and finally the Sun. The distance organization follows a similar movement. We begin with the rose, then beyond is an open field, then trees, another open area, then more trees, and at the edge of the horizon the sunset and the Sun. When we see the difference in size between the near trees and the far ones, we realize that the picture covers a vast distance, with most of the land open fields. Another look reveals that the rose actually floats in the air, high above the Earth.

The traditional version of this trump shows a boy and girl holding hands in a garden. They symbolized the two poles of life brought together. While we do not see any children here we do find a subtle blending of male and female images. In the Lovers, the unicorn, a male symbol appeared above the women, while the rose, a female one, appeared above the man. Here, at the higher levels, the unicorn has returned on the essential female trump, the Moon, while the Sun displays a rose.

In most symbolic systems the Sun represents not only maleness but the "masculine" qualities of rationality over feeling. Traditionally, the Sun signifies the head and the rose, the heart. In this picture, however, the rose, by its roundness, resembles a head. The Sun is a flat disk. Its abstraction may seem removed from our usual ideas of feminine intuition. But the spiral and the labyrinth both appear around the world in carvings and paintings dedicated to the Mother. The term "labyrinth" comes from ancient Crete and derives from "labrys," the two-headed axe which symbolized the Moon Goddess. Modern research on myth and symbolism suggests that spirals and labyrinths signified the uterus of the Goddess, which the initiate entered, to emerge reborn.

Compared to the Moon, the Sun is constant, not shrinking and growing, disappearing and returning. But the Sun also goes through phases and, of course, the most basic cycles—night and day, summer and winter—derive from the Sun. We see this suggested in the glow of red and gold. It implies dawn or sunset, yet the Sun shines above, in a flat blue sky.

The rose also presents a paradox. Its petals give an appearance of age, but the rose has never opened, has never matured. It remains always in potential, a symbol—like the Sun—of eternity. There are twenty-one petals, for the trumps 1–21 of the Major Arcana. The Sun and the rose display a contrast of artistic history. The Sun takes us back to humanity's oldest art, for spirals figure among the earliest images. The more naturalistic rose brings us forward to the style of religious art of the Middle Ages and after.

The rose—and the unicorn—have figured very strongly in Christian symbology as images of purity and mystic revelation. We find the rose in the *Paradiso* of Dante. The rose represents both Christ and Mary. The color indicates Christ's blood and therefore His sacrifice to redeem the world. The thorn suggests the crown of thorns, Christ's suffering. The thorn on the beautiful flower allows the plant to signify pain and joy mixed together, desire joined to pain.

While the Middle Ages saw the rose as Christ, it saw it even more as His mother. The white rose especially represented Mary, for the color symbolized her purity. We shall see in a moment that the red rose belongs to the Goddess. The five petals of a rose, as shown in the picture, connected the flower to the apple, with its five-pointed star. We have seen in the Hierophant how the star made the apple a symbol of the Goddess. In medieval times, people saw the apple-pentacle as a sign of witches, but also of Eve's sin in the garden. Mary, with her rose, replaced Eve. The symbolism may seem merely intellectual to us today, but it affected our lives. The idea of Mary—a white bloodless rose—helped create an ideal for women that separated them from nature, from sexuality, from their own bodies.

The rose, like the apple, goes back to before Christianity. In ancient Greece the rose signified Aphrodite, Goddess of love. In India, it represents the Goddess, known, according to Barbara Walker, as "holy rose." And before it symbolized the blood of Christ, the red rose signified menstrual blood and the blood of childbirth.

In the picture the individual leaves form a *yoni*, a downward-pointing triangle. The arrangement, however, suggests a *lingam*, an upward-pointing triangle. Throughout the card we see a subtle enactment of the basic message shown in the Rune: the merging of opposites, of the Empress and the Emperor (for the Empress is Mary as well as Aphrodite, and the Emperor is Christ as well as Eros), the ecstatic union of body and mind, desire and truth.

DIVINATORY MEANINGS

The traditional meanings of the card stress joy and simplicity. The Sun is shining, life is wonderful. This may come after a time of sorrow or confusion, and then the Sun will indicate a relief. The person has passed through the dark time and the world has become good again.

The Sun supplies the energy that keeps us alive. Therefore, the card of the Sun indicates an energetic time in a person's life. It shows activity, excitement, optimism. The person enjoys doing things, believes in the future.

The Haindl version of the trump is more subtle than most, but it still shows an image of simplicity. In readings, this means a simple approach to situations. The person looks at the basic issues, makes clear decisions, takes action. The card does not just recommend doing this, it says that such an approach will work. The subtleties of this version suggest complexities under the surface. Nevertheless, the path between the trees remains broad and open.

As a symbol of the head, the Sun takes a rational approach to situations. This may not mean the detailed analysis of such cards as Justice. Instead, the Sun's simplicity implies a rationality that looks at the basic facts and decides what to do. We can therefore think of the Sun in contrast to the Moon, where fantasies and emotions tend to make action difficult.

The Sun brings self-confidence. At night we may doubt ourselves, but when the day comes, without clouds or rain, we feel everything will turn out all right. We can do anything.

The Sun suggests sexual desire. This contrasts with the Lovers, which indicates consummation. The Lovers card represents relationships; the Sun represents sexual energy within the person. Though the person will probably act on this desire, it may bring some pain as well as pleasure. Remember the thorn beneath the beautiful flower.

REVERSED

One meaning of the Sun card reversed stresses that the Sun becomes clouded over. The essential joy in life remains, but may become obscured by day-to-day problems or confusion. The problems may be minor, such as too many obligations, or more serious, such as emotional strains in a relationship. Nevertheless, an underlying happiness remains, and the person needs to recognize it.

The reversed Sun may mean a loss of confidence. Think of waking up to a bright morning. With the Sun shining, you feel you can do anything, that life will satisfy all your desires. But as the day wears on, clouds fill the sky. The optimism sinks, and with it the energy to do what needs to be done. The reversed card reminds us that the Sun still shines behind the clouds.

More subtly, the Sun reversed may indicate a time to withdraw slightly from action and responsibility. The person has gone through a Sun period and now needs to become quieter, maybe more introspective. These meanings become stronger in connection with such cards as the Hermit or the High Priestess.

If we see the Sun as desire, then the Sun reversed may mean frustration. Whether this applies would depend on the other cards, such as the Lovers (especially reversed), or some of the Cups and Swords.*

*See Volume II.

XX

AEON (JUDGEMENT)

A EON IS CARD 20, and twenty reduces to two, the High Priestess. We see in Aeon some of the same images as in the High Priestess, though in very different settings: the rain falling down, rivers running between cliffs. Twenty is also 2×10. The Wheel of Fortune dealt with time as a recurring cycle. Aeon is also about time, but in a more apocalyptic way. As Judgement, the traditional versions of this card show the angel Gabriel blowing his horn for the Last Judgement, while a man, a woman and a child rise from their graves. While moving the card away from this specific imagery, the Haindl Tarot still deals with the idea of a radical break with the past.

The Hebrew letter for trump 20 is Shin, which means "Tooth." There is a connection here with age, in the German saying, "the tooth of time," and the English description of an old person as "long in the tooth." Some people describe Shin as a serpent's tooth, joining the letter to the complex of ideas associated with snakes. The bite of a serpent kills. As the higher harmonic of Death, Aeon also shows the death of something limited and worn out. But it goes much further, for what dies here is a whole view of the world, not just the narrow limitations of a personality. And the card goes beyond the dying, to a new birth in the fetus tumblling down in its egg.

In Hebrew all letters bear a number value. Therefore, words also have a number, the sum of the different values of the letters. This enables Kabbalists to make connections between words and letters that have the same values. The letter Shin is 300. The sum of the letters in the phrase "Ruach Elohim," which means "life-breath (Spirit) of God," is also 300. Therefore, Shin, too, means this divine breath, which gives life to an individual soul and to the world. Kabbalists call Shin the "holy letter." Notice, by the way, its three-pronged shape, connecting it to Neptune's trident on the Hanged Man; the Empress; the Triple Goddess; the Christian trinity; the Freudian id, ego and superego; the occult unconscious, conscious and superconscious; and so on.

169

Aeon

The Rune is Peorth, P. The exact meaning of this Rune is not known. Some commentators say it means "secret," which connects us to the esoteric quality of the Tarot in general, and this card in particular. Hermann Haindl describes it as the figure of a man without a head, an image which implies mystery, or a lack of self-knowledge. The head, Haindl points out, appears below, in the glyph for Pluto. Another common meaning for Peorth is "Dice-cup." This does not refer to gambling, but to divination, for in ancient Germany people read the future by casting dice and lots, as well as Runes. Some people today still practice "cleromancy," fortune-telling by dice, with meanings assigned to the possible number combinations. Divination suggests fate, and the card deals witih the fate of the Earth.

The Germans saw fate as a matter of unfolding in time. Their version of the three Fates (another form of the Triple Goddess) was the Norns. According to Runic writer Edred Thorsson, the Norn names—Urdhr, Verthandi and Skuld—meant "that which has become," "that which is becoming" and "that which should become." Now, this resembles strikingly the answer God gives when Moses asks for a name he can bring to Pharaoh. "I am becoming what I am becoming." ("I am what I am," is, according to modern scholarship, a mis-translation.) Both the Norns and YHVH are expressing the idea of events in time as an evolution, an emergence into reality.

The planet for Aeon is Pluto. Astrologers will notice that Haindl has used an uncommon form of the glyph, which usually shows a cross beneath a curve. This version shows a circle—a head, above a curve—a bowl or a sickle. This joins consciousness with the lunar unconscious. It also suggests a beheading, for Pluto, God of the Underworld, deals with death. Pluto means destruction, but also regeneration. This is the same idea we saw in Death. In Pluto it becomes more powerful, more violent. Pluto is said to govern atomic energy and, in fact, the form of uranium (named for Uranus) used for fission is Plutonium.

The element for Aeon is Fire, the Plutonic destruction raining down on our suffering planet. When Haindl painted the red water on the right of the card, he thought, among other things, of the prediction in the Book of Revelations that the rivers will run red in the final battle between Christ and Satan. Shortly after he finished the painting, an accident caused tons of chemical waste to fall into the Rhine, a river which flows close by the Haindls' house. For a time the river really did run red, with poison instead of blood.

Aeon is one of those cards, like Death, that present an accumulation of details. While the bottom shows a clear landscape, the sky is obscured with dark clouds, giving us a sense of an unknown but ominous future. The landscape organizes itself according to distance. The rivers run through canyons, a sign of their great age. On either side, the land is dark but green. On the left we see a blasted tree, on the right, shadows. Beyond the flat land we see hills, and beyond them white mountains, a traditional symbol of purity and abstract truth. In the version of Judgement from the famous Rider Tarot, white peaks rise up behind the resurrected bodies. In the Haindl version, the mountains are not the final image. A dark volcano, symbol of destruction, looms behind the mountains, while above them clouds hide the strange images surrounding the fetus.

Between the shadowed hills and the white mountains we see a single blue hill. If we look closely we can spot a tower on the hilltop.

This is Glastonbury Tor, symbol of divine force protecting the world. We have seen references to the Tor in the Hermit, and in Alchemy, where the circle came from the Glastonbury well cover.

The child may remind people of the end of the film *2001*, where a similar baby approaches the Earth. This movie was essentially an esoteric film in the form of science fiction. It carried a message similar to Aeon—humanity on the edge of suicide, the promise of an evolutionary change that will bring renewal.

To the left of the child, the rain falls. On the right, drops of fire rise up into the sky. The division of blue and red is another reminder of Alchemy, trump 14. In fact, there are fourteen drops on either side. The idea of the fire going up reminds us of the occult idea of movement in two directions. The spirit descends through the soul into matter. But it does not remain there, inactive. Instead, it raises the world of matter to a higher level. When the soul releases itself its experiences—including suffering—have caused it to evolve to a greater understanding.

We saw the same idea at the very beginning of the Major Arcana, in the Fool. There we encountered the universal myth of the Fall. The Fool introduced the theme of suffering nature and the possibility that going through the journey of the Major Arcana would lead to wisdom. The Fool was silent, his mouth closed, for he did not know himself. Here, the baby's lips part, ready to speak. Aeon represents the last stage of the journey, for ourselves and for the planet. It shows a dark, yet fiery passage, with the hope of a new life on the other side. The baby occupies the center of the card. Notice that we see it upside down, like the Hanged Man.

Strange shapes, all obscure, surround the egg. The clouds themselves appear like dark wings, recalling the owls in the card of the Hermit. To the right of the baby, we see claws, or maybe ropes. Behind the clouds looms a single eye in a head so old it becomes impossible to identify. The shape of the head looks vaguely birdlike, but the eye is human. The figure is the Goddess, a woman as the Earth, a bird as the Sky, ancient and suffering.

The card of Aeon presents to us prophecies of the Earth's destruction and renewal. We have seen these themes before—in the swan of the Fool, in the Wheel of Fortune, in the Star—where we saw Erda washing her hair. But whereas the Star gave us an image of hope, Aeon shows an esoteric vision of the process of renewal, filled with danger and an unknown future.

We know very well the disasters facing our planet. The rain in the card may bring fresh life, or it may represent acid rain killing the trees, or fallout poisoning the ground and water. Many people think of all these disasters as a purely modern development. Yet, in cultures as diverse as the Hindu and the Hopi, as well as old Germany (see the following card), people have prophecied the Earth's destruction and rebirth.

The term *aeon* means a vast period of time, and all the prophecies share this image. The Earth gets old, worn out, life runs down. Catastrophes erupt. Some cultures predict the destruction of the cosmos. But then the new creation begins. The card of Aeon shows us an Earth so old the volcanoes have died, the stone merges with the sky (look below the egg—is that a mountain or a cloud?), the trees stand dead, the rivers run through barren cliffs. And yet, there are signs of hope. The white mountains shine with the perfection of eternal truth, the new child tumbles down, the land has begun to turn green again, even if no new trees have sprouted, and in the middle of the landscape, almost hidden, stands Glastonbury Tor, the secret protector.

The prophecies all speak of great destruction. People seem to yearn for this, as if only cataclysm could cleanse our weary lives. In recent years, we have seen, along with the religious texts, predictions by psychics old and new, such as Nostradamus, Edgar Cayce and various lesser-known messengers, of disaster. It seems we long for apocalypse to replace boredom. Or else, we cannot hope for rebirth without the punishment of cataclysm. But the Tarot teaches us that we make our own choices. And the traditional card of Judgement emphasizes that we hear a call within ourselves to rise up, to begin a new existence.

The baby in the egg represents this hope of renewal. The double symbolism corresponds to the ambiguous image above of the woman/bird (a baby from the woman, an egg from the bird). It unites the human and the divine, for we have seen in the Hanged Man and elsewhere how birds connect us to the Gods. The egg appears within the dark clouds. The renewal comes in a time of pain, emerging from the dark. In this idea we find the optimism of all the prophecies, including this one. The upside-down baby recalls the Star as well as the Hanged Man. The legs form a cross, a symbol in many religions (not just the Christian) of the spiritual (the vertical line) meeting the physical (the horizontal). The arms, in turn, form the infinity sign, the sideways figure eight, symbol of existence turning back on itself, continuing forever.

Many of the ancient prophecies view the universe as essentially repetitious. The same cycles, the same gods, even the same events, go on and on. The occult tradition, however, teaches of evolution, especially of consciousness. It takes as its symbol the spiral as much as the circle. Life does not merely return to where it was but emerges at a higher level with each turn of the dance (again, see the next card). The egg and the child return us to the Fool, but the child's mouth is open. Through the lessons and experiences of the Major Arcana—through the pain of our planet—the innocent has learned how to speak.

We have mentioned Glastonbury Tor, the vertical line on the flat landscape. The idea of protection also comes into the prophecies. The changes all occur as part of a divine plan (or rhythm). Therefore, the prophecies tell us, no matter how terrifying the future, take heart, for the Holy Spirit has not abandoned us. To this we can only add the fundamental idea of the Tarot. This Spirit does not exist somewhere out there. It exists in us.

DIVINATORY MEANINGS

The Haindl version of Aeon (Judgement) emphasizes the theme of renewal for the whole planet. When we think of the card in readings we see that this can apply to an individual as well. The card of Aeon is a powerful one. It tells you that this is a time of change. That is, renewal does not mean that things stay the same, but become better. Instead, the person who receives Aeon becomes "reborn" into a new situation. This may involve real change in circumstances—a new job, a move to a new home, a new relationship. Often, the new situation is psychological, a new way of looking at life in which everything becomes fresh.

Because of the imagery here, the rebirth may require a painful period in which the old life, or the old attitudes, become worn out. The person may feel that her or his life just doesn't work any more. Things may be falling apart. This does not have to be the case, and the reader should avoid imposing such an idea on the person. But if the person has been going through such a time, then the card speaks of optimism. For even though it implies an end to old patterns, even though it suggests a painful period of change, the emphasis remains on the baby emerging from the clouds.

Nor does the change come very slowly. An essential quality of Aeon is spontaneity. The person may have been going through a long psychological process, but under the surface. Suddenly everything will crystallize and the person will see the world in a new way. All things become possible, especially ideas or plans which the person might have resisted for a long time. We might recall here the traditional image of Judgement, the older form of the card. The angel Gabriel blows the trumpet and the dead rise from their tombs. Something stirs within us like a sound, a call, and we rise from lives that are fragmented or depressed or confused, into a new world, or rather, into the old world seen through new eyes.

REVERSED

When the card is reversed, the essential experience of Aeon does not change. It still means a rebirth. What changes is the person's reaction. Aeon reversed says that the person resists change. He or she does not want to recognize that the old life has ended. We found something similar with Death, which occupied the same position in the middle sequence. There we discussed the person who finds it hard to give up a life or a situation that is understood and safe, even if it is no longer valid and may even be harmful. In Aeon, however, *the change has already occurred,* only the person resists knowing it. As an example, think of someone in a bad relationship, or a relationship that simply has run down. The person may recognize that he gets nothing valuable from the situation, or that it brings pain. Nevertheless, he stays, afraid he will not be able to survive without it. Aeon says that psychologically he already has moved into a new life. Reversed shows him trying not to acknowledge it. Aeon in a reading can help overcome this resistance.

XXI

THE UNIVERSE (THE WORLD)

THE NUMBER OF the Universe, 21, like twelve, combines the 1 and the 2, the Magician and the High Priestess, light and darkness. It also adds up to three (1 + 2 = 3), the Empress. In that early card, we first saw the snake and learned some of its mythological, esoteric and psychological associations. Here we see the dragon, the grand serpent of the imagination. The number 21 is 3 × 7, the final harmonic of the Chariot's victory. The victory here is one of spiritual liberation.

The Hebrew letter, the final one in the alphabet, is Tav, which means "Signature" or "Mark." Paul Foster Case points out that a signature sets the seal on something. Trump 21 sets the seal on the Tarot's spiritual work. In fact, as the uncoiled dragon shows, it breaks the seal, opening up the mind to the hidden truths of the universe. Tav is related to the Greek letter Tau, which in turn connects to the Egyptian Tau cross, shaped like the letter T and a symbol of eternal life. In some modern Tarot decks the Hanged Man hangs from a Tau cross. In others he hangs from a gallows shaped like the Hebrew letter Tav. The connection reminds us that the traditional versions of the Hanged Man and the World mirror each other. In the Haindl Tarot the connection between the two cards is more subtle, for instance in the mythological connections of Odin (card 12) and the Midgard Serpent (card 21).

Case links the idea of a "mark" with a passage in Ezekiel where God tells the prophet to go through the city and mark the heads of the righteous people who lament the sinning. Therefore, Tav means salvation. Case might have mentioned the more well-known mark, when the Israelites marked their homes with lamb's blood so that the Angel of Death would pass over their houses on his errand to slay the firstborn of all the Egyptians. In traditional religious terms salvation means salvation from death. In the Tarot's esoteric psychology we overcome the fear of death through the Hanged Man's connection to life. The Universe signifies a greater awareness, in

The Universe

which we go beyond all the forms and limitations of the material universe to find eternity, blazing into light, like the fiery breath of the dragon, in every moment.

Just as Aleph, the Fool's letter, begins the Ten Commandments, so Tav begins the word "Torah," the first five books of the Bible. The Torah is God's law, dictated to Moses on Mt. Sinai. Now, the Torah, like the teachings of the Hierophant, tells people how to live their lives. Christianity sees Christ's incarnation as the replacement of a written law with the living reality of God's love. As traditional Jews, the Kabbalists revered the Torah. However, they sometimes described the physical scroll as a reflection of a greater Torah, non-material, existing before the universe. When God wished to created the universe He consulted this eternal Torah. Therefore, Tav—the Universe—signifies an existence beyond the merely physical.

The Rune is another form of Gebo, the gift Rune, found on the

Sun. Runes have more than one written shape, for the Runic alphabets traveled through Germany, England, Friesland (now a part of the Netherlands) and Scandinavia. Where trump 19 showed us the gift of life from the Sun, 21 brings us the gift of truth in the dragon's fire. Remember also that Gebo means ecstasy. The rising of the kundalini snake is exactly that, an ecstatic opening of the self to the entire universe.

The planet is Saturn. In Greek myth, Chronos (Saturn) was the son of Ouranos (Uranus) and the father of Zeus. Snakes were sometimes described as the "spine of Chronos." We have learned how the kundalini, which lies curled at the base of the spine, rises up the spine to the head.

Before the discovery of the three outer planets, Saturn was thought to be the last planet. Therefore, it has acquired the astrological meaning of limitations and restrictions. Many people see Saturn as a teacher that tells how we learn from our difficulties. The Tarot writer Mary Greer, in discussing the connection of Saturn with the world, has described the card as a personal transcendence, "dancing on your limitations." In the Haindl Tarot we also find the idea of transcendence, or breaking open limitations. We see this in the open circle. Compared to the ancient symbol of a snake with its tail in its mouth (called in Greek Ouroboros), the spiral form created by the dragon suggests open possibilities as well as an evolution to a higher level. We shall look at this symbol in more detail in a moment, but here we should note that Chronos means time (the image of Saturn has degenerated in the modern world to a cartoon figure known as "Father Time"), and that the Ouroboros snake means eternity.

In J. L. Borges's *Book of Imaginary Beings* we find an interesting connection between Chronos and Hermann Haindl's vision of the Universe. Borges cites a sixth-century writer, Damscius, who describes an ancient teaching that the first principles were Water and Earth. From these two came a dragon known as Un-aging Chronos, who laid an egg from which the world hatched (remember the egg in Aeon).

The element for the card is Earth. This may seem odd at first, for we have described the trump as transcending the material universe. But transcendence does not mean abandonment. In fact, it means embracing the Earth. In the Tarot we have learned to view the Earth once again as a divine being, the Mother of Life. In the state of awareness described in the Universe, we do not conquer the world but join with it. Every object—a pebble, a leaf, a drop of water—can unite us with all existence. Every moment can open to eternity.

In a film made about the Haindl Tarot the film crew followed Hermann Haindl's creation of this card through its various stages. Compared to many earlier cards, the Universe is a simple design. We see the bottom half of the Earth, with a dragon beneath it. Actually, the dragon circles the planet, as implied by the way the head and tail disappear up the sides of the card. Scandinavian myth described the World Serpent as coiled tightly around the Earth. This dragon has uncoiled. The head appears before the tail, suggesting a spiral. Now, the spiral appears to coil downward, for the head comes below the tail. We can describe this as the spirit returning to ordinary life. In other words, we do not "ascend to heaven" and stay there. At the same time we gain spiritual understanding, we become more ordinary. We go down at the same time we rise up. When Watson, Crick and Franklin discovered the double-helix shape of DNA, the basis of all life, occultists recognized the image as the double spiral basic to esoteric tradition.

We see the bottom half of the Earth, and below it the heavens, filled with other worlds. Usually, pictures of such a scene depict the top half of the globe, with the sky above. This is because we look up to see the stars. We should also note that the Middle Ages considered the human head a microcosm of the planet. Therefore, to see the bottom half instead of the top means that the trump reverses the usual image. If we think of the planet as a head, then it suggests someone upside down. And the idea of reversal, as we know from the Hanged Man, the Star and Aeon, is one of the particular themes of this Tarot.

The dragon and the Earth are both green, the color of new life. The Earth is smooth, not pitted. This indicates that the Earth is both eternal and in a state of renewal. A ring of light surrounds the planet, an indicator of an atmosphere and life. Light rings many of the other planets in the picture as well.

The line from the dragon's head along its body forms a diagonal in the direction of harmony. At the same time, the tail begins on the left, the side of instinct, and coils around the planet to come down on the right, the side of consciousness. There are ten planets below the dragon's body, a link to the Wheel of Fortune. Above the body we find twenty-two planets, the number of trumps in the Major Arcana. In the Kabbalah, the number thirty-two can be said to represent the universe, for it signifies the Tree of Life. There are ten Sephiroth and twenty-two pathways between them.

From between the dragon's eyes strange shapes rise up. They symbolize the experience of the third eye opening. The shapes open from the top of the head, the crown chakra. The highest Sephirah on the Kabbalist Tree, the one that leads back to the divine, is also called the "crown."

Like the dragon in fairy tales, our great serpent breathes fire. The red, color of energy and blood, mixes with white, color of pure thought. Fire here is breath. The English words "spirit" and "inspiration" both derive from Latin *spiritus*, meaning "breath." In Hebrew *ruach* (remember "Ruach Elohim" from Aeon) means both "spirit" and "breath." Breath allows us to live. In many religious traditions God breathes life into humans. Some people believe that when a person dies the soul leaves the body with the last breath. But we do not just breathe in at birth and hold on to it. We breathe in and out, so that if we become conscious of our breathing we will recognize that we constantly exchange energy with the world. The oxygen we breathe in comes from plants. The carbon dioxide we breathe out goes to plants. The ego's belief that it exists separate from the rest of creation is an illusion, disproved by our most common activity. In our time this illusion has become extremely dangerous. For if we cut down the forests, or if holes in the ozone destroy the plankton in the seas, then we destroy the sources of our own breathing.

In the fairy tales, the dragon's breath is danger and destruction. Here we can describe it as burning away illusions. This is not simply a metaphor. To see reality is indeed like breathing in light and fire. The term "enlightenment" does not mean an educated attitude. It means a great flash of truth, like a lightning bolt. When the kundalini energy awakens, people experience heat. In Tibet initiates prove themselves by going out naked at night in the middle of winter. Helpers lay frozen sheets over them and the initiates must melt the ice with their own warmth.

In the Middle Ages people described dragons as combining Air and Earth (spirit and matter), for as a lizard it belonged to the ground, yet it could fly. Our dragon has no wings but the breath combines Air with Fire, while Earth, as we have seen, is the element for the card. Water comes in when we learn that the Ouroboros was described as coiling the planet at the bottom of the seas.

For Hermann Haindl the Ouroboros signifies what he thinks of as the old belief, that existence is closed and repeats itself over and over. In this view people must fulfill their function in life and not strive for anything more. Social patterns remain fixed forever. But the modern world has changed this. We have discovered the possibility of individual activity, of the universe as a place that is always new. This had led to arrogance and danger, but we should not give it up even if we could. The snake has opened the circle. At the same time we do need to return—not to the old rules, but to the genuine truths found in the ancient traditions. We need to return to reverence for the Earth and all Her children. And so the serpent does not rear up, but spirals down.

The World Serpent of Germanic myth was very similar to the Ouroboros. The Serpent lived beneath the sea; Snorri Sturlason, the great preserver of Scandinavian mythology, described the Serpent as biting its own tail. But the stories also described the Serpent as evil, as in the fairy tales. The Serpent gnaws at the base of the World Tree. It fights with an eagle that flies round the top of the tree. An eagle, as we have learned, symbolizes spirituality, and a snake the unconscious. But as we saw in the card of Death, they are actually the same thing. The fear of the unconscious—the fear of our own desires, our own fears and dreams—creates the illusion of the eagle and the snake as opposing energies.

The great enemy of the Serpent is Thor, God of thunder and therefore, along with Odin, similar to Zeus (some myths describe Thor, not Odin, as the father of the Gods, while the Romans identified Thor with Jupiter/Zeus and Odin with Mercury/Hermes). Two stories describe Thor battling the Serpent. In the first, Thor comes to a hall of giants who challenge him to a test of strength. The mighty God agrees and his hosts tell him to pick up a cat lying on the floor. To Thor's embarrassment he can only raise the animal very slightly. The laughing giants tell him the creature was the World Serpent. Now, if the Serpent represents the unconscious, or more broadly, life itself, then Thor in this tale symbolizes the powerful ego trying to conquer the world through the force of its will. The second story follows the first. An angry Thor invites one of the giants to go fishing. Thor's hook catches the Serpent. With all his might he manages to raise the head. Thor readies his hammer to smash the Serpent. The giant, terrified of the end of the world, cuts the line and the Serpent sinks back below the waves.

The ego sees itself as the hero and the unconscious as the poisonous beast. To raise up that energy in order to overcome it invites destruction, for the unconscious is not "out there" but in ourselves. And the simple lesson of every breath teaches that the whole world is inside us, just as we are inside the world. The Scandinavians, like many other people, prophesied the end of the world. Their name for this disaster is *Ragnarok*; in German it is *Gotter-damerrung*, the name Wagner gave to the final opera in his Ring cycle. Many cataclysmic events will signal Ragnarok, including the awakening of the World Serpent. When it uncoils, the water will rise up to engulf the land. Now, we have learned that psychologically the seas are the unconscious, the land the ego. Therefore, the "end of the world" comes when the hidden energy awakens and overwhelms the conscious mind. For if this energy joins us to all of existence, and the ego creates the illusion of an "I" isolated from everything else, then the rising sea really can destroy this tiny island.

In Ragnarok, Thor battles the Serpent for the final time. He destroys it but the venom kills him as well. A similar fate meets the other Gods, and so the world ends, only to begin again after an unimaginable time. Many people have observed the courageous pessimism of this story, the same events always ending in the same destruction. But as we have learned in the Hanged Man, we can choose an alternative to courage and battle. That alternative is surrender, joyously and freely given. If we do not see the world—and our own selves—as enemies, then the dragon, the snake, uncoils like the Shakti, burning away fear as well as illusion.

In the Empress we saw how Marduk declared a great victory by killing Tiamat, his mother. The myth tells how he dismembered her body to create the Sky and the Earth. He then set himself up on a throne to demand obedience. For the arrogant ego, creation means separation, conquest, and strict rules of above and below. Any change in these rules will threaten destruction. But in the card of the Universe, the final triumph of the Major Arcana, we find Tiamat uncoiled. And the message is not of conquest or destruction, but liberation and love.

DIVINATORY MEANINGS

The traditional meaning for trump 21 is success. This may refer to something specific, such as success in business, especially if the person has asked a work-related question. The card can also mean becoming happier, more fulfilled. If the card comes up during a time of struggle, it signals a release, with a better life ahead. The meaning is the same whether the struggles are practical, such as starting a business, or emotional or health-related. The Universe in a reading for a sick person will indicate recovery and a new sense of well-being. If a person asks about a career, the Universe tells of an exciting future.

Usually the card does not mean success only in practical terms. It also implies satisfaction, a feeling of justified pride. Life in general is going well. There is a further sense of using your life well, of not wasting talents or experience.

Sometimes the reading as a whole indicates that success will not come automatically, and that the person must do something. This may mean overcoming resistance from other people. Or it may mean not giving up at initial setbacks. The person might have to overcome apathy or pessimism. The Universe says, "You can achieve great success and happiness if you believe in yourself."

The particular symbolism of the Haindl version—the spiraling dragon—suggests the idea of a person going beyond previous limitations. It shows a life opening up. There is a sense of newness, excitement, new ideas and opportunities.

REVERSED

The reversal of the success card does not mean failure. Usually, it indicates stagnation. The situation—or the person—has gotten stuck in some way. As a result, possibilities for success or happiness have not been realized. Sometimes stagnation results from outside opposition. Often it comes from the person—a fear of taking chances (especially if the Universe reversed should come up with the Fool reversed), a lack of willpower or confidence, or a desire to keep things the way they are, a fear of the future.

The reversed Universe may emphasize the person's limitations, *or* that the person does not try to go beyond them. Limitations may be of education, of finances, of courage, of imagination. In connection with romance, they may mean shyness. Limitations may be self-defined. "I don't dare." "I'm not smart enough." "No one will like me." "It's too late." "I'm too old." "I'm not creative enough." The presence of the Universe in a reading signifies a potential for success and fulfillment. Reversed, the Universe may emphasize resistance or opposition, but the potential remains.

MAJOR ARCANA

Num-ber	Card	Hebrew Letter	Rune Word	Astrological Sign	Ele-ment
0	The Fool	Aleph (ox)	Wynn (joy)	Uranus	Air
1	The Magician	Beth (house)	Peoh (cattle)	Mercury	Air
2	The High Priestess	Gimel (camel)	Ur (aurochs)	Moon	Water
3	The Empress	Daleth (door)	Thorn (thorn)	Venus	Earth
4	The Emperor	Heh (window)	Ansur (mouth)	Aries	Fire
5	The Hierophant	Vav (nail)	Radh (wheel)	Taurus	Earth
6	The Lovers	Zain (sword)	Ken (torch)	Gemini	Water
7	The Chariot	Cheth (fence)	Hagall (hailstone)	Cancer	Water
8	Strength	Teth (snake)	Sigil (sun)	Leo	Fire
9	The Hermit	Yod (hand)	Is (ice)	Virgo	Earth
10	Wheel of Fortune	Kaph (palm)	Jara (year)	Jupiter	Fire
11	Justice	Lamed (ox goad)	Nyd (necessity)	Libra	Air
12	The Hanged Man	Mem (seas)	Tyr (God of war & law)	Neptune	Water
13	Death	Nun (fish)	Ba (birch Goddess)	Scorpio	Water
14	Alchemy	Samekh (tent peg)	Laguz (water)	Sagittarius	Fire
15	The Devil	Ayin (eye)	Eolh-elk (man)	Capricorn	Earth
16	The Tower	Peh (mouth)	Yrr-err (woman)	Mars	Fire
17	The Star	Tzaddi (fishhook)	Eh (horse)	Aquarius	Air
18	The Moon	Kaph (back of head)	Othal (prosperity)	Pisces	Water
19	The Sun	Resh (head)	Gebo (gift)	Sun	Fire
20	Aeon	Shin (tooth)	Peoh (dice cup)	Pluto	Fire
21	The World	Tav (signature)	Gebo (gift)	Saturn	Earth

READINGS

THINK OF THE Tarot as a very special kind of book, one which you can change every time you pick it up. By shuffling and laying out the cards you create a new order, and therefore new relationships between the cards. This widens the meanings of the individual cards, and therefore the whole deck. The Tarot is not just to study; we use the Tarot as a tool for self-knowledge, and for knowledge about the world.

People used to think of Tarot readings as a means of getting hard answers to direct questions: "Will I get the job?" "Will I get the girl?" Today we tend to see a reading more as a complex mirror of ourselves. A question about a relationship may show a person her inner attitudes to lovers and to sex. It may tell her something about how she behaved in past relationships, or how her upbringing has affected her, or what she really wants. At the same time, a reading is not entirely subjective. It does not show only the person's feelings and beliefs; it gives us a sense of what the patterns are in the world around us. What is the other person's attitude to the relationship? Does the moment favor the two of them getting together, or is this simply the wrong time? Among other things, the Tarot (and other oracles, especially the *I Ching*) teaches us to recognize that we exist in a complex pattern with the world around us.

Many people find it difficult to accept that the Tarot can give us any kind of objective view of ourselves, let alone situations. They wonder how a deck of cards can relate to outside reality. And if the person mixes the cards again, won't they say something entirely different? To take the last question first, in practice this tends not to happen. If you do the cards again, you usually get the same message, often with many of the same cards (people who have read through the card descriptions will realize that the meanings of many cards overlap, so that a second reading can give you a similar answer even with somewhat different cards). Very often there will be subtle but important differences between the two readings. In fact, the only reason to do it more than once is to gain greater clarity, or to see the situation from a different angle.

This still leaves the issue of why it should work at all. We should say first of all that the Tarot does not cause anything to happen. The cards do not contain some magic power to compel events. Instead, they reflect the direction events will probably take of their own accord. They show what a person is likely to do and what situations are likely to occur. More important, they give us a greater understanding of the situation right now, so that we can work to shape the future in valuable ways.

At any moment, the world and the people in it form a complex web. Think of the labyrinth radiating from the face of Spider Woman.* There are forces we know of, and many more forces unknown to us. Together, the conditions and actions create reality. Now, a Tarot reading, or an *I Ching* hexagram, or a Rune casting, also creates a pattern. Because this small pattern exists within the larger one, it gives us a picture of the greater reality. It mirrors it. This may strike most people as a radical (and irrational) idea. We have grown up with the belief that events have to have a direct cause. If a tree falls over, something—a wind, or a bulldozer—must have pushed it. If two people in an office have a fight, they must have annoyed each other in some way. Now, the Tarot does not argue against cause and effect. It simply adds another dimension. It suggests that if the tree falls at the same time that the people are fighting, the two events go together. They help form a pattern, along with the other factors that make up that particular moment. By mixing the cards and laying them down, we allow ourselves to create a reflection of our own small part of the overall situation. The problem then becomes to interpret it.

The term "divination" literally means "to communicate with Spirits." We might term this the "archaic" view of readings. Because we do not consciously control the shuffle of the cards, we allow God, or Spirits, to guide our hands. Some people who cast Runes call on Odin to guide them. We do not need to believe in divine help in order to accept the value of a Tarot reading. We simply need to trust that the cards have a message for us, and then try to understand that message in the best way possible.

We should, however, recognize that the Tarot forms a spiritual philosophy. Anyone who has read the descriptions of these cards will understand that. This means that readings do not just advise us

*For more information on the Minor cards discussed in this section, see Volume II.

how to look for a job, or how to behave in a relationship. They also help us to see the world in a sacred way. Any method of creating a random pattern will give us some kind of reading. People have used tea leaves, dice, pebbles thrown on the ground, candle droppings, and so on. The value of the Tarot lies in the depth and subtlety of its messages. Because each card means something valuable in itself, the whole reading gives us greater understanding of the world and our own place in it.

Some people fear that if they believe in the Tarot, they cannot believe in free will. A Tarot reading does not eliminate choice. This is because it does not actually predict anything, not in an absolute way. It shows instead the likelihood of events. It says: given the current conditions, and the forces that shaped them, things are tending in certain directions. Actually, a Tarot reading can and should increase free will. Because it increases our knowledge, it enables us to make better choices. That understanding applies not just to ourselves, but to the moment. A reading may tell a person that conditions do not favor new relationships at this time; she will find greater fulfillment in a Hermit-like peacefulness. We see the idea, especially with the Minor cards, that a person needs to take action at some times, and to wait at other times. A reading shows us two things in particular: the first is our own motives and goals in a situation, and the second is the character of the situation itself.

There are many different ways of laying out the cards. Some people prefer to turn over a group of cards at random and see what they say. Most people, however, prefer to use a "spread," that is, a particular pattern. The cards go in a definite order and place, and the meaning of each card depends on the position as much as on the card itself. We will look at several of these spreads in a moment.

Whichever spread we use, the method of doing the reading remains roughly the same. The first thing is to decide on the question. You do not need to ask something very specific; you may wish to see what the cards have to tell you at this particular moment. However, if you do have a question, you should try to make it clear. This will help you to interpret the meanings. If you are reading for yourself, formulate the question in your mind or even write it down on a piece of paper. If you are reading for someone else, ask the person to tell you the question.

This last suggestion may surprise some people. They are used to the idea of the fortune-teller who guesses at a person's secrets.

It seems like cheating for the reader to know the question. However, we should not look at readings as a kind of game or test. We do them for understanding. If a reader starts off knowing the purpose of the reading, she or he can go much further in interpreting the answer. Still, there are some readers who prefer not to know the question. They wish to keep their minds as clear as possible for the moment when they first look at the cards. Others may wish to know the general area (love, money or spiritual development are the most common), but not any details. When you have gained some experience you will find what works best for you.

We should also point out that some people read only for themselves or only for others. It may sound easier to read for yourself but, in fact, many people find it much harder. First of all, you do not feel as involved when you read for someone else. If a disturbing card appears somewhere in the spread, you are less likely to panic. Or if something very nice appears, you can consider it more objectively when it concerns someone else. Also, when you read for another person you need to explain it. This means going slowly, discussing each card, and trying to find some overall interpretation. Through this process you carry your original impressions much further. You will see new meanings and new relationships between the different cards. When you read for yourself, you might stop at the first ideas that come into your mind. For a long time I never read for myself, but rather traded readings with a good friend. Only after some years did I learn to treat my own readings with the same care I give to others. Even now, I often prefer to ask someone else to read my cards. Doing so gives me an outside perspective on my questions and choices.

When the question has been formulated, the next step is choosing a "significator." This means a card to represent the person in the reading. Usually we choose this card ahead of time and set it on the table, face up, before the person mixes the cards. Traditionally, the significator is one of the Court cards. (Some people use a Major card, most often the Fool. For myself, I prefer to leave all the trumps in the deck.) In ordinary decks we might use a king for an older man, a queen for an older woman, a knight for a younger person of either sex, and a page for a child. In the Haindl Tarot, I would recommend using a Son or a Daughter. The simplest method is to find these cards in the deck and lay them out, face up. Ask the person to choose one, following his or her feelings about the picture. You can also choose the significator astrologically. As we saw in the Major Arcana, each sign belongs to one of the four elements. Therefore, a Leo would use the Daughter or Son of Fire. When the person has selected the significator, lay it on the table face up and return the others to the deck.

Now the time has come to mix the cards. The subject of the reading, sometimes called the "querent," shuffles the deck with the pictures face down. In this book I have given reversed meanings for each card. Therefore, the subject should shuffle the cards in such a way that some of them get turned around. One method involves setting the cards in a pile face down on the table, and then spreading them all around in a jumble, finally bringing them back together.

When the person has mixed the cards, he or she should lay them down again in a neat pile. With the left hand, the person cuts the deck to the left, then cuts the left-hand pile again to the left, making three piles altogether. The reader, also using the left hand, puts them back together with the bottom pile on the top. This separation into three is part of the tradition of readings. In the Haindl Tarot we can also think of it as a way of invoking the power of the Empress, who represents the Triple Goddess.

The reader then lays out the cards in the particular pattern called for by the spread. Some people prefer to turn them over one at a time, others to turn them over all at once in order to get a general impression before interpreting the individual cards. A little experience will show you the best method for yourself. When interpreting the cards, remember that the purpose is understanding, not demonstrating magical or psychic powers. If we trust that the cards have something worthwhile to tell us, then we need to give them the best chance to do so. This may involve discussing a card (or cards) with the querent. If you can see several possibilities, you might want to explore them with the person. Remember to use tact and caution if you think the cards say something difficult. Remember as well that a reading should be a positive experience. If the cards do show problems, try to find a way the person can use the experience. Do not lie or distort what you honestly think the cards are saying, but help the person deal with it in the best way. And remember that you are not infallible. Even if we accept that the cards will always reflect actual situations, this does not mean we will always understand their messages.

When you first begin to do readings, you may find it difficult to understand the cards at all. Many people find they can grasp what a specific card might mean but they cannot connect the different bits into an overall message. Do not get discouraged. Reading Tarot cards is a skill, and like any skill it takes practice. After you have done it for awhile, you will suddenly discover you can see things that would have completely eluded you when you first started.

At the beginning of your work with the cards, get yourself two notebooks. In one, record all the readings you do, with the date and a summary of your interpretation. If you remain in touch with the person, you can see if events match your impressions. And if someone comes back for a further reading, you can look at the previous one to see how the situation is developing. Very often in a series of readings, one or more cards will appear in each one. These cards will take on a special significance for that person.

In the other notebook, write down your own ideas about the cards. When you first get it, set aside several pages for each card. Write down your immediate impressions of the picture itself, and of the meanings given in this book. As ideas come to you about specific cards, add them to your notebook. A reading may suggest a new interpretation, or it may produce some strong feeling. If you meditate with the cards, you might record your experiences. In a separate section of the notebook, write down any thoughts you have about the cards in general. You might want to include pictures or stories suggested by the images. From time to time read over your notes. You will probably find yourself expanding old points that you wrote down months ago. Through this, and through practice with both readings and meditation, you will make the Tarot your own.

SPREADS

There are a great many spreads for laying Tarot cards, and any book on Tarot will describe several. Some books devote themselves entirely to providing various spreads. Layouts include methods to link the Tarot to astrology, or to the calendar, or to Kabbalistic systems such as the Tree of Life, or to other esoteric diagrams. At one time, serious students of the Tarot dismissed readings as crude fortune-telling. Now that readings have developed into a serious tool for self-awareness, many excellent books exist which can help you put your knowledge of the Tarot into practice.

THREE-CARD SPREADS

One of the simplest ways to begin Tarot readings is the use of three cards. The small number will help you see the connections between the cards. At the same time, a pattern of only three cards can sometimes produce remarkably subtle readings.

Here are two layouts, each using three cards. For both, lay the three cards in a row below the significator.

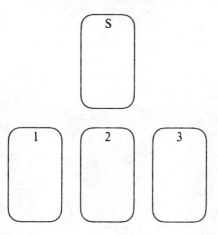

In the first method, card two, the center card, represents the current situation. It shows something happening in the person's life at this moment. Card one, on the left, indicates past experience, something that has led to the current situation. The third card, on the right, shows the future. This does not mean a fixed prediction, but simply the way things are heading. The person can change the direction (or help it along) through understanding the reasons why things are going the way they are going.

The other three-card method involves choices. Again the card in the middle depicts the current situation. This time, however, the cards on either side show two of the choices available to the person. An example will show how this can work in practice.

A person chooses Radha, the Daughter of Wands, as significator. Her question concerns a relationship, and when the reader turns over the cards they come out the Chariot, the Three of Cups reversed and the Daughter of Stones.

Daughter of Wands in the East
Princess of Wands

The Chariot

Three of Cups
Overflowing

Daughter of Stones in the West
Princess of Stones

Take a moment to look at the pictures. Allow the images to affect you. See if you can see their implications together. The following interpretation merely sketches the possibilities in this group of cards. The center card tells her that the situation has become overemotional. The intense feeling between the two people has spilled over into problems and sadness. The Chariot suggests that she can try to ride the wave of emotion, to use all that intensity to explore her own reactions to love and relationships. It implies a strong possibility of victory, that is, getting what she wants. However, she might find it a rough time, requiring courage and will-power. On the other side we find the Daughter of Stones. This would tell her to take a step back from the situation. Buffalo Cow Woman would suggest, first of all, serenity rather than high emotion. Secondly, it would adivse her that she can find this serenity through putting her energy outside the relationship. Service to others may help ground her feelings.

The person in such a reading still might want to know the results of each of the choices. She can do this in two ways. She can do a more complicated reading (for instance, using the Celtic Cross spread described below), with a question such as, "What will happen if I follow the Chariot?" More simply, she can turn over two more cards, one directly under the Chariot, and the other under the Daughter of Stones. These two would then show the likely developments. Let us say the two cards are the Lovers upside down and the Hermit. The reading then would look like this:

Daughter of Wands in the East
Princess of Wands

The Chariot

Overflowing
Three of Cups

Daughter of Stones in the West
Princess of Stones

The Lovers

The Hermit

The Lovers reversed would indicate continuing problems in the relationship. The two people probably would stay together but without harmony. The struggles would continue for some time before they could become smooth again. The Hermit, on the other side, would carry the Daughter of Stones a step further. It would show the person feeling more peaceful, but it would also show her alone. She could feel good about herself and her world but without the other person. Notice that the cards do not offer any easy solutions. The choice remains difficult, but the reading might help to make it more conscious.

The above layouts are only two of the many possibilities for three cards. Another example might be one that shows the situation in the middle; on the left, the behavior of the person; and on the right, the behavior of other people.

CELTIC CROSS

The most popular Tarot spread is probably the Celtic Cross, named for the shape formed by the first six cards. It appears in many books, usually with slight variations in each one. The version given here is one I have used for many years. After a person has mixed the cards in the usual way, turn over the first card and lay it on top of the significator. Lay the second card horizontally across the first.

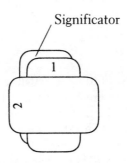

Turn over cards three through ten in the following pattern around the first two cards.

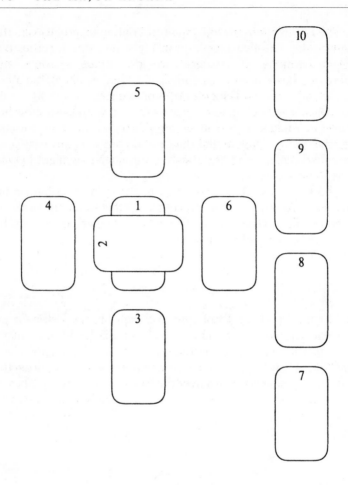

Cards one and two form the "small cross" or "center" cards. Cards three through six are the "cross," while cards seven through ten form the "staff." The meanings of the positions are as follows:

1. The Cover card—This shows the basic situation, the central issue.

2. The Crossing card—This card joins with the first card to state the concerns of the reading. Sometimes it acts as an opposition to card one. For instance, the Star, as a card of hope, might form an Opposition to one of the more negative Swords cards, such as the Five. The Crossing card also may show some result that has developed out of the first card. As an example of a result, suppose the

Cover card is Strength reversed, and the Crossing is the Five of Wands. This would indicate that the person feels weak at this time, and as a result gets into situations of conflict withi the people around him. The Crossing card is always read right side up.

3. Basis—This card depicts some experience, usually in the past, that acts as a root, or cause of the current situation. Though it may indicate some specific event, it usually shows a more general condition that has led to the developments shown in the two center cards. Sometimes this card will reach deeply into the person's life. Once, in a reading about a woman's sexual difficulties, the Emperor in the Basis position brought up the issue of a stifling relationship with her father.

4. Recent Past—This card does not reach as far back as the Basis. It indicates what has been happening recently in terms of the person's question. It may show something that has finished but still affects the person. Or, it may show a continuing situation; in this case, the influence will probably come to an end fairly soon.

5. Possible Outcome—This card shows the *general* way things are heading. In contrast to the last card in the layout, the Outcome (see below), it is less specific and less definite. For instance, an Outcome of the Son of Cups might indicate a decision taken about something, while the Possible Outcome of the Universe suggests that the decision is apt to turn out quite well.

6. Near Future—This card indicates immediate developments. It is not the final result of the situation, but part of its unfolding. Like the recent past, it tends to show conditions that will not last. If the card indicates a problem, the reader can point out that the difficulty will be temporary. If it shows something desirable, the reader can advise the person to make the most of it while it lasts.

7. Self—This card shows what the person contributes to the situation. It may show an attitude or an action. You may find this the key card, as in a reading I once did where the Chariot reversed showed that the person lacked the will to continue in the situation.

8. Environment—This card shows influences from outside the querent. It may refer to some specific person (especially if the reading concerns a relationship), or to the general atmosphere.

9. Hopes and Fears—This card illuminates what the person expects to happen. Often this position greatly affects the Outcome because it shows the person's attitudes and desires. For instance, the Five of Swords here would say that the person fears defeat; such

pessimism can help bring about that defeat. The Star would produce a much more positive result. This position sometimes helps the person confront hidden attitudes.

10. Outcome—This card sums up the other nine. It shows the most likely result, given all the other influences.

We should never consider the result as fixed. We can always change direction, and in fact, the reading itself, becuase it shows the way things are going, can serve as the starting point for change. The very fact of having a reading means that the situation is no longer the same. Still, we should not assume we can alter that situation without any serious effort. A reading may show strong influences on a person's life. Going against those influences can demand conscious work. If the reading should show some sort of undesirable outcome, the reader should help the person find ways to improve the situation.

THE WORK CYCLE

Tarot spreads give you information. At the same time they give you images of your life. You can use these images to focus your efforts at change. However, most readings primarily tell you what is happening. The spread below, developed by myself, emphasizes what you can do in the situation. Unlike most layouts, it also provides a method for turning over more cards if the first line leaves you without a clear answer.

Choose the significator and mix the cards as usual. Lay the first card on top of the significator and the second across it, as in the Celtic Cross. Then turn over the next seven cards in a row below the first two.

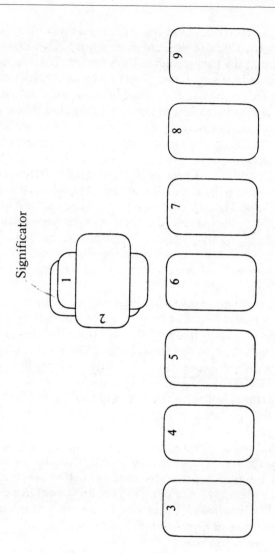

Cards one and two set out the same basic situation as the first two cards in the Celtic cross. Card three refers to Past Experience. It shows part of the background to the situation. It acts somewhat like the Basis in the Celtic Cross. Card four represents Expectations. It indicates the person's attitude, what he or she expects to happen. This helps to identify positive or negative approaches. These are not always conscious. The next three cards, five, six and seven, are read together as the Work. They indicate the opportunities and obstacles facing the person.

The sixth card is the Outcome. It shows what is likely to happen. The seventh card is the Result. It indicates what will happen *because* of the Outcome. For instance, suppose that card six, the Outcome, is the Two of Swords. This indicates a truce between people who may have been having problems. But what will happen after the truce period ends? Will they stay close or go back to quarreling? The Two of Stones as the Result would indicate that the truce allows harmony to develop.

If these cards give you a clear message, then stop there. But if you find yourself still seeking understanding, you can lay out a second line of seven cards underneath cards three through nine. The same positions apply to this second line of cards. As a group, they will show a different aspect of the situation, giving the person a chance to look at it from a different point of view. Often the point of view is defined by the first two cards in the line, the Past Experience and the Expectation. For instance, if these show a realistic attitude then the Work and the Results are likely to be positive. But if the Expectation card indicates over-optimism, or exaggerated fears, then the rest of the line may become distorted as well. The Work may call for the person to see the situation as it really is.

In principle you can lay out up to ten lines, with five cards left over for a "commentary." In practice, I have rarely found the need to go beyond two or three lines. For many readings, the first nine cards will give a firm answer.

This spread works best with questions such as, "What should I do about my problem?" or "What is the best way to handle . . . (a person, an opportunity, etc.)?" You might ask, "What approach can I take to get the job?" or "How can I deal with my lover?"

THE HAGALL SPREAD

A new Tarot should have a new spread. In working with the Haindl Tarot it struck me that one thing that distinguished it was the way the three types of cards had their own character. A layout especially for this Tarot could reflect this, with the Major Arcana and the Minor Arcana Suit cards and Court cards, each shuffled and laid out separately. When I created this layout, and was working out ideas for the Minor Suit cards and the Major cards, I discovered that together they could form the Rune Hagall—so important as a symbol for the entire deck.

To lay out the Hagall spread, first separate the cards into Major, Suit and Court cards. You will then have three piles. The spread does not call for a significator, so you should not remove any cards.

Begin with the Suit cards. Shuffle the forty cards, as usual thinking of your question. When you have mixed them, turn over four cards in a diamond pattern.

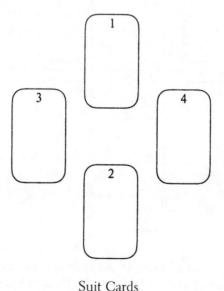

Suit Cards

These cards describe what is happening. Card one indicates the general situation. Card two, below it, shows something you've done, or an experience you've had, that has helped create the current conditions. Card three shows your beliefs—your own impressions and expectations, conscious or subconscious, of the situation and where it's going. Very often, our beliefs shape the situation in a much greater way than we realize. This card can help you see those beliefs and decide if they work for you or against you. You can follow through on them or change them. Card four indicates the likely results of the situation as it stands now.

We next go on to the Major cards. Mix up the twenty-two trumps and lay down three in a triangle above the Minor cards. This creates Hagall.

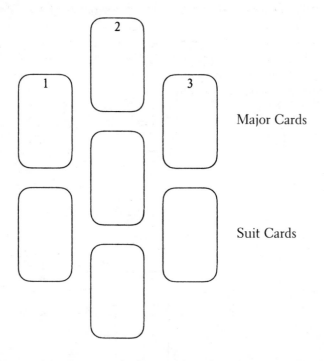

Major Cards

Suit Cards

The Major Arcana indicate our spiritual tasks in life. Some of them challenge us, like the Chariot, the Hanged Man or the Devil. We may have to overcome obstacles, either in ourselves or in the outside world, in order to fulfill these challenges. Other cards, such as the Lovers, or the Star, come to us as wondrous gifts. The task with these cards becomes to appreciate them, and to use them in a way that helps us but also helps the world. In the triangle, card two, on top, signifies the spiritual task at this time. It shows the challenges and opportunities in the current situation as shown in the Suit cards. Card one, on the left, represents spiritual history. It indicates something about how you've behaved in the past, and what you've learned. Card three, on the right, indicates a "metamorphosis." It shows, on a spiritual level, how the situation will change, and the spiritual tasks that will come to you as a result. You might look at it as connected to card four of the Suit cards section, the likely results.

Now we come to the Court cards, possibly the most interesting aspect of this spread. Mix them up and set out three cards in a row below the others. The final pattern will look like this:

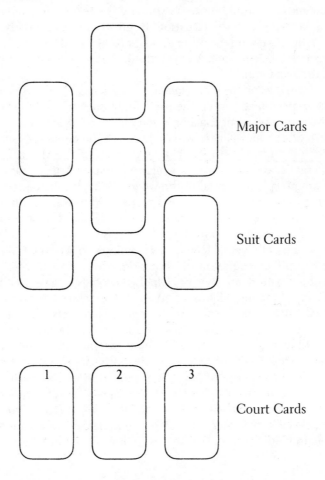

Major Cards

Suit Cards

Court Cards

In this reading, the *Court* cards are always read right side up. If they come out reversed, turn them around before interpreting them. The card in the middle shows you yourself. It indicates what aspect you have taken on in this situation. It does not say you have actually become Radha, or Osiris, but only that you are expressing those qualities at this time. We can describe the Court cards as various ways of being in the world. At different times, and in different situations with different people, we will probably experience all of them. The card in the middle shows you which one you are experiencing now.

Card three, on the right, symbolizes the Teacher. Here we do think of the card as the person. If Brigit comes up here, look at her special qualities and imagine her as an actual Teacher. Imagine the demands she would make on you and the help or instruction she would give you in this situation. Brigit would make a fairly gentle Teacher. Odin, on the other hand, or Kali, would be very demanding, possibly fearsome. And yet, think of all you could learn from a figure like Odin.

Card one, on the left, symbolizes the Helper. Again, visualize the actual person shown on the card. Only now, instead of someone who instructs you or challenges you, this person gives you total support. She or he will help you to deal with the conditions shown in the Suit cards, and the spiritual tasks shown in the Major. Think of the myths and fairy tales in which Athena, or Ariadne, or Merlin, or simply a kind animal in the woods, helps the hero accomplish some impossible errand. As a Teacher, Odin would push us very hard. Because Odin is a trickster, he might put us in situations where we could not know for sure what is happening. As a Helper, however, Odin would lend us his great power. We could allow ourselves to feel magical in the situation, with access to wisdom. By contrast, with Radha as your Helper you could allow yourself to look at everything more lightly. You could feel relaxed and sensual.

Clearly, some Helpers are stronger than others. Parsifal would give you less magic than Kali. But maybe you do not need Kali at this time. Maybe Parsifal, with all his own doubts, is just right for you. To feel that your Helper remains with you, you might carry the card in your pocket, or bag. Or you might draw your own version of it and carry that with you. If you prefer words to pictures, try writing (or telling yourself) a story with the Helper (and perhaps the Teacher) and yourself as characters. This last exercise can be valuable in helping you see fresh possibilities in the situation.

This reading treats the Court cards in a very different way than most spreads. It takes them beyond the strictly psychological and looks at the Gods and Goddesses as living beings. Some people will prefer to see this as aspects of themselves (or people around them). Others may go wholly in the other direction and see them as genuine divinities. Still others might take a middle approach, looking at Spider Woman, or Osiris, or the Goddess of Willendorf, as patterns of energy which we personify in human terms. Remember, too, that one of the three cards indicates yourself. This can help you strike a balance between the personal and the mythological aspects of the images. Whatever your approach, try the Hagall reading and see how it affects you.

MEDITATION

MEDITATION WITH THE Tarot allows us to create a personal bond between ourselves and the cards. Sometimes meditation will come out of a reading. The person lays out the cards and one card strikes her or him as very important. Usually, this will be one of the Major cards, or a Court card, for these pictures present us with powerful mythic images. We see the Magician in our reading, we recognize its importance at this time in our lives, and now we want to go beyond simply understanding what it means; we want to gain a genuine experience of the Magician's creative power. And so we do a meditation with the Magician, and in this way enter into the world of the image.

Meditation does not have to depend on readings. You can choose a card that seems valuable to you at a particular time. Also, many people who study the Major Arcana follow a program of meditating with each card. If they follow a Kabbalist teaching, they will likely connect these meditations to the twenty-two pathways on the Tree of Life. But we do not need to use such a strict program in order to work with the trumps. We can enter into the images of cards one by one, or in groups. One worthwhile meditation with the Haindl Tarot uses the Chariot, the Hanged Man, and the Star as a trio.

Meditation gives us a non-rational experience of the cards. It takes us directly to the heart of the image, allowing us to make it a part of our own lives, our own knowledge. Each card has its own qualities, so that joining with the Moon, for instance, is a different experience than joining with the Magician. Two people doing the same meditation with the same card will not receive the same images and feelings; they will, however, share in the particular values of that card.

Probably, you will not achieve this "joining" right away. You might find in your first tries at meditation that you keep getting distracted, or your mind wanders off in completely irrelevant directions, and nothing at all seems to happen between you and the picture. Unless you actively dislike it, keep trying. Slowly you will discover that your relaxation is deeper, your contact with the cards more intense, and your experiences more personal. Meditation brings many other benefits besides a greater understanding of the Tarot. It gives you a more centered approach to life, a more relaxed attitude to problems, and an opening to the sacred dimensions in your daily life and the world around you. Meditation can widen your perceptions while at the same time grounding you in the immediate reality of your own breath.

There are various kinds of meditation with Tarot cards. However, they all begin with a deep relaxation. This allows you to clear your mind of all the usual thoughts, worries, tensions, excitement, and so on that tend to fill our days. Relaxation brings its own rewards. It calms the nerves, it renews the body and opens up the breath. But it also makes room for the spiritual messages contained within the cards.

To begin your meditation choose a time and place where you can sit comfortably without disturbance by family or visitors or outside noise. For some people, such as parents with little children, this may require a special effort. However, meditation need not take longer than fifteen minutes to half an hour. If you decide to do a regular program of meditation try to do each one at the same time and in the same place. Sit in a comfortable position with your back straight. Try to sit in such a way that you do not draw your knees up to the chest, for this restricts the breathing. You can sit in a straight chair, or cross-legged on the floor. Make sure to find a place and position where you will not feel the need to move constantly, for this will distract you from the meditation. If back pain or some other problem makes it difficult for you to sit comfortably, lie down, preferably on the floor and without a pillow. You want to keep the spine straight.

If you think you might want to end the meditation by writing in a journal, or by drawing something, have whatever you need alongside you. This prevents breaking the meditation by having to get up and search for paper or colored pencils. Some people have a special object that contains for them a sacred power. This could be a ritual object, like a wand or a pentagram, or else a crystal, or a stone. If you have such an object, you might wish to include it in your meditation, placing it alongside the card, or holding it in your hand.

Begin the meditation by letting yourself sit peacefully and calmly. Close your eyes and feel that you are coming to a rest. Let your breathing lengthen out, let it become deeper and easier. Do not force it, but allow the breath to go all the way down to the diaphragm, and when you let it out, release all the breath from your body before you take another one. Continue to focus on your breathing, and with each in-breath allow calm and peace to fill your body. With each out-breath, let all distractions and worries float away from you. Feel yourself begin to relax. Let go of the tension most of us carry in our bodies, especially in places like the shoulders, the neck, the back, the bridge of the nose, the jaw. Let your breathing carry it away from you.

Probably the simplest meditation with the Tarot involves taking the qualities of the card into yourself. This meditation works well with cards that have come up in readings, or cards you feel you need at this time. If your life seems scattered and you find yourself weak, you might choose to meditate with the card of Strength, or the Hanged Man.

When you are sitting comfortably and ready to begin, take the card into your hand. Look at the picture. Do not seek to analyze it or memorize any of its official meanings. Allow yourself to experience its qualities. You might want to think of a time when your life did express this kind of energy, or peacefulness, or wisdom. Imagine what you could do in your life now if these qualities came back to you. Now put the card down again, sit relaxed and close your eyes. As you begin your relaxation do not try to remember everything you were thinking. Release it along with all the other thoughts crowding your mind.

When you feel yourself relaxed, allow the image of the card to come back into your mind. Do not worry about the accuracy of your mental picture. Now as you breathe in, let the qualities of the card fill you with each breath. And as you breathe out, experience those qualities moving through your whole body. Some people like to imagine pure light surrounding them and the card. This helps to deepen the bond between themselves and the image. When you feel you have spent enough time with the card, take a final deep breath, and when you release it open your eyes.

Sit for a while longer before you go back to your regular activities. Pick up the card again and look at the picture. You might want to repeat the meditation several times over a period of days. Eventually you will find that in the middle of other activities you only need to think of this card in order to draw on its special qualities.

A more complex form of Tarot meditation involves a kind of story created with the cards. In the description for the Star, I referred to a meditation I led in Hermann Haindl's studio in Hofheim. In this visualization, which was based on the Hanged Man, the people saw themselves climbing a tree that became larger and larger the higher they climbed, until it opened up into the World Tree itself. When they reached a certain point they imagined themselves tying one foot to the tree branch so they could hang down, with the sky and the branches of the tree behind them. Far below they saw the old woman washing her hair, and as the clear water ran over the rocks they allowed themselves to experience the hope of renewal in their own lives.

Meditations such as this usually require a teacher, not for expert knowledge, but simply because people need someone to act as guide. The meditation works best when you sit or lie without moving or thinking, and open your imagination and feelings to the images given to you by the guide. You want to see the Tree; you want to see yourself in the branches, and the light of the stars shining on your hands. If you have to stop and think of what should come next, you lose that quality of staying completely within the experience. If you wish to do such meditations by yourself, you might find it best to tape the instructions beforehand. Think of the kind of story (myth) you want to create. Do not make up too many details ahead of time or you will leave no room for spontaneous experience. However, you should include directions like, "Feel the bark of the tree under your hands. Smell the air, and hear the sound of the birds." Just as in a written story, these sensual details give the experience a deeper reality. Only here, you will create these details yourself.

When you have worked out the various steps, record them on a tape, speaking softly but in your natural voice. In between the different stages of the story leave time for the spontaneous details to come into your mind. Then, when you wish to do the meditation, simply do a relaxation (the same as described above) and play the tape.

All this will take some experimenting. You will need to find out how fast to speak, how much time to leave, how much description to include, and so on. However, it should not take too long to find the method that works best for you. Various books give transcripts of these kind of meditations. (Other terms you might see are "guided fantasies," "visualizations," or "pathworkings.") You can read them into a tape recorder and then play them back in the usual way. You also might want to form a group with other people studying the Tarot. As well as discussing what you've learned, and reading each other's cards, you can take turns leading meditations. Besides the benefits of the meditations themselves, this will give each person the experience of being a teacher as well as a student.

A meditation that has become a tradition with the Tarot calls for you to enter the card itself. For some people this can mean actually projecting yourself out of your body. Such a drastic exercise is not necessary, however, to gain a valuable experience with the images. Begin your meditation in the usual way, looking at the picture and then setting it down to do a relaxation. When you feel yourself ready, pick up the card again. With the eyes still closed, feel it in your hands. Try to see the image in your mind, creating as much detail as you can. Staying in the meditation, open your eyes and look at the card. Notice any ways in which your image didn't match the actual picture. Now close your eyes again, and once more construct the picture in your mind. When it seems complete to you, let the picture get larger. Imagine it expanding in front of you until it becomes larger than the room. Let it become life-size, not as a two-dimensional card, but as an actual scene, with real people and objects. Without actually moving, imagine yourself getting up and entering the world of the picture.

Take a moment to orient yourself. As with the story meditation above, let your senses awaken to this new place. Feel the ground under you, smell the air, hear whatever sounds there are. Allow the scene to change. Maybe the people are doing something, or talking to you. Maybe someone new will enter the scene. Do not choose consciously what is going to happen; instead let yourself experience whatever comes. If you find yourself taking part allow this also to happen spontaneously. When you sense that the scene and the actions have done what they needed to do, take a step back. Return through the "door" of the picture back to your place in the room. Now see the scene shrink back to the size of a card. When it has done so, let the picture dissolve. Then, when you find yourself ready, take a final breath, and when you release it, open your eyes.

You can use this meditation to create your own Tarot card. Before you begin the meditation, take a large sheet of paper and several colored pencils or felt-tip pens, and set them beside you. When you have returned from the world of the card draw, or write, what you experienced there. Your picture may end up very close to the original version, or something entirely different. You can, if you like, do this for the entire deck, or the trumps, or simply for those few cards which have become most important to you. However you approach this or other meditations, they will give you an understanding of the cards unlike any other.

EPILOGUE

The Haindl Tarot Is the Mirror of a Life-Story

THERE WERE SIGNIFICANT points in his life when Hermann Haindl began the paintings for his Tarot cards. These cards are central to his artistic work and it is useful to take a look at the roots of their development. The Haindl Tarot represents a summary of Hermann Haindl's life. It can be compared to a tree, which lives with its roots and branches through the uncountable places of contact with the material and non-material world.

It was in 1945 that Hermann Haindl, a 17-year-old, fell into the troubled confusion of the last months of World War II. Still a youth, he became a soldier for a brief time. He was captured and then held as a prisoner of war in Russia for four years. He belonged to a generation of young people torn away from home and seemingly discarded. Seldom has a generation of young people been sacrificed in a more criminal manner.

It is difficult to find any philosophically creative meaning in imprisonment: 170 young men had gone off as one company; only three survived. Hermann Haindl was one of the survivors. In the unfolding of his life story, this period of constant closeness to death was of utmost importance. During this critical adolescent phase of forming an identity, Hermann Haindl found himself catapulted to the very edge of physical and psychological existence. During this time he experienced a profound religious conviction of the awareness of the life force within us, the energy we call God. It gave him the strength to live through all the obstacles and horrors he faced. To this day, he has lived his life out of this perpetually full well. While his way of life is often unsettling to others, it is both humble and upright.

If suffering can have a creative meaning, Hermann Haindl's life and work were formed by it. While there is no justification for the insanity through which he acquired his experiences, it gave him a passion for working toward peace and reconciliation with the environment of our planet.

215

Throughout our life together, Hermann has spent long hours telling me about the years of imprisonment. In those times, experiences with death were an everyday occurrence. Once, he had to dig his own grave. Many times, his life was saved by strangers. Between the hope for mere survival and the recognition of a higher life principle lay many small encounters with nature, with other people and with himself. These shaped his life and made inner growth possible. Within him grew an autonomous law of life that gave him independence from the opinions of others.

A central theme in the ever-returning memories of prison is a little birch tree. The barren land of the huge camp was surrounded by high barbed-wire fences and guard towers. Successful escape was unthinkable. Others had fled, only to be brought back and shot before the eyes of their fellow prisoners. The future was uncertain and covered with darkness, but those who gave up died.

One day, as Hermann often tells, he discovered a tiny birch shoot just outside the fence. Day by day its new leaves unfolded and stretched further into the light. Throughout a spring and summer the birch shoot grew into a small tree. For hours at a time Hermann sat and contemplated the young tree. The sun and the rain fell equally on the little birch and on the barbed wire. The tree—growing in the midst of misery and the destruction of human dignity—became a symbol of rebirth and life for Hermann.

The message of the simple birch shoot to the young man behind the barbed wire was fundamental: "Live. Believe out of your center, like I do, in a cosmic energy that gives us strength and abundance."

As a refugee in 1949, the way back into the emerging and already prospering society of post-war Germany was long and difficult. Hermann Haindl never forgot the green leaves of the little tree, even though this memory was often veiled by the ordinary difficulties and worries that can go with making a fresh start. But once acquired, the secret of the profound connection between life and death became a well of strength in him, never to be lost.

At the end of the sixties, Hermann reached an artistic crisis. Since the war, a focus on progress had brought prosperity for many; the years 1968–69 brought up for the first time deeply repressed fears and despair, and—resulting from them—some new hope. Hermann Haindl had been working for a number of years as a stage designer and head of the artistic workshop in the theater in Frankfurt. The intensity of that creative experience became a model for him for action within society. In the face of emerging social turbulence, painting abstract pictures lost its meaning for him. For a whole year he touched neither canvas nor brush.

When he returned to creative work he was a different person. The life and suffering in Russia under extreme circumstances shone through all his work and became a dominating principle. In 1970 the painting "The Eye" was born. This work signifies the beginning of the new creative period that culminated eighteen years later in the Haindl Tarot cards.

By 1985 Hermann and I had lived together in Hofheim for thirty years. In an address at an exhibition celebrating our anniversary, Ingrid Mössinger said: "The first painting after this inner emigration was appropriately named *Eye*, as the window of a new consciousness. Whereas Hermann Haindl's view of the environment was originally fastened on the surface of things, losing itself in increasingly abstract forms, in 1970 he turned his focus intensely to the reality of the environment and of nature. The difference between his earlier and later work is a difference in depth: the focus is not on capturing the part of nature comprehensible to the 'eye,' but on the character of the natural. Rather than an interest in what the individual, physical eye perceives, it is the archetypical in nature that has gained importance. In a manner of speaking Hermann Haindl looks with archaic eyes into the soul of nature. . . . Hermann Haindl turns . . . with the voice of his paintings against prejudice and restrictive thinking. He pleads for unhindered and exuberant growth in nature" (Ingrid Mössinger: Hermann Haindl, 30 Jahre in Hofheim, Catalogue for the exhibition, 1985).

One section of this painting, which stands at the wake of the new beginning, has become the leading motive for the seventy-eight cards of the Haindl Tarot. The eye looks at us from the back of the card. It is not the timeless, seeing eye of a godlike entity—this eye is marked by suffering. Amid the otherwise immaculate beauty and tranquility, an abscess must be endured. The abscessed eye presents a symbol.

Perhaps only through suffering can we reach a higher state of awareness, one in which the language and the message of a birch tree becomes comprehensible.

The Haindl Tarot is also the origin of a further step in the life of Hermann Haindl. In 1980, after exactly thirty years to the day, Hermann Haindl left the theater entirely to begin working on his own. It was a Friday afternoon, and on that same day I received word that I had lost a job that had been promised to me, which was to have supported us for several years. It was quite a shock. Hermann sat with me and comforted me. Two hours later he got a phone call in which he was told that a big commission we had counted on had been given to somebody else. It was a true "Tower" situation. I will never forget that afternoon. But after that sudden collapse of our material security, Hermann said, "This is supposed to happen. Now I will finally have time to paint my own Tarot cards!"

So began one of the most suspenseful phases of our joint lives. In unimaginable intensity, one Major Arcana card after another emerged. Each one was more beautiful and exciting than the last.

Long, intense conversations filled the days and weeks as, with merciless intensity, Hermann pulled all the people close to him into the suction of his constantly growing creation.

The first card to come about was the Wheel of Fortune. Truly, it had whirled us off the ground. This card, very reserved in the colors, shows Hermann Haindl's life principle symbolically. The axis of the wheel is the very center of the personal life. However, to know one's own personal center is to confront pain. Hermann's Wheel of Fortune depicts this theoretical and philosophical concept of life; but in particular it shows a life that has been deeply experienced and suffered through, as some of the consequences of war and imprisonment are ongoing pains and limitations that Hermann Haindl endures.

So far, it has been a basic experience in our life together that whatever we need comes in abundance. Now, not only the paintings that were completed since 1970, but also those from our travels over the past years—to Ireland, Scotland and England, to India, and including the many contacts with the Native American people of North America—turn out to have been part of our journey to the Tarot deck. The puzzle has now come together. In fact, the pieces had always belonged together, but these connections were hidden from us.

A last and very conscious piece completed the picture—a trip to Egypt in early 1988. Our immersion in that culture and the way it touched us were profound and overwhelming. Here were Nut and Ra, Osiris and Isis—out of the exalted sublimity of a 5,000-year-old history emerged faces distinguished by the timeless beauty of the Gods. We saw these faces vividly in the throngs of people everywhere in present-day Egypt. They surrounded us in cities and villages, passed us by, treated us with empathy, and sensed their way into our feelings and understanding. They led us to be aware of the collective human memory hidden deep within every one of us. This archetypal memory is overlaid with all the experiences of our conscious life, which cannot reach where only our preconsciousness can gain entrance. The culture-shock which probably strikes each of us when we lose the safety of our familiar world also created the possibility of our understanding the secret language of symbols in which timeless wisdoms are contained.

The last of the seventy-eight cards painted was the Daughter of the South, the card of Isis. This card is linked to the card of the Daughter of the North, the Celtic Brigid. The Isis painting depicts the head of a woman adorned with symbols of the highest spirituality. With the image of a woman in the final painting for the cards, the essence of this Tarot deck is emphasized. From the first painting, the Wheel of Fortune, to the last, Isis, the theme is one of the common longing for a society that finds its inner harmony again—in the return to equality between man and woman. The balance between male and female energies is a necessary prerequisite for a harmonious society, though in our patriarchal world it seems almost a utopian concept.

In publishing his Tarot deck, Hermann Haindl now stands at another threshold. In this third phase of his life work, he must let go of his creations and allow them to go out into the world. In the absence of a harmonious balance, our nations will not stop destroying each other in war. Our food, the air we breathe and the earth itself will be further poisoned by a society moving away from balance. The Haindl Tarot cannot bring about significant changes in the way we all conduct ourselves. Its positive influence will be almost weightless and barely detectable.

However, there is an ever-expanding network of people who not only fend off that which is destructive, but also go further and nurture that which is spiritual. The Haindl Tarot is a part of this network. Many people will see these cards and be moved by them. In this way the rich experience and understanding captured in these inspired images will help balance the scales—with the weight of a feather.

Erika Haindl

PAINTER'S NOTES
AND ACKNOWLEDGMENTS

I WANT TO DEDICATE the Haindl Tarot to my wife Erika. As these cards are being published and find their way into the public, she and I will have been living together for 33 years:

$$3 = \text{The Empress}$$
$$3 + 3 = \text{The Lovers}$$
$$3 \times 3 = \text{The Hermit.}$$

I am especially indebted to Rachel Pollack who wrote this book. I also want to thank Günther Cherubini, who opened the door to the Tarot for me and who accompanied us, together with Barbara Meyer, to the old places in Ireland. Peter Müller deserves my written thanks for the many years of shared interests. Together with him I was allowed to live in a former Radha temple in Vrindavan, India, for a little while. Also, I want to express my appreciation for Herta and Wolfgang Biersack. They were my companions in Egypt, where I found Nut and Ra, Isis and Osiris.

I am deeply grateful to all our friends in the United States, including Regina Eastman, Brave Buffalo, Martin High Bear, Janet McCloud (Yetsi Blue), and Craig. My gratitude goes to Sandy Lofquist, too. They all opened their homes and hearts to Erika and myself, and we had many long and wonderful conversations about the American Indian world view. I thank my Native American friends who have given me much assistance for this Tarot.

My appreciation also goes out to Zoltán Szabó for his help in organizing the runes for the twenty-two Major Arcana. And thank you to my friends Joachim Faulstich, Gundula Mohr, Christine Gerhards and Thomas Petzold, who were with me during this journey into another world from the beginning. Dr. Diane Battung has enriched my understanding with her vast spiritual knowledge; for that I thank her. Gerhard Riemann, the editor of esoteric works at Knaur, who published the German editions of this book and the Tarot cards, also deserves my appreciation. Our work together developed into a friendship. This is one of the mysteries of Tarot—everything we need, we receive in abundance.

I want to thank both of my mothers and my sons. The conscious experience of being bound in time from yesterday to tomorrow is part of the understanding from which grew this Tarot. The young Emperor, rushing into life, embodies the image of the Sons, the next generation to come. As the Emperor—with the untroubled strength of his youth—becomes an enduring and understanding man throughout the course of the Major Arcana, each generation is given the room to have its own life realization.

As a part of the life circle, each of us needs not only the dialogue with himself, but also—and especially—the exchange with others. Out of the abundance of friendship and love I was allowed to receive comes my deep thankfulness, which includes also those whom I did not mention here, but who helped shape this work.

I thank the Great Spirit.

> Hermann Haindl
> Castagneto Carducci
> 1988

If you are unable to find any Newcastle book or the Haindl Tarot deck at your local bookstore, please write to:

Newcastle Publishing Co., Inc.
13419 Saticoy Street
North Hollywood, CA 91605

The Haindl Tarot, Volume I: The Major Arcana and *The Haindl Tarot, Volume II: The Minor Arcana* are $9.95 each, and The Haindl Tarot deck is $15.00. Please add $2.00 for UPS and handling to the cost of the book or deck for the first item ordered, plus $1.00 for each additional item. California residents please add sales tax with each order.

Free, complete, current catalogues are available upon request. Just send us your name and address and we will send you a catalogue.

Quantity discounts are available to groups, organizations and companies for any Newcastle title. Telephone (213) 873-3191 or FAX your order to Newcastle Publishing Co., Inc. at (818) 780-2007.

Thank you for your interest in Newcastle.

AL SAUNDERS
Publisher